SMASHING

COFFEESCRIPT

PUBLISHER'S ACKNOWLEDGEMENTS

Some of the people who helped bring this book to market include the following:

Editorial and Production
VP Consumer and Technology Publishing Director: Michelle Leete
Associate Director–Book Content Management: Martin Tribe
Associate Publisher: Chris Webb
Executive Commissioning Editor: Birgit Gruber
Associate Commissioning Editor: Ellie Scott
Development Editor: Sydney Argenta
Copy Editor: Melba Hopper
Technical Editor: Kevin Bradwick
Editorial Manager: Jodi Jensen
Senior Project Editor: Sara Shlaer
Editorial Assistant: Annie Sullivan

Marketing
Associate Marketing Director: Louise Breinholt
Marketing Manager: Lorna Mein
Senior Marketing Executive: Kate Parrett
Marketing Assistant: Tash Lee

Composition Services
Compositor: Indianapolis Composition Services
Proofreader: Lindsay Amones
Indexer: Potomac Indexing, LLC

SMASHING COFFEESCRIPT

E. Alex Hudson

WILEY

978-1-118-45437-4

A catalogue record for this book is available from the British Library.
ISBN 978-1-118-45437-4 (paperback); ISBN 978-1-118-45492-3 (ebook);
ISBN 978-1-118-45493-0 (ebook); ISBN 978-1-118-45494-7 (ebook)

Set in 10/12 Minion Pro Regular by Indianapolis Composition Services
Printed in the U.K. by Bell & Bain

For Laura & Ben

ABOUT THE AUTHOR

Alex Hudson's first computers comprised an Amstrad 1512 and Oric Atmos: two peculiarly British machines, coming with slightly odd versions of BASIC. As was the case with most 8-bit machines of that era, they also arrived with programming manuals and assembly language instruction set documentation, and from that point on Alex was hooked.

By his teens, the Internet "had happened": or, at least, dial-up CompuServe access arrived in the UK. With a group of like-minded friends who enjoyed swapping code, now on the peculiarly British Psion 3a portable computer, Alex won one of the first national awards for a school's website—in hindsight, probably due more to lack of competition than technical innovation.

Swapping code on the internet turned out to be the next big thing, and Alex became an active member of the UK free software and open source community, developing applications and libraries and actively contributing to a number of different projects, including Linux, Hula (later Bongo), and later became a Fedora Developer.

Alex has a broad background in information systems. From leading development of innovative foreign language e-learning systems to large databases for Government projects, the common theme in his work life has been digital application development. Having co-founded and advised a number of start-ups, he currently serves as the Chief Technical Officer at mydeco.com, an innovative homewares start-up making big strides in Europe.

ACKNOWLEDGMENTS

To begin with, I'd like to thank the wonderful team at Wiley: firstly, Chris Webb for reaching out to me in the first place but then being incredibly positive about the various ideas I pitched to him. Secondly, to Sydney Jones Argenta, whose tolerance and patience with me has been out-matched only by her skilled leadership of this project, and without whom this book wouldn't have happened. I also need to thank the various editors and reviewers who spent their time on my manuscripts, this book is so much the better for their work.

A large proportion of this book covers CoffeeScript, jQuery, and Spine; software authored largely (to begin with, at least) by three individuals: Jeremy Ashkenas, John Resig and Alex MacCaw, respectively. They deserve not only my thanks for their prolific technical authorship (beyond even those projects mentioned), but broader recognition of their contribution to the Internet and technology in general. The world needs more inspirational coders of their ilk.

Lastly, I need to thank my family for providing the time and space to write. My wife is my constant support, and my parents, sister and various in-laws have all been tremendously encouraging. I have a new-found respect for those who commit to writing a book but also for their families, whose contribution is difficult to overstate.

CONTENTS

INTRODUCTION

If you have bought this book, or at least picked it up because it interested you, then you have at least heard of CoffeeScript and have an inkling of what the language is. In the words of its author, "CoffeeScript is a little language that compiles into JavaScript," and in a sense, that is all you need to know about the language. But a number of more profound ideas follow from that simple concept.

To understand CoffeeScript properly, it's important to understand the history of JavaScript. In the early days of Netscape Navigator, an engineer by the name of Brendan Eich was given the task of writing a scripting language that the browser would interpret, along with only two guiding principles. First, the language needed to look like Java, because that was the cool language at the time. Second, he had only ten days to write a functioning implementation.

That was a tremendously tall order but one that Eich was equal to. He created a small, language that fulfilled looked and acted like Java, called "Mocha". Additionally, he made decisions that set the language apart from others, such as treating functions as first-class objects that could be passed around at will and using prototypical object inheritance rather than the classical style preferred by the likes of C++ and Java. JavaScript, as it was eventually called, saw its first release in 1995 as part of Netscape Navigator 2.0.

In early 2000, Microsoft released a new version of its web e-mail/calendaring client, Outlook Web Access, using HTML and JavaScript. Under the hood, it made use of a new browser control Microsoft had created, the `XMLHttpRequest` API, to talk asynchronously to the server. This object allowed information to flow to and from the browser outside the usual HTTP page request: The user interface updated progressively, rather than the browser viewport blanking as the browser went to the server to fetch a new version of the entire page. This supplied a much smoother experience for users, the web server had to work substantially less, and the system in general scaled much better.

This technique was picked up slowly but surely, but burst into the mainstream when Jesse James Garrett wrote an article describing this architectural approach to web application building and dubbed it *AJAX* (Asynchronous JavaScript and XML). Without realizing it, he'd lit the proverbial blue touch paper.

AJAX as an architectural concept gained adoption quickly, to the point that now browsing the web with JavaScript turned off is virtually impossible. Large applications, such as Google's Gmail, were written to run entirely client-side, and the imperative to create richer browser features led to results such as HTML 5. Browser competition, which had stagnated from the time Internet Explorer 6 was released, quickly heated up again with new entrants such as Mozilla Firefox and, later, Google's Chrome. Most importantly, many of the problems associated with programming applications for the web began to melt away. As the focus on web standards became more important, browser incompatibility was greatly reduced, and renewed emphasis on the speed of JavaScript execution allowed client-side developers to create increasingly sophisticated applications.

Amid all this excitement, and the development of JavaScript-based applications "in the large" (a term coined in 1975 to describe the process of programming and maintaining complex software applications by teams of engineers), the fundamental design of the language that had held up well all these years began to fall short. Because JavaScript is an interpreted language with a dynamic type system, many of the static analysis and compilation tools that come to the aid of the developer are unavailable. The design of the object system within JavaScript is prototypical, and entire swathes of the development community aren't familiar with it. Developers coming from other languages, such as Java, found themselves particularly uneasy without the concept of classes.

In December 2009, Jeremy Ashkenas started writing his solution to these problems—Coffee-Script—and announced the release of an initial version on Christmas Eve. Writing the initial lines of code to the first release took 11 days, echoing, albeit unintentionally, Brendan Eich's efforts almost 15 years previously.

The goals were relatively simple: Expose the better parts of JavaScript, add higher-level functionality, and ignore as many of the warts of the language as possible. Although Ashkenas initially intended CoffeeScript to be as much a thought experiment as a tool in its own right, the little language surged in popularity. This popularity quickly pushed the project forward, and in exactly one year, a stable 1.0 version was reached.

WHY LEARN COFFEESCRIPT?

Why did people flock to the CoffeeScript project in the first place? Although the initial implementation worked, right from the start it was a little rough. In fact, many of the major decisions that came to make the language stand apart from JavaScript hadn't been made yet; even the significant whitespace that would one day be used to mark code blocks, was yet to come. The language and the syntax were initially influenced by Ashkenas's development work on large-scale web applications, but the chorus of feedback from other engineers honed and fine-tuned the language.

The idea that CoffeeScript embodied, though, was that you could write code for the browser in a higher-level and more concise, readily understandable language than JavaScript, but still benefit from the wide deployment of JavaScript by compiling code into JavaScript, similar to the way a C++ suite compiles source into machine code.

Many of the changes contained in the CoffeeScript syntax are directly aimed at web developers, which is different than JavaScript, where the language was heavily influenced by systems programming. Before JavaScript, there wasn't a concept of what a client-side web application might look like, or what types of problems would need to be solved, or even why you would contemplate writing such a thing in the first place. CoffeeScript, on the other hand, was designed with this context in mind and hindsight is 20:20.

BEST PRACTICES, FORMALIZED

As developers started writing larger and larger JavaScript applications, they began to collect idioms and patterns that represented "best practice," which meant a variety of things, including using only features that were broadly supported by browsers but staying away from features that had broad support but questionable value.

As an example of the latter, to this day there are arguments about whether JavaScript statements should end with a semicolon. Although neither the specification nor the implementations require it unless more than one statement is on a line, the rules about how a semicolon may be inserted into code are baroque and difficult to understand. But, many developers prefer not having superfluous semicolons in their code, and omit them.

Global variables were also eschewed, and various object-oriented design patterns became common. In particular, the jQuery library arrived and solved two major problems at the same time. First, working with the browser's Document Object Model (DOM) became vastly easier using jQuery's fluent API rather than the official W3C DOM API; second, virtually all the remaining browser incompatibilities that JavaScript developers had to contend with were effectively eliminated by compensating for them at the library level.

CoffeeScript has been inspired by all of these ideas, and more. Concepts have been borrowed from functional programming languages, such as the increased emphasis on expressions over imperative code, but also from popular systems scripting languages such as Perl, Ruby, and Python, which have developed succinct approaches to common data structure manipulations and explored what it means to be a dynamic language.

As an example of how web programming has influenced CoffeeScript, you need look no further than the humble function. JavaScript made the decision to make functions first-class objects, meaning that you can treat functions as any other data. You can pass them to other functions, you can return them as values from functions, and you can almost create them on the fly. Because web applications need to deal with asynchronous processes (in practice, this means certain functions return before they actually complete their work, such as the XML-HttpRequest API underlying the principles of AJAX), it became natural to use functions as callbacks, a practice familiar to anyone who has developed a GUI on the desktop.

In CoffeeScript, functions not only remain first-class, but are actually about the easiest things to type. The syntax is concise, and you can construct them just about anywhere you please. This neatly demonstrates the whole approach of CoffeeScript: The things you need every day are concise and easily accessible. Programmers rarely, if ever, need to repeat themselves, and the amount of "boilerplate" code is minimal.

Equally, it's surprisingly hard to write invalid CoffeeScript, and certainly by the time the compiler does its work translating the code into JavaScript, the chances of any syntactic or typographic mistakes making it into the output are very small. As an example of how this can make a difference, consider that many JavaScript programmers lay out arrays over multiple lines and start each line but the first with a comma. They do so because it all but prevents a trailing comma being left in the array. This is a well-known mistake that most browsers are willing to tolerate. Internet Explorer, on the other hand, is entirely unforgiving of such an error and will generally decline to run any of the code that follows. Such a mistake is practically impossible to commit in CoffeeScript.

In the short time that it's been available, there are already examples of how CoffeeScript is influencing the design of other languages—including JavaScript, where many of the Coffee-Script features, if not the actual syntax, are being built into proposals for revisions of the language. This is not just a tribute to the design of Jeremy Ashkenas and the CoffeeScript community but also a strong indicator of the momentum to improve the browser platform for web designers and application developers. The brilliance and power of CoffeeScript could be summed up as "tomorrow's web platform, running today."

SOME WORDS ON THE SYNTAX

This book introduces the CoffeeScript syntax gradually through example. Additionally, although the code being run is actually JavaScript, the JavaScript code being generated won't be discussed, mainly because that's a CoffeeScript implementation detail, which can change from version to version.

It's quite possible, although a bit of a crutch, to mentally translate CoffeeScript into the JavaScript that will run. I gently encourage you not to do so, at least while learning the language. The main advantages that CoffeeScript offers come from the developer thinking in a style idiomatic to CoffeeScript, which means leaving the JavaScript behind.

That said, for those of you who want to gain the deepest understanding of the language and who know JavaScript well, it is often instructive to look at how CoffeeScript actually does that translation. For one thing, you'll immediately gain a deep appreciation of how many lines of code the compiler is actually saving you from having to write!

HOW THIS BOOK IS STRUCTURED

In addition to introducing CoffeeScript gradually, I've tried to put this book together in a way that makes sense and progresses technically. Most of the simpler topics are toward the front, and as you work through the book the sophistication of the code and the concepts being discussed increases.

- **Chapter 1—Starting Up Your CoffeeScript Environment:** This is the most crucial chapter, since without it you can't make progress. I recommend making sure you have a working environment in which you can test the code before trying to read too much further.

- **Chapter 2—Using jQuery: DOM Manipulation:** You have likely had contact with jQuery by now, and this chapter serves as an introduction to CoffeeScript through some simple webpage code, and in particular it explores functions.

- **Chapter 3—Working with Forms:** Although not tremendously exciting, forms have been the mainstay of web application development from the start and probably will be for years to come. This chapter also introduces some more advanced CoffeeScript syntax.

- **Chapter 4—AJAX requests:** At this point, the book begins to get a bit more technical, as you examine how browsers create HTTP requests and look at the security of such requests and how to handle network reliability issues.

- **Chapter 5—Object-Oriented Design:** This might be one of the main reasons you've picked up this book: quite early on you'll be looking at how CoffeeScript supplements the JavaScript OO system.

- **Chapter 6—Using JavaScript Libraries:** Although this is primarily a CoffeeScript book, it wouldn't be complete without a look at how JavaScript integrates, and this chapter examines a number of different scenarios.

- **Chapter 7—Testing with Jasmine:** Sometimes thought of as a bit of a passing fashion, test-driven development is extremely important to me, and in this chapter you learn about some of the key testing tools for CoffeeScript applications.

- **Chapter 8—Debugging CoffeeScript:** Despite all the testing done in the previous chapter, bugs are a fact of life, but thankfully, there is a broad repertoire of debugging tools for CoffeeScript, and I'll show you the most important.

- **Chapter 9—Building Resources with cake and hem:** This is the first chapter that will begin to look at developing genuinely large-scale CoffeeScript applications, by first looking at how they might be built and deployed.

- **Chapter 10—Writing Applications with Spine:** As a client-side framework, Spine is among the easiest to learn and use, and as a bonus is written in CoffeeScript. I'll show you how to write Spine applications but also how to get the most out of the Spine framework itself.

- **Chapter 11—Writing jQuery Plug-Ins:** I tend to think that jQuery is still arguably the most important JavaScript library, and although its use has been covered, this chapter is all about extending the library itself, as well as examining some code from its sister project, jQuery UI.

- **Chapter 12—Mobile CoffeeScript Applications:** I'm a firm believer in the importance of mobile devices, which continue to rise in popularity, and this chapter of the book concentrates on developing Spine-style applications for the small devices and touchscreens.

- **Chapter 13—Data Bindings and Form Elements:** Many of the proceeding chapters have concentrated on some interactivity of some sort, but this will explore one of the most difficult areas: binding data to forms within the browser. This is some of the most complex event-driven code in the book.

- **Chapter 14—Server-Side CoffeeScript:** Although there are some small examples of server-side code dotted throughout the book, this is the main introduction to the popular Node.js system and some of the key modules. By no means is this an in-depth exploration, but I hope this will whet your appetite for much more.

- **Chapter 15—Realtime Web with socket.io:** Saving the best for last, this is my favorite chapter: real-time web programming is still very new, and is a fundamentally different style of development to even the AJAX architecture that seems still quite new. I'll show you just how different this area is, but how you can achieve some really interesting results using real-time frameworks.

My goal by the end of the book is not to convert you to a CoffeeScript ideologue, but to show you at least a couple of things that might be new or exciting, and that will make you want to write some code. It might be that you get to the end and decide it's not for you, but I hope to at least make the journey there interesting. And if you decide CoffeeScript does have a role in your future applications, then all the better!

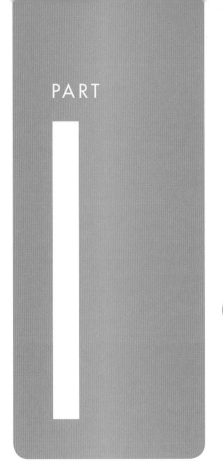

PART

I

COFFEESCRIPT BASICS

1

STARTING UP YOUR COFFEESCRIPT ENVIRONMENT

UNLIKE MANY DEVELOPMENT tools you might already be using, CoffeeScript is an almost entirely build-time affair. There is no plug-in required on the client-side, and no requirement for special versions of JavaScript or other compatibility concerns. Once an application or website is developed, the end user will have little to no idea about it being written in CoffeeScript.

A CoffeeScript developer has enormous freedom with respect to the tools used, and in general, using the latest and greatest CoffeeScript environment is the recommended practice. With no end-user impact to worry about, the remaining concern with version upgrades is whether a new feature or bug-fix is going to affect working production code. The general release policy for CoffeeScript is to ensure that such breaking changes are not made, particularly within a minor release series, and in practice such changes are rare.

The hardest part to CoffeeScript is getting started, and that's what this chapter is all about. As well as setting up a usable development environment, it's important to start becoming familiar with the language, both in terms of the technical syntax and of the overall approach to solving problems with it. This chapter is a basic introduction to the language and also to the practices and coding habits that help avoid problems, particularly for novices.

COFFEESCRIPT IN THE BROWSER

Using CoffeeScript directly in the browser is a quick way to start using the language because the barrier to entry is low, and you can immediately start becoming familiar with the process. There's no need to download any fancy tools or install a web server. Only three things are required:

- **A web browser:** I recommend Mozilla Firefox simply for the developer tools, but at this stage, it doesn't matter which browser you choose.
- **Your preferred text editor:** I use geany, but TextMate, Sublime, vim, and emacs are all popular.
- **A copy of** `coffee-script.js`**:** You can download this file from `http://jash kenas.github.com/coffee-script/extras/coffee-script.js`.

STARTING COFFEESCRIPT IN PLAIN HTML

I start the introduction to the language with a short and trivial script to demonstrate Coffee-Script being loaded and executed by the browser:

```
<!DOCTYPE html>
<html lang="en">
<head>
    <script src="coffee-script.js" type="text/javascript"></script>
    <script type="text/coffeescript">
    runWhenReady = () ->
        textbox = document.getElementById("textbox")
        text = document.createTextNode("Time to make coffee!")
        textbox.appendChild(text)

    window.onload = runWhenReady
    </script>
</head>
<body>
    <div id="textbox"></div>
</body>
</html>
```

Save this as an HTML file in the same directory as the copy of `coffee-script.js` you downloaded, and open it directly in your web browser. You should see the message "Time to make coffee!" in your browser confirming that the code did indeed run.

> *Throughout this book, I'm going to be writing HTML 5 and occasionally some small pieces of CSS. If you've never used HTML/CSS much before, or you're just a bit rusty, I recommend the documentation available at the Mozilla Developer Network, or MDN. A good starting point is here:* `https://developer.mozilla.org/en-US/docs/HTML/Introduction`.
>
> *MDN is an excellent reference resource covering all browers, not just Firefox, and covers all the key technologies and APIs within a browser.*

Most of this content will be familiar to you. There's some stripped-down HTML with just a JavaScript file included in the head and an empty `<div>` in the body. However, the second script tag is interesting: The content type is `text/coffeescript` (which the browser can't execute directly), and the contents are clearly CoffeeScript.

UNDERSTANDING COFFEESCRIPT

You're probably thinking that the script included looks a bit alien, so I'll break this down a bit because most of the key concepts are here. Once you understand these few lines, you're well on your way.

First, I'll talk about the parts that might be familiar to you already. `window.onload` is the standard DOM property that you've probably encountered before. If a function is assigned to it, the browser will run that function once the document has loaded fully and you're also using standard DOM functions, `document.getElementById()` to find your empty element, and then `document.createTextNode()` followed by `.appendChild()` to add content to it.

So far the code is standard, at least in terms of calling the functionality the browser gives you. Standard functions available in JavaScript are also available in CoffeeScript. They can be called identically, and there's no layer in between your code and the browser making it work.

Now, take a look at the parts you might not be so familiar with (although, if you've used a similar language, such as python, you've probably worked some of this out already). The first things to notice are

- Each statement is on its own line, and no terminating semicolons are needed.
- Variable names are not declared before use.
- Indentation produces logical blocks of code—there are no curly braces here, and the block ends when the code unindents back to where it was to begin with.

Last, but not least, is the most important part—the function declaration. Something called `runWhenReady` is defined, which is a function that takes no arguments and contains the DOM manipulations intended to run when the page is loaded. The actual syntax to create the function is simply the `->` operator, sometimes called "thin arrow," taking parameters in parentheses to its left and the definition to its right—either an expression (on the same line) or a logical block of code (below and indented, as in the case here), like this:

```
double = (x) -> x * 2

doubleIfEven = (x) ->
  if (x % 2) == 0
    return (x * 2)
  else
    return x
```

The key concept here is that in CoffeeScript all functions are actually anonymous—that is to say, they don't have a name. So if you want to refer to them sometime after you define them, you need to assign them to a variable to have a name to use. This means `runWhenReady` is not a function name at all; it's just the name of the variable you're using to refer to the function you defined. The previous two examples can also be called as you would expect:

```
double(2)        // this will return 4
doubleIfEven(2)  // this will also return 4
doubleIfEven(3)  // this will return 3
```

For some readers, this distinction will seem odd. Even in languages where functions are treated as first-class citizens, they're usually given names, and an anonymous function— sometimes referred to as a *closure,* or a *lambda,* depending on the language—is a less frequently used variant. However, it quickly becomes second nature if used in practice. The only syntactical difference is an extra = in the function definition.

COMPILING COFFEESCRIPT OUTSIDE THE BROWSER

Now that you've successfully run some CoffeeScript in the browser, I'm going to quickly pull the rug from under your feet: this isn't how to develop using CoffeeScript. What's happening here is that the entire CoffeeScript compiler is being loaded into the browser, with some additional tooling to allow it to look for `<script>` content with the `text/coffeescript` type. When the compiler finds those scripts, it loads the content, compiles it to JavaScript which is then passed to the browser to execute. At this point, you're bound to realize that this isn't the most efficient process.

So, what should happen instead? The simple answer is that it's generally best to compile CoffeeScript into JavaScript and then deliver it to the browser in the same way JavaScript is delivered. For those projects consisting mainly of static files, this approach requires a small amount of extra work; for more significant projects, the compilation process can be integrated into existing media delivery systems, alongside other steps, such as automatic code checkers, test suite harnesses, and delivery compression, which I cover later on.

WHAT IS NPM?

Throughout this book, you'll be calling on the services of a variety of tools and libraries (not least of all CoffeeScript), most of which are developed by different people as part of different projects. Ordinarily, using a diverse tool set like this would be a pain. First, you'd have to track down the tool you want and go through the process of installing it, making sure that it works with the other tools you've installed. Then you'd need to keep the tool up-to-date, and new features would require you to go and find other tools and install those before updating the first tool. This problem has often been dubbed *dependency hell* in development circles.

Enter the package manager, npm, used to manage additional libraries or utilities that your project might need. Although not officially or historically an abbreviation of "node.js package manager", it was developed within the node.js project (a JavaScript execution environment for servers) to allow developers to download and install "packages" of software alongside their own applications, and maintain the list of packages (or "dependencies") required to run the application.

npm provides you with solutions to all these types of problems:

- Instead of making you search for different tools, npm has a single public directory that anyone can search (and even publish code to!).
- Instead of making you download dependencies that a tool requires, npm can automatically fetch the dependencies and install them for you.
- Instead of making you manually update the installed tools, npm can automatically refresh them to the latest version upon request.

If you've used a packaged operating system before, such as one of the GNU/Linux distributions or one of the many "ports" style systems on Mac OS X or Windows, this type of setup will be immediately familiar. Like many of the better package managers, npm gives you another key option: You can install tools globally, but also locally—that is, you can make the tools available on a per-project basis. It's entirely possible to use a cutting-edge version of a tool in one project and an older one in another, giving you control over when updates to production tools happen.

INSTALLING COFFEE USING NPM

Because npm is a key part of the node.js project, by far the easiest way to get npm is simply to install node.js. Doing so installs the package manager and gives you a command-line Java-Script environment through which you can execute CoffeeScript and the various build tools you'll be using later on.

The latest node.js download options can be found here: `http://nodejs.org/download/`.

For Windows and Mac OS X, there are standard binary installers that install the various node.js tools for you. On other operating systems, there are various third-party binary packages or installers that are generally preferable to attempting to compile node.js from source.

A QUICK TOUR OF NPM

npm is designed to be used from the command line. On Windows, you can choose Command Prompt from the Accessories section of the Start menu to access the command line. On Mac OS X, the application is called Terminal and lives in the Utilities folder.

For those of you who aren't command-line interface (CLI) aficionados, don't worry; although npm is text-based, it's difficult to get lost in. To begin with, it's always useful to know where the help is. Type **npm help** at the command prompt to retrieve a list of available commands and **npm help <command>** to get more guidance on a specific command.

Searching for Packages

The first thing most people want to do is look around and see what's available. The way to accomplish this is as obvious as you might hope. Type **npm search <searchterm>** at the command prompt:

```
$ npm search coffee-script
npm http GET https://registry.npmjs.org/-/all/since?..m
npm http 200 https://registry.npmjs.org/-/all/since?..
NAME              DESCRIPTION
[..]
coffee-script     Unfancy JavaScript
[..]
```

I've removed most of the lines describing different packages from this search result. Quite often when a search is requested, a lot of results come back. npm has a big directory with utilities, libraries, and tools of all sorts. Although originally aimed at server-side code for node.js users, the directory has since blossomed to include client-side code as well, so familiar libraries such as jQuery are also included. Many developers end up using npm to manage most third-party libraries simply because of ease of use.

The first time a search command is run, npm downloads a search index. In the previous example, a search was run before, so the first two lines of the log show that the existing search index is just being updated.

Installing Packages

As mentioned earlier, installation is a breeze, but you need to decide whether packages will be installed globally or locally. Global generally means for every user on your computer, and you will usually need some form of administrative permission to install globally, but that's often the easiest way to get up and running. You use local installation to install dependencies for a specific project, and the dependencies live in the project folder, so no systemwide installation occurs, and no administrative permission is generally required.

Local installation is slightly more advanced. The main problem is that if you use it to install tools, the tools generally aren't available in the shell immediately because they're installed in a nonstandard location where the shell will never look.

INSTALLING COFFEESCRIPT

Typing **npm install <packagename>** at the command prompt asks npm to install the given package, and usually the package name will be discovered with a search. Go ahead and install CoffeeScript with the following command:

```
$ npm install -g coffee-script
npm http GET https://registry.npmjs.org/coffee-script
npm http 304 https://registry.npmjs.org/coffee-script
coffee-script@1.4.0 /usr/lib/nodejs/npm/node_modules/coffee-script
```

In this example, on the last line, npm gives you some really useful information. First, it tells you that you've downloaded CoffeeScript version 1.4.0; second, it gives you the path to the directory where CoffeeScript version 1.4.0 is installed.

You can verify that it's installed correctly by running it—by default an interactive shell, or Read Evaluate Print Loop (REPL), starts at the command line, where you can write directly in CoffeeScript and have it run. Type **coffee** at the command prompt to start the interpreter:

```
$ coffee
coffee> sayHello = (name) -> console.log("Hello, #{ name }!")
[Function]
coffee> sayHello "CoffeeScript user"
Hello, CoffeeScript user!
undefined
coffee>
```

The first line creates a function and assigns it to the variable `sayHello`. Notice that in interactive mode, `console.log()` is available for output as in a web browser and that Coffee natively supports string interpolation. Every time an expression is evaluated in this loop, the result of the evaluation is printed. In this case, `[Function]` indicates that the expression evaluated to a function.

The second line calls the function referred to by `sayHello`. Notice that the parentheses are missing; that line could be written `sayHello("CoffeeScript user")`, and it would function identically. In the same way that parentheses can be used in numerical expressions to make the order of evaluation clear, they are used in CoffeeScript to disambiguate the parameters to a function call. They're not always necessary or desirable.

Finally, where did that last `undefined` come from? It's simply the return value of the `console.log()` call. Although output was sent to the terminal, all functions return a value, and if the value is not explicit, it's simply not defined. The interactive loop is still going to evaluate the function call and print the result, hence it outputs `undefined`.

COMPILING COFFEESCRIPT CODE

Now that the `coffee-script` package is installed the `coffee` utility is available, and you can use it to compile scripts before they're delivered to the web browser. Recall that the browser cannot execute CoffeeScript directly, but the compiler can turn CoffeeScript into JavaScript that a browser will understand. This "compilation" process takes the `.coffee` source file and generates a `.js` equivalent that can then be refered to from the HTML code on the web page.

In any non-trivial projects, the compilation step will be part of a more general build system, but for less sophisticated projects simpler processes can be used to generate the `.js` files.

Understanding how compilation works when invoked manually is a useful first step. With the same idea as earlier—waiting for the page to load and then placing some text on the page to demonstrate the code is running—save this code in a file named `trivial.coffee`:

```
window.onload = ->
  textbox = document.getElementById "textbox"
  textbox.appendChild(document.createTextNode("Time for coffee!"))
```

This functionally is equivalent to what was directly inserted into the HTML before, but a couple of lines have been simplified by removing extraneous parentheses and assigning an anonymous function to be called on page load directly rather than "naming" it first.

For the browser to execute this code, it first needs to be compiled into JavaScript, and this is done using the `coffee` utility:

```
$ coffee -c trivial.coffee
```

If all goes well, `coffee` will output nothing on the command line. If it encounters an error, you'll get a number of lines of output showing you exactly where it thinks things went wrong. The result of this process is `trivial.js` (it uses the same file name but changes the extension, and writes the compiled JavaScript there), so have a look at the JavaScript it produced:

```
// Generated by CoffeeScript 1.4.0
(function() {

  window.onload = function() {
    var textbox;
    textbox = document.getElementById("textbox");
    return textbox.appendChild(document.createTextNode("Time to make coffee!"));
  };

}).call(this);
```

Immediately, it's clear that the original CoffeeScript is more concise that the resulting Java-Script—in general, this will be true of most, if not all, CoffeeScript you write. The JavaScript experts will have also picked up that the entire output is wrapped in an anonymous function, which ensures that, among other things, the end result is self-contained and can't affect code you may have included elsewhere on a page. This type of best practice is arduous boiler-plate if you have to write it yourself, but coffee does this for you!

> *As an aside, the file extension is* `.coffee` *by community convention. This does seem a bit overly verbose to a newcomer, and not necessarily friendly to Windows users. Unfortunately, the more concise* `.cs` *was already in use by the C# crowd by the time CoffeeScript arrived on the scene.*

PUTTING IT TOGETHER

Now that the result is compiled into a JavaScript file, you can easily update the HTML to make use of the new code:

```
<!DOCTYPE html>
<html lang="en">
```

```
<head>
    <script src="trivial.js" type="text/javascript"></script>
</head>
<body>
    <div id="textbox"></div>
</body>
</html>
```

The inline script has been removed, so the reference to `coffee-script.js` can therefore also be removed. By compiling the CoffeeScript first the script file being loaded is truly native JavaScript, so there's no reason to have the compiler itself also loaded on the page.

AUTOMATIC COMPILATION

Running a coffee compile command every time you've edited your code and want to see the result is, frankly, a pain. It would be tempting to use the in-browser compilation system to make the process of editing the code and viewing the result less painful, but luckily there's a better way: coffee's special *watch* mode.

The idea is simple: Ask coffee to compile your source and give it the extra parameter `-w` or `--watch`. This time, coffee doesn't exit as it would have, but continues running. As the file changes on disk (when you save the file in your editor) coffee will automatically recompile the file into JavaScript. This happens very quickly. By the time you've moved from the editor to the web browser, the compilation will have occurred, and you can reload the page to see what changed.

One of the neatest parts of this is that you can ask coffee to watch an entire directory:

```
$ mkdir coffee
$ coffee --watch --compile ./coffee/
14:45:11 - compiled ./coffee/main.coffee
14:48:32 - compiled ./coffee/main.coffee
```

In this example, coffee is watching a directory called `coffee` and recompiling the Coffee-Script sources that it sees. As though that's not good enough, the "watch" doesn't just extend to the files that were there when you started running it; if you add new files to a directory being watched, it will compile those as well.

AVOIDING COFFEESCRIPT ERRORS

Most people make errors in their code at the best of times, and particularly in the beginning you may well find yourself getting the syntax slightly wrong—as CoffeeScript is quite terse, even a single character in the wrong place will change the entire meaning of a piece of code. Look at how coffee responds to a missing thin arrow to declare a function (the specifics of the message will vary):

```
Error: In broken.coffee, Parse error on line 3: Unexpected 'TERMINATOR'
    at Object.parseError (./coffee-script/lib/coffee-script/parser.js:477:11)
    at Object.parse (./coffee-script/lib/coffee-script/parser.js:554:22)
```

```
     at Object.compile (./coffee-script/lib/coffee-script/coffee-script.js:43:20)
     at ./coffee-script/lib/coffee-script/command.js:180:33
     at ./coffee-script/lib/coffee-script/command.js:150:18
     at [object Object].<anonymous> (fs.js:123:5)
     at [object Object].emit (events.js:64:17)
     at Object.oncomplete (fs.js:1187:12)
```

The error message—`Unexpected 'TERMINATOR'`—sounds pretty terrible. It's followed by a number of lines of back-trace from files you likely didn't even know existed. This looks more frightening than it actually is; the error message is on the first line, and the other lines are more for the benefit of the CoffeeScript developers. In this example, all that's happened is that coffee hasn't been able to parse the code according to the CoffeeScript grammar. Specifically, it encountered the end of a line where it was expecting to see more code and doesn't know what to do.

CODING IN GOOD STYLE

You can do a number of things to help avoid errors right from the start, and some tools can be brought to bear on the problem. It's excellent practice in general to detect problems or errors as early as possible, but you will probably pick and choose among these different techniques to find those that work best in your projects.

To avoid common pitfalls, I recommend you follow a number of basic rules, and they're all about how you actually format your code. Of course, coding style is a touchy topic among professionals. Most developers have their own preferred style, and you are free to break these rules, but they reflect common practice and more importantly, are backed up with some solid reasoning.

- **Use spaces to indent your code.** CoffeeScript uses indentation to control the logical flow of code. This means that whitespace at the start of each line is critically important, and I recommend that you use spaces and indent at two-space intervals. By all means, use the Tab key to indent code—this is entirely natural!—but have your text editor insert spaces. Mixing tabs and spaces leads to trouble in a single file or project, and consistency really is king here.
- **Make sure you have space around operators.** For example, a+b is a valid CoffeeScript expression, but a +b (note the single extra space after a) is not. The preferred form, to avoid that kind of error, is to have space on both sides of the operator: a + b.
- **Use a code editor that displays whitespace,** usually with a light dot in the center of the character. In particular, this immediately shows that spaces have been used to indent, which makes mistakes in a file obvious before you attempt to run the code.
- **Only omit outer parentheses for readability.** It's often useful to omit parentheses because the extra bit of white space in the code can make it less dense and slightly more readable. However, that readability should never be at the cost of ambiguity—if you have to think about what code is doing, it's becoming unreadable! Take this example:

```
[x, y] = [2, -3]

biggest = Math.max(Math.abs x, Math.abs y)
```

This looks straightforward: two variables are assigned and an expression is evaluated to work out which one is actually the largest value in absolute terms (this could be evaluating the margins of objects on the page, for example). Since the parentheses have been removed from the inner function calls, it's not obvious that the expression is actually equivalent to this:

```
Math.max(Math.abs(x, Math.abs(y)))
```

When you define functions that take no arguments, feel free to leave off the parentheses. Similarly, if you have a line that consists of only a function call, you can leave them off—but if you need to think about whether they should be there, it's best to leave them. Implicit parentheses don't close until the expression is finished: so for clarity I recommend only omitting the outermost pair:

```
biggest = Math.max Math.abs(x), Math.abs(y)
```

It's readable and difficult to get wrong.

- **Adopt consistent naming:** The CoffeeScript standard is to use `camelCaseNaming` for variables and attributes (and, therefore, functions—because they're referenced using variables). Classes, as a special case, take a capitalized first letter as well, `LikeThis`. Constants in code are `ALL_UPPER_CASE` and "private" functions have `_leadingUnderscores`.

  This is the most arguable rule presented here, but if you're planning on reusing code from the community or contributing yourself via npm, it's useful if for no other reason than community consistency.

More Style Guidelines

The code in this book is laid out according to the preceding rules, along with other rules. These rules are heavily influenced by, and in places identical to, those generally agreed to by the CoffeeScript community at large. In turn, those rules have been influenced by many years of experience of developers in other communities, such as Python, Ruby, and JavaScript, and reflect years of coding practice.

Many code editing environments also have the ability to syntax highlight code: if yours has that feature, and it can correctly highlight CoffeeScript, I encourage you to enable it. My experience is that the sooner an error is detected the easier it is to fix, and a good highlighter is a lot of help.

Edit your code in small bursts, particularly to begin with. It's incredibly frustrating to spend tens of minutes writing some code only to find it doesn't even compile, and can be time consuming to go back and figure out what went wrong. Save often, use `coffee -watch` and check its output regularly: it will alert you when things start going wrong and it's always easier to fix a mistake just made.

If you've never used a language that is white-space sensitive, you will find the indenting rules particularly difficult. I strongly encourage you to invest the effort in following them. They've helped my coding style enormously, and I hope you discover the same value in them. Throughout this book, I will continue to point out guidelines and rules as appropriate.

COFFEELINT WILL PICK UP ERRORS

You can use the tool coffeelint to pick up some style errors. Installation with npm is easy:

```
$ npm install -g coffeelint
```

And running it over good or bad files is equally easy:

```
$ coffeelint good.coffee bad.coffee

  y good.coffee
  x bad.coffee
     x #4: Line contains inconsistent indentation. Expected 2 got 1.
     x #4: Line contains tab indentation.

x Lint! » 2 errors and 0 warnings in 2 files
```

In this instance, coffeelint has recognized that the indentation in the second file is incorrect—tabs have been used. Unfortunately, it hasn't gone as far as to correct the problem, but you do have the line numbers, which is the next best thing.

SUMMARY

As a language CoffeeScript is easy to pick up, but as with most things taking the first few steps can be the hardest so congratulations on making it to the end of the first chapter! If you have only read the text up to now, I encourage you to get online to download CoffeeScript and start testing it out before going too much further. The subjects I've covered are basic but essential:

- Installing CoffeeScript tools and libraries using npm
- Exploring some of the basic syntax of CoffeeScript and writing simple functions
- Executing CoffeeScript code in the browser by importing the CoffeeScript compiler
- Compiling CoffeeScript offline using the coffee utility and loading the resulting JavaScript into the browser
- Using some of the tools to check code and looking at the coding practices that help you avoid making errors

In the next chapter, I'll show you how to use CoffeeScript and jQuery together to perform common tasks, which should be comfortable ground for most readers. Make sure you're happy writing CoffeeScript, compiling it to JavaScript and referencing it from HTML documents before proceeding!

USING JQUERY: DOM MANIPULATION

JQUERY IS CONSIDERED the pre-eminent library for creating and manipulating HTML. This chapter is dedicated to demonstrating how to use jQuery on CoffeeScript projects. Although designed originally for use from JavaScript, the fluent API that jQuery offers works incredibly well in CoffeeScript—arguably, it's easier to use than in the native JavaScript.

jQuery came to prominence for its straightforward approach to manipulating web pages, but has quickly become more of a utility library than that. As well as smoothing out various browser differences, it provides a range of additional functionality, to the extent that jQuery has almost become a platform itself.

JQUERY'S FLUENT API

Arguably the finest decision made when authoring jQuery was the use of the fluent API. Coined in 2005 by design pattern gurus Martin Fowler and Eric Evans, the term "fluent" is associated with a method-chaining style of code structure. Although as a design pattern it had been in use decades by that point, it was particularly appropriate to dynamic languages.

Within each web browser, there is something called the Document Object Model, or DOM. But what is the DOM? It's almost like a window into the internal functioning of the browser: it represents the internal data structure of how the browser has interpreted the HTML document, and any assets mentioned in the document, but does so in a standard way which for the most part is the same in every browser. The browser parses the HTML document into a pyramid-like structure—with the <html> node at the top, the <head> and <body> nodes underneath that, so on and so forth—and from this it creates the DOM.

jQuery gives you a number of tools to manipulate this document structure. If you haven't used jQuery before, the basic rules of the API are simple to state:

- There is a function defined called jQuery(), but most people call it $()—that's an alias for it to save you from having to type the full name each time,
- If you pass DOM nodes or a CSS selector, jQuery() will return a list of the selected nodes, and the list will be wrapped with jQuery functions,
- jQuery() has a variety of functions as attributes that make up the main API and which you can call on DOM nodes.

Here's a fragment of a simple HTML document:

```
<body>
  <h2>Staff Directory</h2>
  <ul>
    <li class="executive">Jim Jones
    <li class="executive">Alice Arnold</li>
    <li class="admin">Laura Lansbury
    <li class="admin">Paul Peterson</li>
  </ul>
</body>
```

Within the DOM, this would be structured as a <body> node with two children nodes: <h2> and <ul>. The <ul> would have four children, the <li> nodes. You may have noticed that some of the list item tags are not well-formed: they are not closed. From a DOM perspective, that actually doesn't matter: once a document has been parsed a node is a node, and the mark-up of the document matters only if any error within it causes the browser to structure the DOM in a way that was not intended; for example, turning the list item into an unintended sub-list.

With that basic understanding, it's time to dive into using jQuery with CoffeeScript to see how this works in practice, and why the fluent interface is a really great thing. Say that you wanted to add a cheesy effect to this staff directory page: when the visitor arrives, you'd like the names to fade in quickly rather than simply appear. You can do this in one line with jQuery; don't worry if this single line looks unintelligible right now, I'll break it down piece by piece:

```
$ -> $("li").hide().fadeIn(300)
```

There's actually a lot of combined magic here: some jQuery, and some CoffeeScript. Leave the `$ ->` idiom to one side for a moment; you look at how it actually works later. For now, all you need to know is that it means "here's some code to run after the DOM is ready". This part is really important. If this code runs as soon as the browser is able to execute it, the DOM would probably not be complete. The browser would not finish parsing the document (depending on where you placed the `<script>` tag referencing the code, amongst other factors).

So although you might want to alter the list items on the page, if the list items are not in the DOM yet you don't actually have anything to manipulate! You need to wait until the DOM is ready, and handily, the browser has a specific signal built in to trigger that.

The next part of the expression is no less magical:

```
$("li").hide().fadeIn(300)
```

There are four list items on the page, but apparently only one command here. You would ordinarily use a loop of some sort to address each list item one at a time (this is called iteration).

The basic secret here is that when you use a CSS-like selector with jQuery, it always returns a list of nodes. It might be an empty list, in which case nothing is found, or it might be a list with a single item, in which case only one node is found, but it will always be a list. When `$("li")` is called it returns a list of all the `<li>` nodes, and the list is "wrapped" in a jQuery object—so you can then call `hide()` and then `fadeIn()` on that returned list, and internally jQuery is performing the requested function on each node in the list. The loop is there—it's just hidden within jQuery.

Putting all this information together and translating it into rough English, this one line of CoffeeScript is saying, "When the DOM is ready, find every `<li>` node and hide it, then fade each one in."

THE "DOM READY" HANDLER

Earlier, I set the `$ ->` expression aside, and now it's time to come back and explain it fully. There are a couple of twists you haven't seen yet. The first is a little piece of jQuery magic: although you usually give `$()` a selector or set of DOM nodes, in one special case you can pass it a function instead.

Since virtually all scripts need to wait for the browser to get the DOM into a ready state, at some point, you can use jQuery's event handler support to do this. `document` is the name the browser gives the DOM structure and when the browser has finished parsing the HTML `document` receives a "ready" event.

To be notified of the event a handler needs to be attached to document, and a handler is simply a function that contains the code you want executed when the event happens. In this example the handler can look like this:

```
callback = -> $("li").hide().fadeIn(300)
```

This says that callback is a function that takes no arguments. When called the callback function manipulates the list on the page. To attach it to the DOM-ready event you just call $(document).ready(callback), and the browser is then responsible for calling the function when the DOM is ready.

This is such a common pattern, or idiom, that it has a special case: if you pass a function into $, jQuery assumes the function is a DOM-ready callback. That makes these two expressions equivalent:

```
$(document).ready(callback)
```

```
$(callback)
```

You now have virtually all the pieces of the puzzle. The last piece is that the callback function doesn't need to be assigned to a variable. Because you don't need to give it a name, it can be passed into jQuery directly:

```
$(-> $("li").hide().fadeIn(300))
```

Since the outer parentheses enclose the entire function definition they can be left out (ensuring you leave a space between $ and -> !) and finally you arrive at the original code.

You might be forgiven for wondering whether all this combined cleverness was worth it; sure, the code is short, but at what expense? In my opinion, this illustrates the natural fit of CoffeeScript to web programming and particularly when partnered with jQuery: in general, the lean syntax doesn't have much impact on readability or comprehension in these types of situations. Common patterns were designed to be terse simply because they are used time and again. There are some idioms in CoffeeScript that take some time to get used to; once you're over that particular hump things quickly start to feel natural, and you'll find the expressive power of the language is probably its key feature.

SELECTORS, NOW EVEN MORE USABLE

To recap one of the key pieces of the jQuery API: When you're selecting nodes from the DOM, you always get back a list (also called an array), no matter whether there are no nodes, one node, or many nodes. Fundamentally, a lot of jQuery functions operate on lists, and while chaining jQuery functions together hides that fact somewhat, that's what is happening underneath.

Sometimes the jQuery functions are not enough, and you need to step outside of the jQuery API. A common requirement is to operate in a more sophisticated way on a set of nodes, or to build data structures from them.

To demonstrate how CoffeeScript can make such tasks easier, take a look at something that you already know how to do in jQuery. Operating again on the staff directory document from earlier, this time the important executive names will fade in faster than the lowly admin staff:

```
$ ->
   for listitem in $("li")
       timer = if $(listitem).hasClass("executive") then 300 else 900
       $(listitem).hide().fadeIn(timer)
```

Instead of calling jQuery functions on the result of `$("li")` this code is manually iterating over the list of nodes returned. It's worth pointing out here that although the returned list is wrapped in a jQuery object, the individual nodes within the list are not. Therefore, you have to pass each node back into jQuery to start operating on it again, which is why `$(listitem)` is used and not simply `listitem`.

This code is quite clear and the way it works is obvious: It looks at every list item node it finds, and if the CSS class "executive" is set on the node, it reduces the fade-in timer to 300 milliseconds. It then hides the list items and fades them in as before.

However, notice the `if` clause being used as an expression! This highlights one of the slightly unusual features of CoffeeScript: Practically everything is an expression. Other languages often have two forms of `if`: the common form, used to control the flow of execution, and a less common one used in expressions. JavaScript, for example, uses `?:` as this second form, often called the ternary operator. In CoffeeScript, there is only one form, and you can use it as an expression.

COMPREHENSIONS

Now is the time for me to introduce an important CoffeeScript feature: comprehensions. If you haven't used a language with comprehensions before, they may take a little bit of time to get used to, but you'll find them to be one of the most useful tools in the toolbox.

At its heart, a list comprehension is a simple thing. It's an operation on a list, which often returns another list. The comprehension is similar to a standard loop, and if you've come across map functions in other languages you'll recognize familiar traits. The previous code could be rewritten with a list comprehension like this:

```
$(listitem).hide().fadeIn(
    if $(listitem).hasClass("executive") then 300 else 900
) for listitem in $("li")
```

At first glance, you might think that all that happened is that the loop has been described inside-out: The loop body comes first, and after it the expression creating the loop. However, the real power of the comprehension becomes clear when you need to iterate over a list of nodes (or any other list) and save the results somehow.

As an example, say you wanted to create a list of staff members by looking at the text nodes on your staff directory. The easy loop-based approach might look like this:

```
staff = []
for listitem in $("li")
    staff.push $(listitem).text()
```

This approach is the same kind of approach used in many other languages. First, you define a result variable which is an empty list, then iterate over the list of items you want to examine. For each iteration, you add to your result list. In this case, you pull the text out of the page, so that you end up with an array that looks like:

```
["Jim Jones", "Alice Arnold", "Laura Lansbury", "Paul Peterson"]
```

However, with a list comprehension, you can create this array more concisely and, arguably, using syntax that more closely matches your actual intention:

```
staff = ($(listitem).text() for listitem in $("li"))
```

The result of the list comprehension is stored in a variable that you haven't had to "pre-declare" in any way, and the code states pretty clearly the intention: `staff` is an array of the textual contents of each of the list item nodes you find.

This is such an important CoffeeScript idiom that you need to grasp it as early as possible, particularly when you're using jQuery. While I would not advise attempting to turn every loop in your code into a comprehension—that way madness lies—it is definitely worth asking "could this be a comprehension?" every time you write a loop, particularly if the loop is iterating over lists of nodes.

WORKING WITH FUNCTIONS

When you first start learning a new language, particularly if you don't have many under your belt already, you may think much about how to define your variables. The tendency is to use global scope, which means making the variable accessible anywhere in the code. You define it once, and then you can use it anywhere else.

It becomes quite hard to manage all your variable names once the code gets to a certain length, but more importantly it's very easy to re-use a variable accidentally and introduce bugs into the code. This style of coding is not maintainable.

In CoffeeScript, functions play two important roles. The first is to group blocks of code into reusable blocks that you can call, but the second is to introduce a new "scope" into the program: a way of restricting the visibility of variables. Here's a contrived example:

```
alterThing = ->
    thing = 1

alterThingAgain = ->
    thing = 2

alterThing()
```

```
alterThingAgain()

console.log thing
```

In this really simple code, two functions are defined, both of which set `thing` to a value, and both functions are called. The browser is then asked to output the value of `thing`. But what should the value be?

If you use global scope, the variable called `thing` would be the same variable everywhere. So first it would get set to 1, and next it would get set to 2, so when the browser outputs its value, it would output 2.

However, CoffeeScript doesn't use global scope. Variables are "scoped" to the enclosing function and although `alterThing` and `alterThingAgain` both alter a variable called `thing`, it's actually a different variable in each case. In fact, when the browser comes to output the value of `thing`, it's referring to a third variable that was never even defined, so the output is `undefined`.

Making a couple of changes to this contrived example demonstrates the really neat, useful property of "lexical scope" (which is the fancy name for this feature):

```
alter = ->
    thing = 0

    alterThing = ->
        thing = 1

    alterThingAgain = ->
        thing = 2

    alterThing()
    alterThingAgain()
    console.log thing   # outputs 2

alter()
console.log thing   # outputs undefined
```

When a function is defined in CoffeeScript, the variables it uses are declared as its inner scope. Then, when a child function is defined within a function, only those variables not already declared are created, giving the child function the ability to see the variables declared in its parent. The variables declared in the child are not visible to the parent, though.

In the previous example, the variable `thing` is created in the inner scope of the function `alter()`, and therefore is visible in the two functions defined within `alter()`. Thus, when you define `alterThing()`, it can "see" `thing` (set to 0 at the time you defined the function) and modify its value also. Functions inherit the scope from their parent.

Thus, when you call `alter()`, `thing` is set to 0 initially, then set to 1 by the call to `alterThing()`, and then set to 2 by the call to `alterThingAgain()`. When you output `thing` for the first time, the value is 2.

However, by the time you come to output thing again, it's no longer in your scope. The variable was defined within the scope of `alter()`. So the second `console.log()` call simply outputs `undefined`.

It's this last scenario that's actually the most interesting: by defining variables within the scope of a function, you can effectively hide those variables from the rest of the code. Hiding it means that you can't accidentally trample on the value in another section of the code, but it also means that you can't purposefully change it either.

This is the first example using "nested" functions. Depending on what languages you've used before, this nesting could be a novelty, but this is part of what it means to treat functions as first class citizens within the language. You can define a function practically anywhere, including within expressions.

Remember previously when I said that functions don't get names in CoffeeScript, and that you have to assign them to variables to call them by a name? Hopefully the implication of lexical scoping is clear: since functions in CoffeeScript can be referenced only after declaration by assigning them to variables, the scope of that variable name holding the function is the same as any other variable. In the previous example, although you could call `alter()`, you can't call `alterThing()` or `alterThingAgain()` from that same point in the code—for the same reason that thing itself was `undefined`.

FUNCTIONS FOR ENCAPSULATION

The general technical term for this kind of feature is *encapsulation*: that is to say, you can use these lexical scoping rules as a way of binding data (variables) and code (functions) together, so that you can treat them as black boxes—opaque blocks of logic that code outside can't really see into. You can place code like this on a web page with a good degree of certainty that it's not going to interfere with other code on the page (unless you designed it that way).

Commonly, you would use this system as a way of defining a web page *widget*—some single self-contained piece of UI and/or logic. It could be a piece of navigation such as a menu, or a more sophisticated interactive tool; it doesn't matter what the functionality is, the important point is that this is a really common pattern that you'll want to use again and again for this kind of work.

Frequently on websites, particularly on home pages, you'll see what's now called an "image slider" or gallery. Now look at how one can be created. The HTML to use is relatively simple and semantic; you don't need anything more than a list of the "slides" you want to show:

```
<!DOCTYPE html>
<html lang="en">
<head>
    <meta charset="utf-8">
    <title>Example CoffeeScript Slideshow</title>
    <script src="jquery-1.7.2.min.js" type="text/javascript"></script>
    <link rel="stylesheet" href="slideshow.css" type="text/css" />
    <script src="slideshow.js" type="text/javascript"></script>
```

```
</head>
<body>
    <ul class="slideshow">
        <li>
            <h1>Slide one</h1>
            <p>Some text here.</p>
        </li>
        <li>
            <h1>Slide two</h1>
            <p>This is great!.</p>
        </li>
        <li>
            <h1>Slide three</h1>
            <p>Do what?</p>
        </li>
    </ul>
</body>
</html>
```

In addition to defining an unordered list, references to jQuery and some CSS styles have been included on the page, as well as a notional slideshow.js that will be the result of the code compiled to JavaScript. The source `slideshow.coffee` might look like this, initially:

```
$ ->
    panels = $(".slideshow").find('li')
    active = 0  # which panel are we showing

    # initial panel positioning
    panels.css({left: '-400px'})
    $(panels[0]).css({left: '0px'})

    doRotation = ->
        # which panel to show next?
        next = if active == (panels.length - 1) then 0 else active + 1

        # move the active panel off-screen
        $(panels[active]).animate({left: '-400px'}, 1000)

        # put the next panel in position, and animate on-screen
        $(panels[next]).css({left: '400px'})
        $(panels[next]).animate({left: '0px'}, 1000)

        # treat this next panel as the 'active' one next loop
        active = next

    window.setInterval(doRotation, 4000)
```

There's quite a lot to like about this initial implementation: it's quite short and to the point. When the page loads and the DOM is ready it finds the panels you want to include in the slideshow and gives them an initial position: assuming that the slideshow is 400px wide (and yes, you'll revisit that assumption later!), it stacks them like cards to the left—effectively, off-screen.

A function called `doRotation()` is defined, and this is where the images on the page are swapped over. First, it starts a jQuery animation to move the current panel to the left—back onto the deck. Then, it starts by moving the next panel off-screen to the right (which happens immediately), and then animates this panel to move to the left also—this time, into the active window the user can see. The resulting "sliding" effect is shown in Figure 2-1.

Finally, a timer is set up so that the `doRotation()` function is called every 4 seconds, which ensures that the image slideshow continues round and round, forever, or at least until the browser window is closed.

Figure 2-1: This slideshow has two images mid-slide.

Source: Mozilla Firefox on Microsoft Windows 7

So, what are the problems with this implementation? Well, it's not very well encapsulated: although the code is in the DOM ready handler, it would be better to wrap it in its own function so that you could expand the ready handler to include other code without having to worry about the interaction. Generally, a single ready handler is better than having multiple separate ones: in particular, it makes the order of execution of code much clearer.

There are also a lot of assumptions built into the code. The code essentially presumes that there is only one slideshow on the page, that it is of a specific fixed width, and has specific fixed timings. It also assumes the slideshow works in a single direction. All of these things could be valid assumptions, but equally, you could design it to be slightly more generalized: if you're going to the effort of encapsulating the slideshow, you can also parameterize many of these characteristics so that you could change them later without having to change the code.

It's always good to challenge assumptions built into code. Quite often, an assumption in the code represents a potential bug. There's a good example in the slideshow: how many slides will the slideshow have? By referring to `panels.length` you're not assuming a specific number of panels, but by having a concept of "active panel" and "next panel" you are assuming that there are at least two panels. There is no check for this, and a single panel slideshow would certainly not work very well with this code!

KEEPING CODE DRY

One of the big advantages of parameterization is that it keeps the code DRY. If you haven't heard that term before, let me expand the acronym for you: Don't Repeat Yourself. Whenever you see code that looks the same or similar repeated, or the same value or expression repeated within the code, it means that there is an opportunity to remove some repetitiveness.

As an obvious example, the 400px width assumption is not only built into the code for the image slideshow, but it's there in three different places. At some point later, you might decide you want to change it to 600px: that would mean changing each reference, and if you missed a reference it would likely introduce a bug. That's why it's good to make it DRY.

Now have a look at a better—and DRYer—version of the slideshow. There are a number of new CoffeeScript-isms here too, so I'll take this piece by piece. The first thing to do, then, is to define an overall function to wrap this slideshow into a single neat package. It's going to be called `rotator()`, and to start a slideshow you pass it an arbitrary list node on which to work:

```
rotator = (slideshow) ->
    panels = $(slideshow).find('li')
    return if panels.length < 2  # can't rotate with fewer than 2 panels!
```

So far so simple: it looks for panels (the list items) and refuses to run if there are not enough to start a slideshow. Notice that the return call is conditional, and the expression to determine whether you do return can come after. You can write this type of code either way, but often simple statements like this read better in the suffixed-expression style.

Next, to parameterize this a bit further, you set up some configuration variables and read some data into them:

```
    # configurable attributes
    active = $(slideshow).data('start') ? 0
    direction = $(slideshow).data('direction') ? 1
    duration = $(slideshow).data('duration') ? 4000
    speed = $(slideshow).data('speed') ? 1000
```

If you haven't seen data attributes before, they're a new feature in HTML 5 which allows you to write custom attributes on nodes. In this example, it means that you can write the slideshow HTML as follows:

```
<ul class= "slideshow" data-start="3">
    <li
```

```
            <h1>Slide one</h1>
            <p>Some text here.</p>
        </li>
</ul>
```

Based on that example, the call to `$(slideshow).data("start")` returns the value 3. You can have as many data attributes as you like, and you can set them at run-time too. I stress only that they should be descriptive in nature; don't use them as a general-purpose data passing mechanism.

FUNCTION PARAMETERS AND EXISTENTIAL OPERATORS

The usual way of passing data into a function is to use the arguments of the function, and CoffeeScript offers some useful features that make function parameters even more powerful. Like other languages, CoffeeScript allows functions to be defined with "default" parameters:

```
default_greeting = "Hello"

greet = (greeting = default_greeting) ->
  console.log "#{greeting}!"

greet()    # outputs Hello!
greet "Hi" # outputs Hi!
```

Unlike other languages, CoffeeScript allows the default value of a parameter to be any expression: it could be a fixed value like a number or a string, but it could also be a variable (as above), a calculation, or even a call to another function. The expression is evaluated at run-time, every time the function is called.

The function parameters are not always the most appropriate place to construct a default value, but there are plenty of times when a default value is needed. In the previous example of parameterizing the slide show, the code looked like this:

```
    # configurable attributes
    active = $(slideshow).data('start') ? 0
```

Note at the end of the line the use of an existential operator: ?. You will likely have come across Boolean logic in expressions before; for example, `false or true` is a valid Coffee-Script expression and it evaluates to `true`. What is actually happening is that `or` first evaluates the truth of the expression to its left. If it's true, the entire expression evaluates to `true` automatically. If it's `false`, the entire expression evaluates to the truth of the expression on the right.

? operates in the same way as `or`, except that instead of testing for truth, it tests for existence: `true ? false` is a valid expression that evaluates to true, because the left-hand side is defined. The expression `false ? true` evaluates differently to the `or` equivalent though: since `false` is also defined, the expression evaluates to `false`.

This might seem like an academic difference, but for something like setting a sensible default to a variable it's crucial. A JavaScript developer might write an expression like `var test = $(node).data('test') || 1;` as a way of setting a default, and many times that works fine. However, because logical `or` tests for truth, not existence, it means that you can never override a default setting that evaluates to `true` with anything that evaluates to `false`—the most common example being `0`. With logical `or`, it is impossible to set test to `0`.

USING UTILITY FUNCTIONS

Functions in CoffeeScript are so easy to define they quickly become ubiquitous: written in good style, a non-trivial CoffeeScript program often uses a lot of small functions to make repetitive tasks easier. I call these *utility functions*, although there's nothing special about them in terms of CoffeeScript: it's just a natural consequence of the language.

Within this slideshow, you need to be able to change CSS attributes at run-time: the images can slide in either direction. By convention in this code, a direction of 1 means "slide from left to right", while any other value means "slide from right to left". Rather than hard-coding a specific set of styles for each direction it would be better to parameterize the CSS, but at this point you run into a problem with CoffeeScript.

As a convenience, CoffeeScript automatically quotes the keys within objects. Most of the time this is incredibly useful:

```
css = {left: '-400px'}
console.log css.left  # outputs -400px
```

However, it means you can't write code like this:

```
direction = "left"
css = {direction: "0px"}

console.log css.direction   # outputs 0px
console.log css.left        # undefined
console.log css[direction]  # undefined, equivalent to css.left
```

The key cannot be evaluated when defining the object, only when accessing values (when in fact any expression can be used). This slideshow will be updating the CSS attributes a lot though, so it makes sense to wrap this logic into a utility function:

```
css_setting = (value) ->
    style = {}
    style[if direction == 1 then 'left' else 'right'] = value
    return style
```

Calling this function with a specific value returns the object with that value set under the key `left` or `right`, depending on the direction the slideshow is set up for. Instead of hard-coding the object `{left: '-400px'}` (for example) you can now write `css_setting '-400px'` which is slightly longer but more powerful.

With this utility function available, you can now move the slideshow panels into their initial position on either the left or the right, depending which direction they need to slide. As in the original slide example, panels that are off screen stack on one side like a set of cards:

```
# move panels into initial position
$(panel).css(css_setting '100%') for panel in panels
$(panels[active]).css(css_setting '0px')
```

Now, the code moves all of the panels off-screen and then specifically moves the active one back to where it was. Since active is now a configurable variable, you can choose which panel is the one to start with, and it could be any of them, from first to last.

Finally, you're back to defining the function which does the main work. The first line of the function deserves a little bit of description:

```
doRotation = ->
    # which panel to show next?
    next = (active + direction + panels.length) % panels.length
```

The calculation for which panel should be next has become a lot more complicated, because you need to take into account the fact that you could be working through the panels backwards! This can be broken into separate steps:

1. Calculate next as active + direction.
2. Check that next isn't greater than panels.length (and reset to 0 if it is).
3. Check that next isn't less than 0 (and reset to panels.length if it is).

This type of range-checking is the typical ground for an off-by-one bug, so instead an expression is used, relying on the modulo operator % to provide the bounds checking.

If you haven't seen modulo before, its primary useful property is that it can be used to wrap a number series between 0 and some maximum. For example, when counting from 0 to 7, the resulting series modulo 4 would go from 0 to 3 twice (0%4 is 0, 3%4 is 3, 4%4 is 0 again, 5%4 is 1 again). This is often used in web development where repetitive patterns are used—a loop value modulo 2 is often used to color the alternate rows in a table, for example.

In this example, calculating the result modulo the number of panels ensures the counter never runs off the positive end of the array: It's always wrapped back to 0. When working backwards through the panels though, modulo itself doesn't offer much help—it's quite happy to work through negative numbers, rather than wrapping –1 back to the number of panels. To stop this from happening, the number of panels is added before taking the modulo, ensuring that the counter is positive and doesn't affect the result. (You might want to play with some of these numbers on the CoffeeScript REPL to convince yourself this is correct!)

The basic CSS movement and animation is much like the original, except that you use the various parameters instead of fixed values, and instead of using a fixed width you use the value 100%:

```
    # move the active panel off-screen
    $(panels[active]).animate(css_setting '-100%', speed)
    # put the next panel in position, and animate on-screen
    $(panels[next])
        .css(css_setting '100%')
        .animate(css_setting '0px', speed)

    # treat the next panel as the 'active' one next loop
    active = next

  window.setInterval(doRotation, duration)
```

That's the entirety of the slideshow code; the only thing remaining is to find slideshow nodes on the page after the page has loaded, and apply the slideshow:

```
$ -> rotator(slideshow) for slideshow in $.find(".slideshow")
```

This slideshow widget is much, much better. The page can have multiple slideshows, illustrated in Figure 2-2, running in different directions, at different speeds, and with different panels. All of that is entirely configurable, and the slide shows don't interact with each other at all. The API for all of this is all extremely simple as well: it's straightforward to set up a slideshow on a node in the DOM, and the configuration can be stated simply in the HTML.

Figure 2-2: This page has multiple slideshows, moving in different directions at different speeds.

Source: Mozilla Firefox on Microsoft Windows 7

CLEANER CLICK HANDLERS

Encapsulation is all well and good, and keeping things in opaque boxes is a nice technique for ensuring that one part of a web page cannot interfere with another. However, that's not always what you want: most pages are more interactive than that, and to interact with something you need a way in, as it were. You can provide this and still keep the code nicely encapsulated.

Ever since JavaScript was first built into the browser, there has been a way to trigger JavaScript functions from clicks on a page from links, buttons, or other page elements. A link with such a click trigger would have looked something like this:

```
<a href="javascript: doSomething();">…</a>
```

This method worked relatively well, but it came with a downside: it put code in the HTML markup, which meant that if you ever wanted to change the name of the function you had to do it in a few places.

Better ways were developed, and the current state of the art is the jQuery event handler that can be applied to a variety of page nodes, not just links and buttons. Like most other jQuery features, you find the nodes you're interested in by using a selector, and the `click()` function allows you to attach your own click handler directly to them, looking something like this:

```
$("a#clickable").click (event) ->
    event.preventDefault()
    console.log "Clicked!"
```

This click handler would be attached to a node written in HTML as `<a href="..." id="clickable">...</a>`. Usually, when you click a link the browser takes you to the URL specified in the `href` attribute. However, when a specific click handler is attached that's usually undesirable behavior, so the first thing the handler does is prevent the default action from occurring.

The great thing about these types of handlers is that you can define them within other functions, and they inherit the parent scope! Handlers like these can be used to interact with encapsulated pieces of functionality, so let's take a look at exactly how that can work. Going back to the encapsulated image slideshow, say that you want to add a button to the page that will allow you to pause and then un-pause the slideshow at any given time.

The main rotation function can stay as currently written. The main thing to change is the way that it gets run. Recall that it doesn't run constantly; rather, you have a timer setup that calls it every once in a while:

```
window.setInterval(doRotation, duration)
```

This code runs forever and is not suitable for what you want: certainly a way of starting the slideshow is needed, but you also need a way of stopping it again later. You can provide a button for triggering the stop, and for ease-of-use you can make the text on the button reflect the action that occurs if it is clicked. First place a button on the page to control this:

```
control = $('<button></button>').insertAfter(slideshow)
```

You haven't seen jQuery called like this before now: You've seen nodes passed to it, you've seen CSS selectors passed to it, and you've also seen the special case of passing a function to it. But in this instance a fragment of HTML markup is being passed in as a string. What's that doing? This is another nifty jQuery shortcut: in the same way that a browser parses an HTML document into a DOM tree, this shortcut parses an HTML fragment into a DOM fragment, ready to insert into the DOM. The call to `insertAfter()` does what you would expect: it takes the DOM fragment that was just created, and inserts it into the DOM after the slideshow node that was originally passed into the `rotator()` function.

With the control button in place, you can now create functions to start and stop the timer, which calls the slideshow rotator. `setInterval()` passes back a reference to the timer when it is created and can later be used to cancel it:

```
timer = null

doStart = ->
    timer = window.setInterval(doRotation, duration)
    control.text("Pause")

doStop = ->
    window.clearInterval timer
    timer = null
    control.text("Unpause")
```

The variable timer is set to `null` to begin with to ensure that you have it in scope. Without that, with the lexical scoping rules, timer in `doStart()` would be a different variable to `timer` in `doStop()`, and the whole thing would not work.

All that is left to do is set up the click handler and set the slideshow in motion at the start:

```
$(control).click ->
    if timer then doStop() else doStart()

doStart()
```

No `preventDefault()` is needed on this handler, because a plain `<button>` has no default action. By defining a specific internal function to start the slideshow itself, the startup and the click handler are quite DRY as well. At only one point in the code is the slideshow actually started, even though that might start in two different circumstances.

GENERAL EVENT HANDLING

As you might imagine, there are many different types of events other than simple mouse clicks. The click handler setup is actually a shortcut to a more general form of event handler:

```
$(control).on "click", (event) ->
    if timer then doStop() else doStart()
```

jQuery's on() function is incredibly flexible, handling not only clicks and double-clicks, but other types of mouse movement or input, form submission, and other browser events; it's really worth working through the jQuery API in this area and taking in all of the available events.

There is another jQuery feature worth mentioning at this point. Most events on a page bubble: The user clicks on a button, and that button receives the click event, but that click event also registers against the button's DOM parent, and against the parent's parent, so on and so forth unless some piece of code deliberately prevents the event from bubbling further.

jQuery ensures that the bubbling happens consistently on the various browsers and allows you to attach handlers to nodes so that the handlers pick up these events from children nodes. This gives you two great options at the same time:

- An ability to write a single handler that can process events from a variety of different DOM nodes beneath it, and
- An ability to listen for events from DOM nodes that will be created later on in the code.

Generally, the fewer handlers a page has, the better the performance; although an event that has to bubble up through a number of nodes before it reaches a handler will have a negative impact on performance. It's good to strike a balance here.

As an example, this is what a click handler on the slideshow panels could look like:

```
$(slideshow).on "click", "li", (event) ->
    # do something
```

The handler is placed on the slideshow node itself, but as well as giving jQuery the event you want to receive ("click") you also give it a CSS selector. Now, any click event on a child node of slideshow that matches that CSS selector triggers this event handler.

If at any stage you find yourself adding handlers to sets of nodes using jQuery, particularly where the number of potential nodes is very high, see if you can use this delegated event handler style instead. This is a very efficient method of handling events.

PAGE EVENTS

You've seen a variety of different ways of incorporating events into your code, but there's an important class of event that hasn't been covered yet: synthetic events. Although most events in a browser occur because the user has done something—clicked a button, entered some information into a form—it's possible for the code on the page to generate and receive custom events unrelated to any specific DOM node on the page.

These types of events have a number of different uses, but the use case discussed here is the ability to pass messages in and out of encapsulated code.

Not all types of page interactivity are like the slideshow developed earlier in this chapter. Not only is the code encapsulated, but the user interface to it is pretty encapsulated too. It exists in a specific area on the page, and doesn't interact with another part of the page. It's nice to have a feature that can be that well isolated, but it's not always possible to isolate a feature so completely.

As an example, say you have a page that contains three different slideshows, but that you need a single button that can pause all of them. The naïve approach to this would be to create a button before any of the slideshows are created, and then pass this button to each slideshow so that it can attach a click handler to it or agree on some common selector so that each slideshow can find it. Either would work, but it would be a bit messy, and it's not an approach that will scale well to more complicated page interactions.

This is where custom events come in. Instead of attaching separate handlers to one button, you can simply have the slideshows listen for a custom event, and have your single controlling button issue this custom event.

On the slideshow itself, you can implement those controls with two simple listeners for some custom events:

```
$('body').bind 'slideshow.start', ->
    doStart()

$('body').bind 'slideshow.stop', ->
    doStop()
```

These event handlers look like any other event handlers, except that the event being listened for is specific to the slideshow code. The event handler is attached to the <body> node on the page by convention: To listen for the events, the handler needs to be attached to a node on the DOM. <body> is convenient because it's always going to be on the page, and if events are triggered on it but not caught by any listener they don't end up bubbling very far; there should be only one parent. It's useful to choose a different node if the events should somehow be private within a piece of code, but the page body is generally a good choice.

Using these custom events makes it quite easy to place a single control on the page to control every slideshow. To stop all the slideshows you can now do this:

```
control = $('<button>Stop all</button>')
$('body').append(control)
$(control).click ->
    $('body').trigger("slideshow.stop")
```

A button is created, placed on the page, and a click handler attached to it which triggers the custom event—it's as simple as that. This really straightforward mechanism lets you plug different pieces of code together. It's even possible to send additional information through with the custom event:

```
$('body').on 'custom', (event, num, obj) ->
  console.log num  # outputs 1
  console.log obj  # outputs {2=3}


$('body').trigger 'custom', [1, {2: 3}]
```

Are there downsides to custom events? Admittedly, yes. When developing code using custom events, be aware that the event names and any data that you pass through with the event effectively become a kind of API for the code—a contract between caller and callee. If the name of the custom event is changed, any existing triggers no longer make it work. As with any other kind of API, a public function, such as events used in this style, should ideally be documented and the convention for triggering it should change rarely.

Be aware that triggering and listening for custom events is creating a kind of coupling between different pieces of code. The coupling is quite loose, but it's there nonetheless. Custom events are best used in scenarios where the event may not be triggered and, more especially, when the event may not be heard or may be heard by many handlers. When events are triggered by a single specific piece of code, and heard by another specific piece of code, they're becoming surrogates for function calls and that's generally a sign of bad design.

FEATURE DETECTION FOR PRACTICAL POLYFILL

Before I finish this chapter on some of the specifics of jQuery, it's important to talk about one final tool for the toolbox: the polyfill. Inspired by the legions of home improvers the world over, the term *polyfill* is used to describe small pieces of code that cover up the deficiencies of specific browsers: literally, filling in the cracks.

Modern web browsers have come a long way, but people still use older versions that don't directly support features that are available in up-to-date software. The general idea with a polyfill is to provide a piece of code as a fallback for these older browsers that either implements a feature or provides an effective substitute.

This type of approach is not to be confused with browser-sniffing. That practice, examining the browser's version and enabling (or disabling) features for specific browsers, is quite rightly frowned upon. It prevents code from being broadly forward compatible, and relies on the original developer having detected the browser correctly. It also misses the point: The problem isn't the browser version per se, but the ability (or not) for a browser to support a specific feature.

So, rather than attempt to sniff the browser, the better approach is to use feature detection, where you detect whether a browser supports a particular feature before attempting to use it.

DETECTING CSS FEATURES

One of the latest and greatest features from CSS3 that has begun to see wide support is the concept of the CSS Transition. Transitions allow you to write specific types of simple animation with no code. You simply define them within a page's stylesheet.

The benefits of this type of approach are numerous: Controlling animation from within the browser's JavaScript engine requires code to execute many times per second to "run" the animation and position elements correctly for the next frame, which means less time for running other parts of the code. Additionally, browsers tend to have access to graphical acceleration hardware, which means that the animation effect can often be offloaded to the graphics card, reducing the load created by the browser but also making the effect smoother.

The general approach for detecting a CSS feature is simply to examine the DOM and look to see if a specific CSS style is available, and this is easy to do in CoffeeScript, making liberal use of the existential operators.

Picking a node on the DOM is the first step, so that you can examine the various properties available within `node.style`. That makes up the first few steps of the feature detection function. It's possible that you can't find a DOM node, although it would be highly unusual within a browser. But it is more possible in an environment outside of a browser such as node.js. It is also possible that the DOM node doesn't have CSS styles defined, so the function returns `false` early in either of those eventualities. The existential operator can be used to test whether a node has been found and then whether it has a style property:

```
supportsCss = (property) ->
    node = document.body ? document.documentElement
    return false if not node?.style?
```

If the code gets past that, it can test for specific CSS feature support. In the first instance, that's easy: if the property asked for exists, return `true`. However, CSS isn't quite that simple! A feature could be implemented but hidden behind a vendor prefix. This is often done when a feature is being tested, or if the support is not yet 100% complete. It's up to you to determine whether to test for vendor prefixed styles, but this is how you do it:

```
    return true if node.style[property]?

    prefixes = ['Moz', 'Webkit', 'Khtml', 'O', 'ms', 'Icab']
    return true for prefix in prefixes when node.style["#{prefix}#{property}"]?

    return false
```

Testing the various prefixes uses the most complex list comprehension you've seen yet, and it's worth fully understanding what that line is doing. The when clause is filtering out the prefixed properties that do not exist; if a prefixed property does exist the return clause is triggered. And, if none of the properties tested exists, the function simply returns `false`.

It's straightforward to use a piece of detection like this in practice. Generally, you have the code that you want to run and a fallback. Imagine a version of the slideshow that defines doCssRotate() to do a pure CSS Transition instead of a jQuery animation. Here is the implementation of doStart() that would use this:

```
animator = if cssSupport('Transition') then doCssRotate else doRotate

doStart = ->
    timer = window.setInterval(animator, duration)
    control.text("Pause")
```

You wouldn't implement your own polyfill every time you needed one. To do so would be a bit wasteful. It is essential, however, to know how they're used and when to use them. For a much more in-depth system for polyfill, take a look at the modernizr library at http://modernizr.com/.

SUMMARY

jQuery is an excellent library and quite worthy of a book in its own right, so needless to say the coverage I can give it in a chapter of this size is only the tip of the iceberg. CoffeeScript was designed for interactive event-driven web application code like this, and I hope it is beginning to seem clear why I think it's such a great fit for jQuery users.

A lot of this chapter is devoted to the use of functions. It's probably a stretch to label Coffee-Script as "functional programming" in the true sense of the word, but using functions appropriately is crucial to good CoffeeScript style and will certainly make you think about problems in a more functional way if you don't already.

3

WORKING WITH FORMS

BY NO MEANS are forms the most exciting part of web development. Indeed, although data entry is probably one of the least exciting technological fields, it's still one of the most crucial. And armed with a few smart techniques and CoffeeScript, you can do a lot with forms with very little effort.

For a number of years, it seemed as though the technical standards for web forms had stagnated. Although forms were implemented consistently across browsers and could generally be styled using CSS in any way a developer pleased, there were also a number of missing features that led people to develop client-side solutions, using JavaScript, to address many of the shortcomings.

HTML 5 has changed that, and new features for data form features available in recent browsers can be adapted for older clients, using standard polyfill techniques. However, form logic for the client-side definitely still plays a role, and this chapter covers the tools and techniques of CoffeeScript and jQuery as they apply to forms. By the end of the chapter, you'll know how to create interactive forms with sophisticated features to improve the user experience and how to apply these techniques to a variety of forms commonly implemented on websites.

BASIC HTML5 FORMS

Before looking at how to work with forms in CoffeeScript, take a look at the forms themselves and how to implement them in HTML 5. Giving users the ability to log in to a website by providing a username and password is a common feature, and the form for that isn't complicated:

```
<body>
    <fieldset>
        <legend>Enter your username &amp; password to log in</legend>

        <form method="POST" id="login">
            <p><label>Username:
                <input type="text" name="username" autofocus required>
            </label></p>

            <p><label>Password:
                <input type="password" name="password" required>
            </label></p>

            <p><input type="submit" value="Log In"></p>
        </form>
    </fieldset>
</body>
```

Most of this is valid HTML 4 as well, so one immediately apparent feature is that HTML 5 forms are very backward-compatible. That is, new features are added in a way that allows browsers to work even if they don't understand the new features. For you, as a developer, this is excellent news—HTML 5 form features can be deployed today, and where the new features are crucial to the functioning of the form, they can be polyfilled on older browsers.

Two specific HTML 5 features are used on the previous form. First, setting the `autofocus` attribute on the username field asks the browser to immediately focus the username field for data entry. This saves users from having to select the input before they start typing. Second, both input fields have the `required` attribute set, indicating to the browser that they must be filled in before the form can be submitted. Before HTML 5, both of these new features would have required some form of client-side JavaScript.

COLLECTING FORM DATA

The first step to using a form in any way is to be able to see what data the form holds. This can happen at a number of stages. It's possible for the browser to watch the data as the user enters it and to intercept the submission of the form data before it's sent to the web server. It's also possible to take the process of data collection and form submission entirely away from the browser and to handle it manually using AJAX techniques.

To begin with, check the tools jQuery provides to investigate the data held within a form. The most immediately useful feature is `$.serializeArray()`, which returns the data held in the form as an array. On the login form, the data returned could look like this:

```
[
    { 'name': 'username', 'value': 'alex' },
    { 'name': 'password', 'value': 'notverysecure' }
]
```

This is an array of objects, each with a name and value, and each corresponding to a single
`<input>` on the form. At first glance, this isn't the most useful representation. The more
obvious structure for this data is

```
{ 'username': 'alex', 'password': 'notverysecure' }
```

A single object with direct keys and values from the form initially makes some sense. However, it's not always the case that a form includes only a single input with a given name. Some
types of `<select>` can have multiple values, and in fact it's also possible to have other types
of input with duplicate names—check boxes, for example.

Because different forms need to be handled in different ways, jQuery doesn't hold a particular
opinion on how your data should be structured. It simply returns an object for each input
with a value set, and you get back the list of objects.

Thankfully, CoffeeScript makes it very easy to process this data and turn it into a form that's
more useful, and as you might have guessed, the easiest tool to use for this is the comprehension. The list of objects can be "flattened" to a single object:

```
data = {}
data[input.name] = input.value for input in form.serializeArray()
```

This is a useful step to take for most simple forms; the alternative involves searching through
the array of objects returned by `serializeArray()` something like this:

```
inputs = form.serializeArray()
username = input.value for input in inputs when input.name == "username"
password = input.value for input in inputs when input.name == "password"
```

As well as not being terribly pretty code, and certainly not DRY, this is an inefficient solution.
It's often easy to forget that a comprehension is, at heart, a loop. Every time an input value is
pulled out of the list like this, it means that the entire list has been looped over—a lot of work
with little end result.

VALIDATING FORM DATA

Usually, the first requirement you have when adding a form to a page is to do a minimal
amount of validation. This could be for a number of reasons. For example, it's usually not
sensible to allow an empty form to be submitted, but more than that, if it looks as though the
user has entered data that isn't suitable for some reason, it's good practice to give the user
feedback as quickly as possible.

HTML 5 has a number of useful validation features. The `required` attribute does what it says and ensures that specific form elements must be complete before being submitted. Also, new input types are available, such as `email`, `url`, `tel`, `number`, `date`, and `search`. Primarily, the new input types allow the browser to alter its user interface to suit the user. For example, on a mobile phone, when data is entered into an `<input type="tel">`, the virtual keyboard that pops up will likely contain only numbers, and may also offer the ability to look up a telephone number in the user's address book. But, as a secondary feature, these new types of form input also offer some amount of validation (varying from browser to browser) that the data entered is of the right type.

As good as HTML 5 is, client-side validation still has a role in scripting. In some instances, there will be requirements for data that cannot be expressed in the HTML—for example, requiring that at least one of two inputs be filled in. Nothing prevents you from using both the HTML 5 markup and client-side validation at the same time, though—they're complementary techniques and usually don't interfere with each other.

Here's one way to validate the login form using scripting. This code also ensures that the password is a certain length and contains numeric as well as alphabetical characters. Generally, this kind of stringency is applied to the registration form rather than the login form, but it demonstrates the principle:

```coffeescript
$ ->
    form = $('form#login')

    form.submit (event) ->
        data = {}
        data[input.name] = input.value for input in form.serializeArray()

        if data.password.length < 6
            invalid_reason = "Password is too short!"
        if not /\d/.test(data.password)
            invalid_reason = "Password must contain a number!"
        if not /\w/.test(data.password)
            invalid_reason = "Password must contain a letter!"

        if invalid_reason?
            event.preventDefault()
            alert invalid_reason
```

As usual, the code waits for the DOM to be ready and then attaches a submission event handler to the form. When the user attempts to submit the form, this event handler will run.

The validation process is straightforward: Collect the data as it's entered into the form and then check data items you're interested in. If the validation fails, let the user know why and prevent submission of the form.

This example uses validation as a type of security measure. By checking that the password meets the system rules, it can pick up typos and missed characters before the data is submitted to the server. You'll see similar rules put in place for the user registration example later on. It's important to note that client-side validation is to help the user only; it doesn't and cannot form part of any security system, because it's trivial to bypass. Don't ever rely on this type of validation to enforce security on a system you develop!

SYSTEMATIZING VALIDATION

It's tempting to write a function to validate a specific form and attach that as a submission handler to perform validation, but this approach tends to lead to repetitive code. A better approach is to think about the separate components of validation and how they can be joined up.

Working from the bottom up, clearly validation functions are needed. They will take a value and return true or false based on whether the value can be validated. Some sort of description or mapping is needed to determine which validation functions need to be used on which form elements, and lastly some overall function is needed to pull the whole thing together.

The description or mapping is the first place to start because it can describe the validation you want to do as a simple data structure:

```
loginValidation = [
  {
    name: 'password'
    humanName: 'Password'
    valid: [
        {type: 'length', config: {min: 6} },
        {type: 'regex', config: {regex: /\d/,
                                 message: 'must contain a number'}},
        {type: 'regex', config: {regex: /\w/,
                                 message: 'must contain a letter'}},
    ]
  }
]
```

It's often worth thinking about a problem first by considering sensible data structures that will be needed to solve the problem. In this example, the validation rules, or *schema,* are simply an array of objects, and the intention is to have one object per each piece of data that needs to be validated. However, each piece of data might need to be validated against a few rules; hence, each object has an array called `valid` that contains each rule you want to validate the piece of data against.

Each validator needs different information in order to perform the validation, which is why there is a `config` object on each rule—the specifics of each validation are pushed down against each rule.

The next pieces needed are the functions that will validate the individual values. These functions will need to be given the value, of course, and they'll also need to receive that config object to know exactly how to validate the date. It's possible to make them return true or false based on whether the value validates. In this case, I'm making it a bit more sophisticated by also returning a reason for the validation failure, where appropriate:

```coffeescript
validateLength = (value, config) ->
    if config.min?
        return [false, 'too short'] if value.length < config.min
    if config.max?
        return [false, 'too long'] if value.length > config.max
    return [true, '']

validateRegex = (value, config) ->
    return [false, config.message] if not config.regex.test(value)
    return [true, '']
```

It's important that the validators have the same *function signature*. That is to say, they take the same arguments. The code decides at runtime, based on the schema, which validator to call, and if each validator needs to be called differently, a great deal of complexity is created. Now I wrap these validators into a single object, where the key is the name of the validator and the value is the validation function itself:

```coffeescript
validators =
    length: validateLength
    regex: validateRegex
```

In the schema, instead of referencing the functions directly, I've referenced them by a name. This `validators` object is mapping the name to the actual function call. It's also possible to define the validation functions first and then use the function names directly in the schema; however, that couples the code closely into the data structure and makes it more difficult to encapsulate the validation later.

The pieces for the validator are now all in place. The validation functions themselves have been defined, and there's a format for the schema that describes which functions to call on what data. The validator needs both the data items to validate and the schema by which to validate it:

```coffeescript
validate = (data, schema) ->
    valid = true
    messages = []

    for input in schema
        for test in input.valid
            result = validators[test.type](data[input.name], test.config)
            if not result[0]  # value is not valid
                valid = false
                messages.push("#{input.humanName} #{result[1]}")
    return [valid, messages]
```

The main body of the validator is not doing much. It iterates through every input object in the schema, looking at each rule attached to it in turn. If the data does not validate, it sets the entire result to false and adds the reason the validation failed to a list of messages. When it's done, it returns the result and the list of messages (which hopefully are empty).

It's now really simple to attach the validation schema to the form, and this is done after the DOM is ready, as usual:

```
$ ->
    form = $('form#login')

    form.submit (event) ->
        data = {}
        data[input.name] = input.value for input in form.serializeArray()

        result = validate(data, loginValidation)

        if not result[0]
            event.preventDefault()
            alert result[1].join(", ")
```

The submission handler is a lot simpler now. It collects the data from the form, sends it to the validator along with the validation schema, and if the result is not true, it displays the reason—or reasons!—why, and halts the form submission.

Overall, there's a lot more up-front code in this validator than the simple validation function originally attached as the submission handler. Most of this code is entirely reusable though. To validate another form, you just need to define a new schema for the validation and add the validator as a submission handler. The validation can be used again and again on many different forms, and as it's reused, the overall amount of code will be much less.

COMMON FORM TECHNIQUES

So far the focus of this chapter has been on collecting and validating form data and the basic knowledge of forms required to make use of them. Now it's time to go a bit further. Client-side scripting is useful for providing validation beyond the capability of the browser, but it's capable of a lot more than that. This section looks at how you can extend form functionality to enhance the user experience even further, using the techniques already covered.

DISPLAYING VALIDATION RESULTS INLINE

Validation is a process that gives users information. The point is not to get in their way (although from users' perspectives, it might seem like that sometimes), but to make sure that, as far as possible, the data they submit to the server is correct.

The code examples covered so far do a reasonable job of validating the data, but they do a poor job of communicating problems back to the user. Utilizing the generally despised native `alert()` dialog when validation fails doesn't result in an excellent user interface.

A much better idea is to provide feedback to the user, which you can do using a combination of validation and supporting CSS styles. A common scheme that you may have seen before uses colored borders around input elements to denote their current validation status, as shown here:

- No border on an empty element indicates that it hasn't been validated and isn't a required input.
- A yellow border on an empty element indicates it hasn't been validated but is a required input.
- A red border, with associated warning message, indicates that validation failed on the input.
- A green border with a green tick following the input indicates validation is successful.

That last point is crucial. Relying on colors alone for this type of task is generally a bad idea, but particularly so in this case because a percentage of the population are red-green color blind. Not being able to easily distinguish "valid" and "invalid" states would be a poor user experience indeed! (See Figure 3-1.)

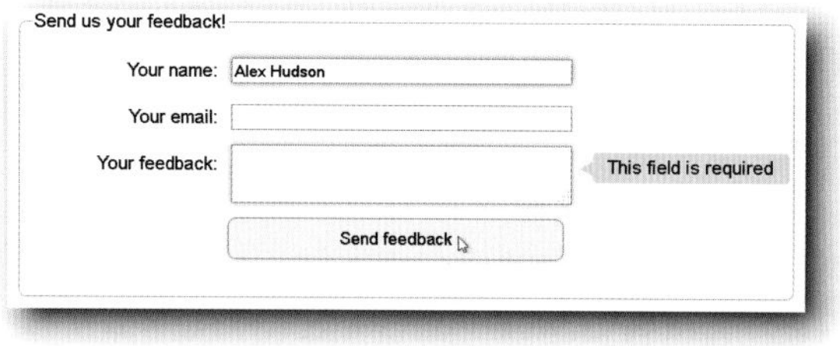

Figure 3-1: This is one way your input form might look.

Source: Mozilla Firefox on Microsoft Windows 7

Most of the validation states can be controlled directly with CSS classes, and jQuery provides the capability to set and unset these states from the code. In order to display helpful messages, though, an additional capability to insert the messages into the DOM is required. You can use a utility function like this:

```
addWarning = (node, message) ->
    label = $("<label role='alert' for='#{node.name}'>#{message}</label>")
    $(label).insertBefore(node)
```

This function does little more than insert another label before a given form input, which itself can be styled using CSS to make it appear in the correct position. `role='alert'` is a little piece of accessibility coding to give users on speaking web browsers a chance to understand why this label has suddenly popped up.

The core validation function is going to change substantially. Instead of passing in a set of data, the first change is to pass in the form so that invalid inputs can be identified and warning labels placed against them. In some instances, an empty but required input will also deserve a warning, so an additional parameter is added to the function, defaulting to false:

```
validate = (form, schema, warnRequired=false) ->
    valid = true
```

The goal of this validator is to alter the user interface of the form to reflect the current validation state. So, the first order of business is to undo any previous changes, because they may be out of date now:

```
    # remove any validation UI
    form.find('label[role="alert"]').remove()
    form.find(':input').removeClass('valid invalid')
```

jQuery's `:input` selector is incredibly useful. It matches any form input, whether it's an `<input>` node or something more exotic like a `<select>`. The code doesn't use `$(':input')`, though, because it would select literally all form inputs on the page. Using `find()` means you're looking only at those DOM nodes that are children of the form node.

The next step is to work through the validation schema again, performing the validation tests but now adding CSS classes where appropriate:

```
    for input in schema
        messages = []

        inputNode = form.find("input[name=#{input.name}]")
        value = inputNode.val()
        if value == "" and not inputNode.attr('required')
            next  # empty, optional, inputs are valid

        for test in input.valid
            result = validators[test.type](value, test.config)
            if not result[0]  # value is not valid
                valid = false
                messages.push("#{input.humanName} #{result[1]}")

        if messages.length > 0  # then this input is invalid
            addWarning inputNode, messages.join(", ")
            inputNode.addClass("invalid")
        else
            inputNode.addClass("valid")
```

Because the validator is now operating directly on the form, most of the code is concerned with querying or adjusting the DOM node associated with the form input. The core validation test is the same as before, but it's skipped on empty optional inputs, so that the validator can be activated before the user has finished the form. Without this skipping, the validator will complain that inputs the user hasn't reached yet haven't been completed—annoying users, rather than helping them.

One validation task remains: to find inputs that are required but that don't have a specific entry in the schema associated with them. If they've been completed, you need to ensure they are marked as valid:

```
# find any non-validated required fields, and mark them valid if filled
for inputNode in form.find(':input[required]')
    value = $(inputNode).val()
    if value != "" and not $(inputNode).hasClass("invalid")
        $(inputNode).addClass("valid")
    else if value == ""
        valid = false
        if warnRequired
            addWarning inputNode, "This field is required"

return valid
```

Note the new `warnRequired` parameter. If set to `true`, it marks empty but required input with a warning as though the input were invalid. This alerts users about missed inputs when they attempt to submit the form, but users shouldn't be bothered with these warnings before they've finished the form—the input is already marked with a yellow border, indicating that it's required.

The final change is that this validator simply returns true or false, rather than return the various validation messages. Because the messages are now being inserted directly into the page, there's no need to pass them back.

CONTINUOUS VALIDATION

Triggering validation on form submissions makes a lot of sense. After users input all the data that they think is required, checking their work before sending it back to the server is logical. That's not the only way of validating, though. Running validation earlier gives the user an opportunity to correct data they've just entered.

The validation code just discussed goes to some pains to avoid unnecessary pop-up warnings. It can be triggered at any point, and it should adjust the form so that potential problems with the data entered are highlighted, but it won't complain about data not yet entered.

Because the validator can now run at any point, it makes sense to run it early and often, as shown here:

```
$ ->
    form = $('form#feedback')

    validationHandler = (event) ->
        warnRequired = event?.type == "submit"
        if not validate(form, loginValidation, warnRequired)
            event?.preventDefault()
```

```
form.submit validationHandler
form.on 'keyup', ':input', validationHandler
validationHandler()
```

The `validationHandler()` utility function is new and slightly more sophisticated than event handlers covered previously. Notice that references to `event` have an existential property accessor embedded—`event?.type` is used instead of `event.type`.

Without the existential operator, attempting to access `event.type` is essentially asking for the `type` property of the `undefined` value, which will generate an error in most browsers. You can write this instead:

```
warnRequired = if event then event.type ==  "submit" else false
```

This is such a common pattern that CoffeeScript provides another idiom: using `?` to say "give me this object property, but if this object isn't defined, just give me undefined". This process is called "soaking" because it "soaks up" the errors that would otherwise be generated without testing the object first. This allows you to call this utility function directly or as a normal event handler. When called directly, no event object exists, so the soaked access ensures errors are not thrown.

Before moving on from this validator, one of the event bindings deserves special mention:

```
form.on 'keyup', ':input', validationHandler
```

This is a delegated event handler. The handler is attached to the form node and listens for any children that match the given selector—that is to say, any input on the form. Every keyup event now triggers the validation handler.

In practice, this means that as users fill out input, it's validated as they type. Changes to the input are picked up almost immediately, and users get instant feedback about what they've entered. (See Figure 3-2.)

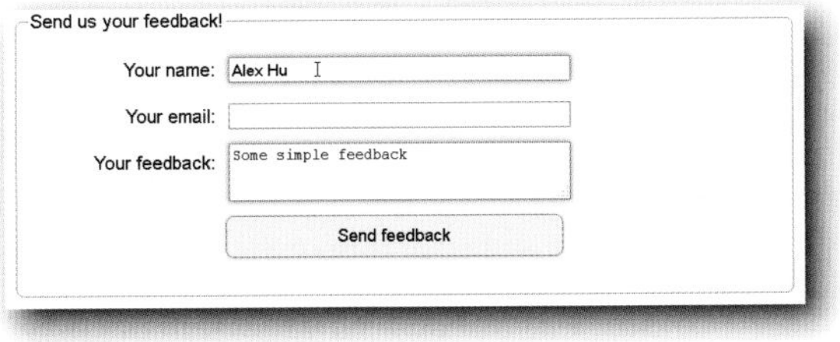

Figure 3-2: Feedback is validated as the user enters information.

Source: Mozilla Firefox on Microsoft Windows 7

CONTROLLING SUBMIT BUTTON INTERACTION

The validation function needs an extra parameter—`warnRequired`—to indicate that the user was attempting to submit the form, and mark any empty but required inputs with a validation error.

Another approach to the same problem is to prevent the user from submitting the form before the entire form has been validated. This simplifies the validator slightly, removing the parameter `warnRequired` and the logic required to implement it, thus making the event handler logic more straightforward:

```
$ ->
    form = $('form#feedback')

    validationHandler = (event) ->
        disable_submit = false
        if not validate(form, loginValidation)
            disable_submit = true
            event?.preventDefault()
        form.find('input[type="submit"]').attr('disabled', disable_submit)

    form.submit validationHandler
    form.on 'keyup', ':input', validationHandler
    validationHandler()
```

The result of this validation is to disable the submission button if the form doesn't validate (or to enable the button if the form does validate) so that, if the form is invalid, the user can no longer click the submission button to submit the form. The submit event handler remains attached because there are other methods of submitting the form (on many browsers, users can press the Enter key to submit a form), but the special logic for form submission is removed.

Whether this is a reasonable approach is up to you and the context in which the form needs to operate. Generally, it's not good practice to prevent users from taking actions without telling them why the actions aren't possible.

PREPOPULATING FORM ELEMENTS

Occasionally, it's useful to prepopulate form elements. You can do so by settings values manually in the HTML or on the server-side generating the HTML, but it can also be done on the client-side. This is both easy and useful in a number of different scenarios, such as reviewing and editing data already held on a system.

```
populate = (form, data) ->
    for key, value of data
        form.find(":input[name=#{key}]").val(value)

$ ->
    form = $('form')
    populate(form, {name: 'Joe User', email: 'joe@example.com'})
```

Setting form data is in many ways easier than getting the data in the first place; it's simplified by jQuery's excellent `:input` selector and `val()` function, which can write values as well as read them.

One notable new CoffeeScript feature used here is the loop over an object. Compare the syntax of looping over a list to the syntax of looping over an object:

```
for value in some_list
for key, value of some_object
```

They work in very similar ways. At this point, you *must* be sure that you recognize the difference between `in` (looping on a list) and `of` (looping on an object). Array and property membership can also be tested with these operators:

```
some_list = [1..10]
some_object = {one: 1, two: 2}

5 in some_list   # true
11 in some_list  # false

'one' of some_object   # true
'three' of some_object  # false
```

MULTI-STEP FORMS

For many projects, small single-area forms are enough. For example, there's often little requirement for expanding forms like simple login boxes and user registrations, or even some of the more complex forms used in content management and other sophisticated applications.

Occasionally, though, it's useful to break down a form into multiple steps. For example, a form may be too large to comfortably display on a page—a significant rationale for developers targeting mobile devices. Also, you might construct the form as separate steps if they form logical blocks, and tasks such as validation can be performed in pieces. Quite often, this is a usability enhancement, as it allows mistakes to be corrected more easily as the user progresses through the steps. Additionally, if a form is made more reactive to the information already entered, it can be possible to customize or even omit entirely later sections of a form based on responses already received—a significant benefit to the end user.

SELECTIVE FORM DISPLAY

Using existing form state to display or adjust on-page elements (which cannot logically be selected, or to highlight most likely options) leads to highly interactive and often easy-to-use user interfaces, and you can use a number of different technical approaches to achieve this level of interactivity.

From the start, differentiate among the various concerns within form-handling code. It's tempting to take the logic used to validate a form, for example, and add sections of code to control how parts of the form display, or to set up individual event handlers on various form elements, triggering logic to turn the display of other elements on and off.

Both of these ideas are born of simplicity, but neither represents good design practice. The logic to control the display of part of a form is effectively a piece of state, and as the amount of state grows and the rules to change the state increase, managing the logic to control the state of the form becomes increasingly difficult.

Now, take a look at an example form that might be used to register visitors to a conference on CoffeeScript. Although it's a two-day conference, many visitors will attend only one day, so there's no point for them to register for talks on the day they will not attend. This is an ideal use case for selective form display.

The HTML looks quite straightforward:

```html
<body>
    <h1>Register for CoffeeScript convention</h1>
    <form id="event">
        <fieldset>
            <legend>Your Details</legend>
            <p><label for="name">Your name:</label>
                <input type="text" name="name" autofocus required>
            </p>

            <p>Days you will attend:</p>

            <ul class="checklist">
                <li><label>
                    Saturday <input type="checkbox" name="attend"
value="sat">
                </label></li>
                <li><label>
                    Sunday <input type="checkbox" name="attend" value="sun">
                </label></li>
            </ul>
        </fieldset>

        <fieldset id="attend-sat">
            <legend>Programme for Saturday</legend>

            <ul class="checklist">
                <li><label>
                    Getting started with HTML <input type="checkbox"
```

```
                  name="talk" value="html">
                </label></li>
                <li><label>
                    Advanced jQuery <input type="checkbox" name="talk"
        value="advjquery">
                </label></li>
                <li><label>
                    Working with Node.JS <input type="checkbox" name="talk"
        value="node">
                </label></li>
            </ul>
        </fieldset>

        <fieldset id="attend-sun">
            <legend>Programme for Sunday</legend>

            <ul class="checklist">
                <li><label>
                    CSS 3 and jQuery <input type="checkbox" name="talk"
        value="css3jquery">
                </label></li>

                <li><label>
                    Debugging Coffeescript <input type="checkbox" name="talk"
         value="debugging">
                </label></li>

                <li><label>After-show party <input type="checkbox"
        name="talk" value="party">
                </label></li>
            </ul>
        </fieldset>

        <p><input type="submit" value="Register for event"></p>
    </form>
</body>
```

A way of separating out the various pieces of form to individually control them is needed, and `<fieldset>` plays this role ideally. This style of form creation can gracefully degrade to scriptless implementation, as well as be semantically meaningful.

The goal here is to display the lists of talks only to those visitors who have indicated they will be visiting that day. (See Figure 3-3.)

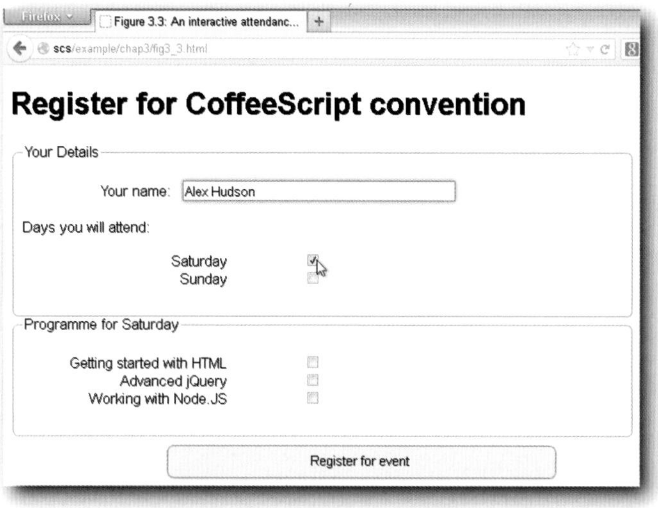

Figure 3-3: This interactive attendance form adjusts to user input.

Source: Mozilla Firefox on Microsoft Windows 7

Putting together a function to control the state of the form is straightforward:

```
updateFormState = (form) ->
    data = form.serializeArray()
    attend = {}
    for input in data
        if input.name == 'attend'
            attend[input.value] = true

    $('#attend-sat').toggle(attend?.sat == true)
    $('#attend-sun').toggle(attend?.sun == true)
```

This can be split into two phases. The first phase is gathering the existing form data and computing the required state variables from it. Sometimes a state variable might be whether or not an input has been filled in, as in the preceding code—but it could be a more complex expression, such as "Has the user checked at least three check boxes from each section of ten?"

The second phase is to react according to the computed state. In this example, the elements to show (or not) are directly modified—sometimes it's simpler to reset a form to a known state and then make the required minimal changes. I generally recommend whichever approach leads to the simplest code, particularly where the state calculations become complex and/or reference other state variables.

Once a function to control the visibility of the parts of the form has been written, it's then a simple exercise to attach it to the form:

```
$ ->
    form = $('form#event')
    form.on 'change', ':input', ->
        updateFormState form
    updateFormState form
```

This works similarly to how a form validator might be attached. Indeed, in some circumstances, it may make sense to allow a form state to be updated only from data that has been validated as correct.

VALIDATING PARTIAL FORM DATA

Although I've recommended not mixing validation and form display state, it's clear that at times the two tasks may need to operate somewhat hand-in-hand:

- If parts of a form are hidden, that doesn't mean the inputs contained within are suddenly either empty or valid—and nothing will be more infuriating to users than a validation problem in an area of the form they can't see!
- Equally, a form that was previously valid may become invalid simply by a new part being opened, so a validator needs to operate over an entire form at once, not just a single input.

To some extent, it's not even clear what should happen first. If the form state should react only to valid input, the validator needs to run before the state of the form is altered. But then the state of the form may impact whether a form is valid—there's a chicken-and-egg situation here, at least in theory.

In practice, it's a bit different. A good compromise is to run the validator first and then to either never allow invalid form items to be hidden or to ensure that they're optional or otherwise resettable to a valid state. Which approach to choose depends on what the best user experience would be. Resetting input state can effectively lose data, which is usually a bad thing, although it can be mitigated by caching the information elsewhere and repopulating the form if needed later on.

MODAL FORM UI

In many circumstances, it's good practice to force the user to complete something before going further. This could be an entire form, where the user must submit more information before continuing, or it could be a small part of a form. A modal UI essentially disables the rest of a page, focusing the user's attention on a significant area, although it's ripe for abuse— to show adverts or other information the user would not ordinarily focus on, for example.

A common use case for this feature as part of a form is to introduce information that could entirely change the form. For example, forms that ask for data that may already be part of a user's login profile may offer unknown users the ability to log in first, so that the existing information stored for them might be re-used, saving them from filling in the same information again. (See Figure 3-4.)

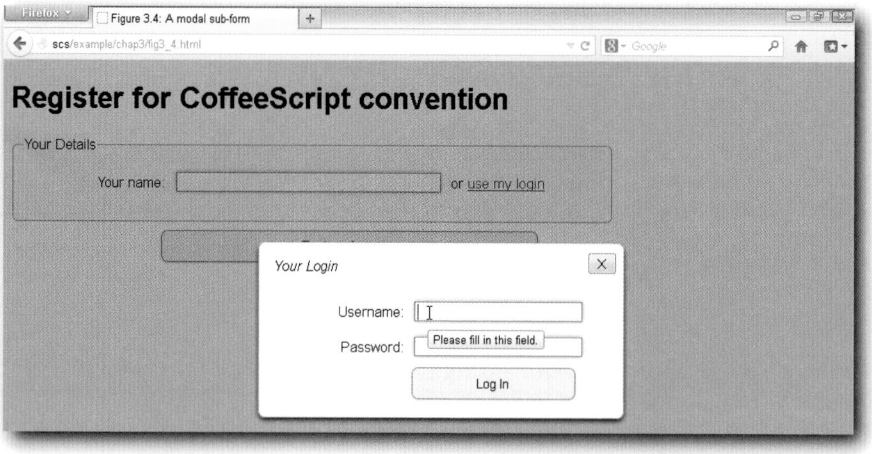

Figure 3-4: A modal login prompt appears over a registration form.

Source: Mozilla Firefox on Microsoft Windows 7

Modal UI is very easy to achieve. This is a complete modal login form:

```
<div id="modal" style="display: none;">
    <div id="modal-bg"></div>
    <div id="modal-form">
        <div class="modal-close"><a href="#">[ Close ]</a></div>
        <form id="login">
            <fieldset>
                <legend>Your Login</legend>
                <p><label for="name">Username:</label>
                    <input type="text" name="username"
autofocus required>
                </p>
                <p><label for="name">Password:</label>
                    <input type="password" name="password"
autofocus required>
                </p>
                <p><input type="submit" value="Log In"></p>
            </fieldset>
        </form>
    </div>
</div>
```

This mark-up has only three significant differences: The form is entirely self-contained within a hidden <div>, there is an empty "modal background" <div>, and a Close button is placed on the form. This button is important because there must always be an obvious way to get out of a modal form.

To achieve the modal function, the form relies on the page styles. First, the modal background must, in fact, overlay everything on the page—effectively disabling it, by ensuring that clicks and other input do not get to the elements behind it. Second, the form must sit just on top of the background:

```
#modal-bg {
       position: fixed;
       width: 100%;
       height: 100%;
       top: 0;
       left: 0;
       z-index: 1000;
       background: rgba(0, 0, 0, 0.4);
}

#modal-form {
       position: fixed;
       z-index: 1001;
       background: #fff;
}
```

Calling up the modal form is simple:

```
$('.modal-close').click ->
    $('#modal').hide()

$('#use-login').click ->
    $('#modal').show()
    $('#modal-form').css
        left: ($(window).width() - $('#modal-form').width()) / 2
        top: ($(window).height() - $('#modal-form').height()) / 2
```

In addition to showing and hiding the form appropriately, of primary interest in this code is the dynamic calculation of the size of the form. This calculation must happen after the form is "shown," because hidden elements generally have a page size of 0 but the browser won't actually display the changes until the script has finished the click handler.

USING SUBFORMS AS DATA HELPERS

With a modal form, there are a number of different options for handling the form submission. You can simply use a standard HTML form submission, in which case, any form underneath will be lost. This approach generally isn't useful, although in some circumstances, it could make sense. More often, the form will have a `submit()` handler attached to it, which will then work in the background. (I cover these background-style AJAX form submission methods in more detail in Chapter 4.)

The question remains of what to do with the form's results once they've been received. Again, there's a temptation to take a slightly easier route and directly manipulate the page from the subform. I recommend, instead, to treat these types of subforms as independent widgets, with a small API that makes them reusable.

jQuery's custom events are an ideal mechanism for this and can be used to show, hide, and receive data from subforms. The setup form can then be wrapped up in a single function and the events used to "communicate":

```
setupModal = ->
    $('body').on 'modal-form-state', (event) ->
        $('#modal').toggle event.data
        if event.data
            $('#modal-form').css
                left: ($(window).width() - $('#modal-form').width()) / 2
                top: ($(window).height() - $('#modal-form').height()) / 2

    $('form#login').submit (event) ->
        event.preventDefault()
        # submit data, process, etc… then:
        $('body').triggerHandler 'modal-form-data', data
```

The API is two custom events: `modal-form-state` to control whether the form is on-screen and `modal-form-data`, which fires when data is entered and perhaps when response from the server is gathered.

Within the body of the page, using the form is a matter of setting it up and then listening for or calling the appropriate events:

```
    setupModal()

    $('.modal-close').click ->
        $('body').triggerHandler 'modal-form-state', false

    $('#use-login').click ->
        $('body').triggerHandler 'modal-form-state', true

    $('body').on 'modal-form-data', (event) ->
        # process event.data - populate the form, etc.
```

SUMMARY

Although not an inspiring area of web development, use of forms and validation of data is one of the most important to get right. Throughout this chapter, I demonstrated some different approaches to common problems and discussed the different forms of user interface. Validation is sometimes thought of as a simple problem, but in fact it's quite complex—at least, to do it in a manner that doesn't annoy the end user.

More importantly, I covered most of the important aspects of the CoffeeScript syntax by now, with the additions of loops and logic constructs introduced in this chapter. While there are still new language features to come, the CoffeeScript learned so far is more than enough to start coding some serious applications.

AJAX REQUESTS

NO MATTER HOW interactive they are, there is a limit to what websites or applications can do without somehow saving information. To begin with, developers use forms to send information back and forth from the server, which works but can be clunky in terms of the user experience.

AJAX requests, which are executed by the browser in the background, give end users a smooth experience and also allow you, as a developer, to simplify the amount of logic that must be shared between the client-side and server-side of an application.

To get the most out of AJAX as an architecture, you need to understand what's going on underneath the covers, so in this chapter I'll dig into not only how to make AJAX requests but what's happening, and some of the security implications all developers need to be aware of.

GETTING DATA TO AND FROM THE SERVER

You'll recall from the introduction that the XHR API was first introduced by Microsoft in Internet Explorer largely for the use of their webmail product. By then, users had become used to their computers opening a pop-up when new mail arrived, and Microsoft realized there was no way to do that within the existing browser architecture without constantly refreshing the page.

The XHR API has essentially a single function: It allows client-side code to make requests to the server without having to refresh the page. Whether it's checking for mail, or downloading large amounts of data, it allows a developer to write an application that loads on a single page, and that page then never needs to be refreshed. This style of architecture, called AJAX (Advanced JavaScript and XML) initially, and sometimes called Rich Internet Application (RIA) now, is a very different approach to building web applications.

As in previous chapters, I utilize the jQuery library throughout this chapter to provide many of the basic functions used to transfer data. Although the basic XHR API in each browser is similar, jQuery takes care of many of the nuts and bolts of performing AJAX requests and really does provide a very consistent interface across all browsers.

Before delving into how to create such requests, I want to recap a bit about how HTTP requests work under the hood. Requests made to the server using the XHR methods are virtually identical to any other request issued by a browser, such as the request to load a page, and much of the knowledge about how forms work (for example) is immediately transferrable.

HTTP REQUESTS

Each HTTP request is made up of a few key pieces of information: the path that the browser is attempting to access, the hostname of the site wanted, and the method (sometimes called the "verb"). Consider a URL such as `http://www.example.com/index.html`. It is divided into the path (`/index.html`) and the hostname (`www.example.com`), and the default method chosen is GET.

Those key pieces of information are placed in the request headers, along with a variety of other information (for example, identification of the type of browser making the request and sending over any cookies that might have been set). The request is made up of those headers and a request body.

One last crucial piece of information is usually added to a request, the MIME type, which tells recipients what type of data they're receiving. HTML files usually have a MIME type of `text/html`, for example. However, not only do responses from the server have a type set, the request to the server has one, too.

Many methods are available for your use, but only four of them are commonly used by web applications: GET, POST, PUT, and DELETE. Though for many of you this will be recap, the basics of how these methods work follows.

GET and POST

Of the four commonly used verbs, these are the two most important ones. It's not too wide of the mark to think of these as being roughly analogous to "read" and "write/modify" in terms of their use.

The requested URL, as a whole, should generally identify a resource on a server. In terms of static content the URLs are files, but they could also refer to the contents of a database, for example—and the GET request is effectively the browser asking for the content of that resource. It's important to note that a GET request is supposed to be *idempotent*—that's a fancy way of saying that if a browser makes such a request, there should be no modification on the server-side, so that (in general) if the browser makes two requests in a row, it will get exactly the same response.

Usually, when making a GET request, the request body is entirely empty and any additional data that the browser wants to send consists of encoded parameters appended to the URL.

Because it's designed to modify a resource on the server, a POST request isn't idempotent. The point of such a request is that the state of the server may (or may not!) change. The request body is generally used to send across additional data. Much more data can be encoded into this section than can be appended to the URL, making this request type suitable for even big jobs like uploading files.

PUT and DELETE

Closely related to the POST type is the PUT request. They function virtually identically, but PUT's role is more akin to "create" than "modify." Although it arguably modifies server state, PUT is an idempotent operation. Using PUT with the same resource twice should have the same effect as doing so once.

DELETE is relatively obvious. It's intended purpose is to remove resources on the server. It definitely modifies server state, but the effect of doing so twice in a row should be the same as doing it once, so DELETE is also idempotent. Like GET, there is usually no use of the request body.

Understanding Caching

Why is it important to understand how these methods work and whether they're idempotent? The key issue for you, as the developer, is actually caching, whether it's caching on the server, caching in the browser, or caching in a proxy in between (or, worse, caching at each of those locations).

It can take some time for servers to generate output, so it's not a good idea to have them spend time re-creating data they've already created for each and every visitor. Also, if a browser has already downloaded a file and a good copy is available, it's not worth spending the time downloading it again. Caching like this is altogether good for performance.

Although good for performance, caching can wreak havoc if not properly controlled. For example, if a stock ticker application is continually pulling back stock market quotes that have been cached and are hours old, the application is rendered useless for all users.

The rules over what HTTP requests can be cached, and for how long, are quite complex. However, it's generally enough to understand that POST, PUT, and DELETE will invalidate cache entries, but that GET requests can happily be cached at various points from the browser to the end server.

EASILY RETRIEVING INFORMATION

Having reviewed some of the intricacies of making HTTP requests, it's time to look at how requests are made in practice. For all the complexity of the problem, the first few steps are actually satisfyingly simple. Consider a staff directory, where the information is returned from a server. The page itself is quite straightforward:

```html
<!DOCTYPE html>
<html lang="en">
<head>
  <script src="jquery.js" type="text/javascript"></script>
  <script src="directory.js" type="text/javascript"></script>
</head>
<body>

<h1>Staff List</h1>

<ul id="staff"></ul>

</body>
</html>
```

It's not always the case that the page must be initially empty and the data retrieved later, but for the purposes of this example, that's the intention. When the user loads the page, the code does an AJAX callback against the server to load the initial list of users.

Now, to make this demo work, it's not necessary to set up an actual server at this stage. That would be a relatively huge amount of work for a small win! Instead, because browsers are capable of loading files from the local system, you can use some static data. Save this content in the same directory as a file called testdata.json:

```json
{
    "name": "Staff List",
    "members": [
        { "id": 1, "type": "executive", "name": "Jim Jones" },
        { "id": 2, "type": "executive", "name": "Alice Arnold" },
        { "id": 3, "type": "admin", "name": "Laura Lansbury" },
        { "id": 4, "type": "admin", "name": "Paul Peterson" }
    ]
}
```

XHR requests can return data in any format that the browser can handle. You can use an HTML response, for example, but one of the most common patterns within the community now is to simply return structured data in the form of JSON.

The content of `directory.coffee` that is going to power this directory is not complicated, although you will find it helpful to go through it line by line:

```
$ ->
    $.ajax
        url: './testdata.json'
        type: 'GET'
        dataType: 'json'
    .done (data) ->
        $('#staff').append("<li>#{ m.name }</li>") for m in data.members
```

jQuery provides a number of functions to do XHR requests, such as `$.get()` and `$.post()`, which are simple wrappers over `$.ajax()`. I used `$.ajax()` here because the wrappers, in all honesty, are not really worth using. They simplify life by a very small amount, but they needlessly limit the ability to do basic tasks such as detect errors.

The API to `$.ajax()` is nice and simple: An object is passed in to configure the request being made, and generally there is no need to pass more information than in the previous example:

- `url`: Where to send the request
- `type`: Which HTTP method to use in the request
- `dataType`: The type of data expected in the response

Sending the request is easy, and the next step is to wait for the response and act on it. `$.ajax()` returns what jQuery refers to as a *jqXHR object,* which is the jQuery abstraction over the XHR API of the browser it's running on. More importantly, though, it implements what's known as the *Promise* interface, which is much more interesting in this context.

Because the requests are asynchronous, the code making a request doesn't wait for the response. Instead, the idea is to set up various handlers that will be triggered when the response finally comes back. This is just like setting up a handler to register a potential future click on a button. The Promise interface provides the ability to set these handlers that are later triggered, as well as various features to manage those handlers.

For XHR requests, a couple of parts of the Promise interface are of interest:

- `done()`: To set handlers to be called on successful completion of the request
- `fail()`: To set handlers that handle errors
- `then()`: To set handlers to be called on either success or failure

You can set more than one handler, and of course it's not always necessary to set a handler for every eventuality. I recommend, though, that you always set some sort of error handler. Otherwise, it's easy to miss errors, particularly in a development environment.

Looking back at the success handler set on the previous request:

```
.done (data) ->
    $('#staff').append("<li>#{ m.name }</li>") for m in data.members
```

This is just a simple function expecting data in the same structure as the `testdata.json` file contents. Since `$.ajax()` was set up to expect a JSON response to the request, the response body (the `testdata.json` file contents) is automatically parsed into an actual structure.

CROSS-ORIGIN REQUEST HANDLING

At this point, I want to comment on some of the security features found in modern browsers. Early in the process of developing the XHR APIs in different browsers, it was clear that there were substantial security concerns. Consider this scenario:

1. A user called Joe visits www.nefarious.com.
2. A script on nefarious.com attempts to make an XHR request to popular-email.com, on the basis that many people use it and remain logged in.
3. Joe, unfortunately, is a popular-email.com user and is indeed logged in.
4. The XHR request to Joe's inbox succeeds, and the script makes another XHR request to send his private emails on to the operator of the nefarious.com website.

Without some type of security measure in place, this scenario would be an easy setup for attack, and with many popular websites available—not just for e-mail but also for e-commerce and banking—before too long a user of one of those sites would likely get caught.

Early on in the standardization process, this type of scenario and many others were discussed by the various browser manufacturers, who recognized that by allowing client-side code to make requests to any server it liked, there was a fundamental security problem that the end-user could not be protected from.

Instead of allowing this possibility, the browser developers decided that browsers should restrict XHR requests to the same place the script came from—a security measure called *same origin restriction*.

UNDERSTANDING BROWSER REQUEST SECURITY

The *origin* is defined as the combination of the hostname, the protocol, and the port number (if given). So `http://example.com/test.js` has the same origin as `http://example.com/testdata.json`, but it doesn't have the same origin as `http://popular-email.com/inbox/` or even `https://example.com/testdata.json` (note the different protocol).

Requests to resources on different origins are denied by the browser. Generally, and most annoyingly, the browser will not issue a warning, either to the code making the XHR request that has been denied or even to the browser user. The request simply fails. This is another reason I always recommend an error handler on XHR requests. The error handler fires in recognition of the denied request, even if it doesn't indicate why the request was denied.

JSONP REQUESTS

Although having additional browser security is rarely a bad thing, in some instances it does get in the way. It's not always the case that resources in other origins should be treated as being protected. So, although by default they're blocked by browsers, with some work, it is possible to make requests that aren't restricted.

You've always been able to place scripts from different origins on a single HTML page, and allow them to interact—for example, hosting web analytics scripts or other third-party tools. By making use of this feature and injecting additional scripts into the page after the page load, you enable the browser to make a GET request in a similar style to XHR but without equivalent restrictions.

Browsers do not provide an event to let a script know that another new script has been loaded onto the page, so the callback is provided by the remote server: It wraps the data being returned in a function call, usually according to a URL parameter given by the client.

This system is a little bit complex, and best illustrated with an example. Among the many public JSONP APIs available, Twitter provides a public feed. Next, you look at how to use that feed.

Querying the twitter.com Timeline

The framework for this query is straightforward in terms of the HTML: A form is being used to get the name of the Twitter user to query, but there is nothing irregular here:

```
<body>

  <form id="search">
    <p>
      <label for="username">Twitter username:</label>
      <input type="text" id="username" name="username" value="ealexhudson">
    </p>
    <p><button id="getTweets">Get Tweets</button></p>
  </form>

  <ol id="tweets"></ol>

</body>
```

For the purposes of this exercise, the act of actually fetching the tweets from the remote service is a manual one. The username is entered into the form, the user clicks Get Tweets, and a call to the Twitter API, which is most definitely on another origin, is made.

Setting up a click handler is easy:

```
$ ->
    $('#getTweets').click (e) ->
        e.preventDefault()
        fetchTweets()
```

The main body of the logic is here:

```
fetchTweets = ->
    username = $('#username').val()
    call = $.ajax
        url: 'http://api.twitter.com/1/statuses/user_timeline.json/'
        type: 'GET'
        dataType: 'jsonp'
        timeout: 3500
        data:
            screen_name: username,
            include_rts: true,
            count: 10,
            include_entities: true
    .done (data) ->
        $('#tweets').empty()
        window.clearInterval timer
        for tweet in data
            $('#tweets').append($("""<li>
                #{ tweet.text } - <small>#{ tweet.created_at }</small>
            </li>"""))

    timer = window.setInterval ->
        call.abort()
        window.clearInterval timer
        $('#tweets').empty().append("<li>Couldn't retrieve tweets</li>")
    , 4000
```

First, examine the changes to the $.ajax() call:

- The data type is JSONP rather than JSON; jQuery handles many of the details of the JSONP request for you.
- A 3.5-second timeout on the request has been set.
- An object containing data has been passed to the request.

Because this is a GET request, the data being passed to the service is encoded in the URL rather than in the request body, so the actual URL of the request ends:

```
user_timeline.json/?screen_name=username&include_rts=1&count=10&include
_entities=1
```

This is how the Twitter service identifies which user's tweets and how many of them are being requested.

The success handler is a simple function that is passed data from Twitter, which is already parsed into a structure ready for use. Using the data, the handler then just performs a number of jQuery calls to create the user interface.

I recommended previously to always include an error handler. However, note that I didn't set the `fail()` handler in previous code because of the nature of JSONP requests and because the browser doesn't issue events when these calls (which are, underneath, simply adding new script tags to the page) complete or fail. A successful event is produced by jQuery when the JSONP callback function is triggered, but if the request fails, there is no error event.

Thus, the only way to detect that a JSONP request has failed is to time it out. You set a 3.5-second timeout on the main AJAX call and also set up a 4-second timer to notify the user. If the call succeeds, the timer showing the error message is cancelled.

CROSS-ORIGIN RESOURCE SHARING

JSONP as a system works well, but in many ways, it's less than ideal. It forces requests to return data as script content, relies on randomly generated function names not clashing, and is essentially limited to GET requests. A more recent method of allowing such requests, *Cross-Origin Resource Sharing* (more commonly referred to as *CORS*), doesn't suffer from these problems.

CORS is an opt-in system where the HTTP server indicates that specific resources can be accessed from other origins by including additional headers in the response. To make a resource available from any origin, a server just needs to include this header:

```
Access-Control-Allow-Origin: *
```

As with many security get-outs, you need to remain aware of a number of limitations:

- The request headers from a browser to a resource on another origin are generally "cleansed" before sending, so, for example, cookies aren't sent automatically.
- Additional headers can be requested, such as cookies and other information, but this requires further resource configuration on the server.
- CORS is not yet consistently supported by all browsers, and in particular, versions of Microsoft Internet Explorer previous to version 10 have terrible support.

For these reasons, CORS is not yet a complete answer, but for those browsers that support it, CORS is an excellent solution.

EXAMPLE: USER REGISTRATION FORM

AJAX can be used in a variety of different circumstances, but most of the interesting work happens when data is retrieved from a server, manipulated somehow, and then modified on the server. Almost all AJAX applications are patterned in this way. To demonstrate this point more thoroughly, in this section, I've put together a real-world example of how the front-end and back-end services are connected to provide a user registration service.

To explore the world of AJAX a bit more thoroughly at this point, it's necessary to have a server available on which some requests can be made. Luckily, the node.js system that you installed at the same time you installed CoffeeScript at the beginning of this book is an excellent web server system.

I don't intend to cover the process of writing server-side code in depth at this point—that will come in Chapter 14. For now, you just need to take a look at the code and how to run it to gain a rough understanding of what it's doing:

```coffeescript
http = require 'http'
fs = require 'fs'
url = require 'url'
restify = require 'restify'
port = 8080

users = [
    username: 'alexh'
    password: 'alexh'
    email: 'alexh@example.com',
]

checkUsername = (username) ->
    valid = true
    for user in users
        valid = false if user.username == username
    return {
        'valid':  valid,
        'reason': if valid then '' else 'Username already taken'
    }

respond = (req, res, next) ->
    res.send 'hello ' + req.params.name
    return next

server = restify.createServer()
server.use restify.bodyParser()

server.post '/registration/', (req, res, next) ->
    result = checkUsername req.params.username
    result.var = 'username'

    invalid = (foo for foo in [result] when not result.valid)
    if invalid.length > 0
        res.send 401, invalid
    else
        res.send 200, { 'status': 'ok' }
    return next()

server.post '/registration/username', (req, res, next) ->
    result = checkUsername req.params.username
```

```
    code = if result.valid then 200 else 401
    res.send code, result
    return next()

server.listen port, "localhost", ->
    console.log "#{ server.name } listening at #{ server.url }"
```

Save this code as `server.coffee`. Before running this, you may first need to install a dependency:

```
$ npm install restify
```

Then, you can run this code simply by executing `coffee server.coffee`, at which point, it will (assuming node.js is properly installed) output a URL on which it's listening. The server will continue to run and respond to any incoming requests, until stopped with Ctrl+C.

By default, the base URL for the server will be `http://127.0.0.1:8080/`, which is a local address accessible only on the computer it's running on. A couple of URLs are defined on which it will return specific responses, though.

A request to `/registration/username` checks whether the user is registered with the server. As a simple server, it has only a simple array that contains a single initial user—`alexh`—which is reset when you restart the server. You use `/registration/` to add new entries to that array.

This is typical of URL schemes used in registration services. But by consuming and producing only JSON data, implementing the service is much easier than implementing the equivalent "old style" service that created HTML pages from templates.

A Simple Front End

With the data logic happening on the back end and requests occurring asynchronously, a variety of templates aren't needed. The HTML for this registration form can be modified in response to requests being performed:

```
<!DOCTYPE html>
<html lang="en">
<head>
    <meta charset="utf-8">
    <title>User registration</title>
    <script src="jquery.js" type="text/javascript"></script>
    <script src="user-registration.js" type="text/javascript"></script>
    <link rel="stylesheet" type="text/css" href="form-style.css">
</head>
<body>
    <fieldset>
        <legend>Create your Account</legend>

        <form id="registration" novalidate>
```

```
        <p><label for="username">Preferred username:</label>
            <input type="text" name="username" autofocus required>
        </p>

        <p><label for="name">Your name:</label>
            <input type="text" name="name" autofocus required>
        </p>

        <p><label for="email">Your email:</label>
            <input type="email" name="email">
        </p>

        <p><input type="submit" value="Register"></p>
    </form>
  </fieldset>
</body>
</html>
```

The main part of the interface is a standard form, and the complexity of the front-end logic is contained within the registration code. Note especially that the form makes no reference to the back-end AJAX service. There is no `action` or `method` attribute here, because the CoffeeScript code will handle the entire process of making the request to the server.

Now, examine the front-end script piece by piece. This is the code that will be compiled to `user-registration.js` referenced in the HTML just previous:

```
registrationValidation = [
    {name: 'name'
    humanName: 'Name'
    valid: [
        { type: 'length', config: { min: 6 } }
    ]},
    {name: 'username'
    humanName: 'User name'
    valid: [
        { type: 'ajax', config:
            { url: 'http://localhost:8080/registration/username' }}
    ]}
]
```

First, a schema for validation is defined, and the restriction on the name—that it must have at least six characters—is similar to the form validation methods seen previously. However, the username validation is novel. This validator is going to make an AJAX call back to the server to check whether a username has already been used.

This distinction is important. Although it's possible to provide the client with a long list of the users already registered on the system, doing so involves a lot of data and a design that's not scalable. More importantly, an approach such as this one lets all and sundry see the various users already registered on the system—a real security issue.

The validation code comes next, and for consistency, now all the validators are defined asynchronously in terms of jQuery's Promise interface. Consider the length validator first:

```
validators =
    length: (name, value, config) ->
        promise = $.Deferred()
        if config.min? and value.length < config.min
            promise.reject({ valid: false, reason: 'Too short'})
        else if config.max? and value.length > config.max
            promise.reject({ valid: false, reason: 'Too long'})
        else
            promise.resolve({ valid: true })
        return promise
```

Implementation of the interface used earlier when making AJAX calls gave you the likes of `.done()` and `.fail()`, which allow the caller to set handlers to receive the success (or otherwise) status of an XHR request. In the preceding code, the other side of the Promise interface is used: `.resolve()` and `.reject()` are used to decide success, or otherwise, which is then reported to the handlers that have been set.

This is one of the most important aspects of asynchronous design: When using an asynchronous interface, there's not always a delay between asking a question and getting an answer.

With the validator in the preceding code, the validation happens immediately, and on many browsers, it's probably synchronous, too. However, by reusing the asynchronous API, it's easier to later mix in alternatives that will experience a delay between question and answer, such as an XHR request:

```
ajax: (name, value, config) ->
    promise = $.Deferred()
    data = {}
    data[name] = value
    $.ajax
        url: "#{ config.url }"
        type: 'POST'
        dataType: 'json'
        timeout: 2000
        data: data
    .done (data) ->
        promise.resolve data
    .fail (data) ->
        data = { valid: false, reason: 'Server error' }
        try
            data = JSON.parse data.responseText
        promise.reject data
    return promise
```

`$.ajax()` already returns an object that implements Promise, so why is that rewrapped in another one here? The key reason is the error path: There are actually two types of errors.

The first type of error is returned from the server. When a username is checked, it returns two types of HTTP responses. If the username doesn't exist, the HTTP return code is 201, which indicates success. If the username does exist, the return code is 401, indicating failure. This change in return code dictates whether the handler on `done()` or `fail()` is called.

However, the second type of error is different. It may be returned by the server when something has actually gone wrong (for example, an HTTP response with return code 500, indicating an internal error), or it might be that the request itself just failed (in which case, there's literally no response).

So, the handler set on the `fail()` callback has to handle two types of errors: the expected errors, which represent failure to validate, and unexpected errors, which indicate a technical issue.

Here's how these two eventualities are handled: If the callback can parse the body of the response into a JSON structure, it's a validation error from the server and the promise can be rejected on that basis. If the response body can't be parsed, something else went wrong, and a generic server error response is given as the promise rejection data.

Next, here's how to use some user interface helpers to communicate messages to the end user:

```
addWarning = (node, message) ->
    label = $("<label role='alert' for='#{node.name}'>#{message}</label>")
    $(label).insertBefore(node)

setValidationState = (input, valid, reason) ->
    input.addClass(if valid then "valid" else "invalid")
    if not valid
        addWarning input, reason

validateElement = (inputNode, schema) ->
    rule = r for r in schema when r.name == inputNode.name
    return if not rule
    input = $(inputNode)

    # remove any validation UI
    input.parent().find('label[role="alert"]').remove()
    input.removeClass('valid invalid')

    callback = (data) -> setValidationState input, data.valid, data.reason

    for test in rule.valid
        promise = validators[test.type](rule.name, input.val(), test.config)
        promise.done(callback).fail(callback)
```

Much like previous validators, the logic here is quite simple. For each element that has validation rules set in the schema, check whether it's still valid and if not, alert the user. The main change here is that instead of receiving those results directly and synchronously, the validator receives a promise, onto which it attaches a callback that interprets the result and alters the user interface accordingly.

In this example, the same callback is used to handle both success and failure, which is possible because the data being resolved through the promise is under control in every situation, including the AJAX error handler effectively creating a new error when the communication with the server fails. In other situations, where the promise is not under such close control, it's more common to have at least two different callbacks.

As much as possible, the actual validation state is communicated through the use of CSS classes and visual changes in the user interface. However, readable messages are also being returned, and those are inserted into the interface. It's handy to have that kind of flexibility built into an interface, because it allows the back end to produce more useful error messages in different circumstances.

For example, if the server is later connected to a database that needs maintenance every Monday morning between 9 a.m. and 10 a.m., registrations might be rejected with an error communicating that maintenance window of time to the user. This is helpful because it tells the user two key things: first, that retrying is highly unlikely to be successful; second, when the service will become available again.

There's not much script left to look at. The form validation is set up first:

```
$ ->
    form = $('form#registration')

    validateItem = (event) ->
        validateElement event.target, registrationValidation

    form.on 'change', ':input', validateItem
```

Validation is set to occur every time a form element changes, again warning the user as soon as a problem is spotted.

The final thing to do is to perform the actual registration request when users are satisfied with the data they've entered:

```
    form.submit (event) ->
        event.preventDefault()
        data = form.serializeArray()
        form.find('label[role="alert"]').remove()
        form.find(':input').removeClass('valid invalid')

        $.ajax
            url: 'http://localhost:8080/registration/'
            type: 'POST'
            data: data
            dataType: 'json'
```

```
            timeout: 2000
        .done (data) ->
            alert "Registered"
        .fail (data) ->
            problems = []
            try
                problems = JSON.parse data.responseText
            for problem in problems
                input = form.find(":input[name='#{ problem.var }']")
                setValidationState input, problem.valid, problem.reason
```

The `$.ajax()` call here is making the actual user registration call, and the server is revalidating the username before registration. As with all proper form validation schemes, giving information to the user and doing quick validation on the client-side is excellent, but it's not a replacement for server-side validation.

ERROR HANDLING

As discussed previously, when making `$.ajax()` calls, knowing what a `.done()` handler should look like and what to do when the request succeeds is pretty straightforward; however, handling error cases correctly is much more murky, because such a variety of errors can occur!

Examine a really simple piece of code that makes XHR calls in response to a button being clicked:

```
setResult = (text) ->
    $('#result').text(text)


makeRequest = ->
    $.ajax
        url: 'http://localhost:8081/'
        type: 'GET'
        dataType: 'json'
        timeout: 4000
    .done (data) ->
        setResult "Succeeded"
    .fail (data) ->
        setResult "Fail!"


$ ->
    $('#start').click (e) ->
        makeRequest()
```

There's not much wrong with the success handler, but plenty of improvements could be made to the error handler. These are the key questions to ask:

- Why did the call fail?
- Was it a temporary failure or a permanent one?

- Is there something you can ask the user to do to improve the chances of success?
- What's going to happen if the code fails here?

Too often, developers fling their hands up at the idea of checking for errors. After all, they rarely happen in deployed systems. But often steps can be taken to mitigate or even solve errors.

XHR requests can fail for a number of reasons. Sometimes, they fail because some of the network traffic is interrupted momentarily, sometimes for other transient reasons—for example, they time out, and the user gets bored waiting and tries to reload the page, and it works the second time.

Particularly maddening for users, though, is when they spend time entering data into a system, only to have the final save fail and the application carry on regardless, effectively throwing away their carefully crafted information.

GENERATING ERRORS

It might sound strange, but one of the most positive things you can do is use an environment in which errors can be created. Because errors rarely happen, waiting around for one to occur and to see how an application fails isn't very efficient. Worse, once they're written, error handlers aren't often tested again, and although they may have worked originally, the fateful "bit rot" (where once working code stops behaving correctly, even though it hasn't been changed) sets in, and they cease to work as designed.

Creating errors and testing how to handle them on an ongoing basis is a really useful technique. So that you can properly explore different ways of handling errors, allow me to introduce here another bit of the CoffeeScript server code:

```coffeescript
http = require 'http'
fs = require 'fs'
url = require 'url'
port = 8081

calls = 0

http.createServer (request, response) ->
    query = url.parse(request.url, true).query
    type = query.type ? ""

    # CORS responses
    headers =
        'Access-Control-Allow-Origin': '*',
        'Access-Control-Allow-Credentials': true,
        'Access-Control-Allow-Methods': 'POST, GET, PUT, DELETE, OPTIONS',
        'Access-Control-Allow-Headers': 'Content-Type',
        'Content-Type': 'text/javascript'

    # write back data, or fail
```

```
    if calls % 2 == 1
        response.writeHead 200, headers
        response.end JSON.stringify({ "result": "ok!" }), "utf-8"
    else
        response.end
    calls++

.listen(port);

console.log "Server running at http://127.0.0.1:#{ port }/"
```

The key piece of this server is commented. It counts the number of requests that have been made to it, and it deliberately doesn't answer every other request. In fact, no response is given, simulating a failed XHR request that times out on the browser side.

So, any XHR request can be made against this server, and the first one will succeed, the next one will time out, the one after that will succeed, the next one will time out, and so on. (Incidentally, it would be possible to introduce a wider variety of errors—such as permission denied, internal server error, file not found, and so on—and make them controllable or even totally random. The use of random error generation is a particularly powerful technique, but for obvious reasons, it can make debugging difficult, too!)

To further demonstrate the generation of errors, trying using the bit of CoffeeScript code at the beginning of this section against this server.

DETECTING ERRORS

In the case of standard XHR requests—as opposed to JSONP requests—it's assured that if something goes wrong, the handlers set via `.fail()` will be triggered. Take a look now at how to determine the different types of errors in the handlers, because different types of errors may have different remedies.

The full function signature of a handler passed to `.fail()` actually looks like this:

```
(jqxhr, status, error) ->
```

These three parameters represent

- jQuery's abstract XHR API object
- A string representing the type of error (which could be null or either `timeout`, `abort`, `parsererror`, or simply `error`)
- The error string of the HTTP response (or null, if there wasn't a response)

The last parameter is generally useful only for debugging faulty HTTP servers—the error text varies from server to server and isn't nearly as useful as the status code from the HTTP response, which in this instance is available as `jqxhr.status`. For example, if a resource cannot be found, the status will always be 404, but the error string could read "Not found," or "Document not found," or any other variation of that concept.

The second parameter is more useful. If it's `timeout`, the browser is waiting for a response and didn't get one; if it's `abort`, the request was terminated before a response was received. `parsererror` means the request succeeded but jQuery could not make sense of it (for example, it was told it was receiving JSON but the server sent XML instead), and `error` covers any other error response.

It's often possible to decide a strategy to respond to the error on the basis of the second parameter:

- `timeout` is likely a networking problem and may be temporary. If the request should be idempotent, it's worth retrying it.
- `abort`, if not called by the script itself, often indicates a request not meeting the security expectations of the browser. This isn't likely to work now or in the future. If the script has the ability to abort requests, though, this probably isn't an error and can just be ignored.
- `parsererror` indicates some kind of fault on the server and usually isn't worth retrying.
- `error` can indicate a variety of faults. Select HTTP error codes might indicate different responses. For example, 403 indicates that the user is not authorized. If the user needs to log in to access the service, perhaps the login has expired. 502 is an internal server error code, but indicates a temporary problem, meaning the original request could be worth retrying.

Unfortunately, advising a good general strategy that's useful in every case isn't possible. How to respond to errors depends on the type of service being accessed, which error conditions are more important to look for, and whether there are alternatives that can be used instead.

What is clear, though, is that there's a wealth of information available here, and it's often worth spending time creating the error handlers and also on the means to emulate errors to test those handlers. The end result is significantly more robust code that responds much better to changes in real-world conditions.

RETRYING IN CASE OF TEMPORARY ERRORS

The best and most obvious course of action in the face of a temporary error is to try again. In this instance, it's not a case of practice makes perfect but that when writing software that relies on unpredictable networks, you need to expect the unexpected. In some circles, this is referred to as *defensive programming*.

Calling this the usual case probably isn't accurate. Personally, I've found it rare to come across code that attempts to handle unreliability in the network, but retrying an XHR request is such a useful feature that jQuery makes it incredibly easy to do.

This is how `makeRequest()` shown earlier can be rewritten to do basic retry:

```
makeRequest = ->
    requests = 0

    onSuccess = (data) ->
        setResult "Succeeded"
```

```
$.ajax
    url: 'http://localhost:8081/'
    type: 'GET'
    dataType: 'json'
    timeout: 4000
.fail (data) ->
    requests++
    if requests < 3
        $.ajax(this).done onSuccess
    else
        setResult "Fail!"
.done onSuccess
```

To simplify the logic a little, I removed decision making about when to retry a request based on the type of failure—in practice, it's not always a great idea to simply retry every failed request.

The retry logic is pretty straightforward. If the decision is to retry the request, the error handler doesn't need to re-create the entire request. The special variable this in the context of a failure handler is effectively a copy of the original request. Only the original success handler needs to be reset on what will be a new promise.

Although this logic retries every failure mode, it only attempts to do so three times. Without a limit of some kind, the code could get into an infinite loop, and if the requests were failing very quickly, rather than timing out (for example), the loop will quickly render a page quite unresponsive.

The requirement to reset the promise is slightly bothersome, and if the promise is being sent elsewhere or having other handlers set on it later, the retry logic becomes increasingly complex. However, you can easily wrap the $.ajax() call to provide a consistent promise with inclusive retry logic:

```
requestCache = {}

doAjax = (options) ->
    if options.url not in requestCache
        requestCache[options.url] =
            promise: $.Deferred(),
            tries: 0

    promise = requestCache[options.url].promise

    extended_options = $.extend({
        success: (data) ->
            promise.resolve data
        error: (data) ->
            requestCache[options.url].tries++
            if requestCache[options.url].tries < 3
                $.ajax(this)
            else
```

```
            promise.reject()
    }, options)

    $.ajax extended_options

    return promise
```

Implementing roughly the same logic, but more abstractly, the `doAjax()` wrapper behaves almost identically to `$.ajax()` and can be a drop-in replacement. However, instead of returning a promise based on the XHR request, it returns an entirely different one that is later resolved using the `success()` and `error()` events of the `$.ajax()` call.

Until now, the Promise interface has been used exclusively and `success()`/`error()` are new; however, they are, roughly speaking, the previous less-flexible implementations that promises have superseded. In this case, though, using them simplifies things, and the ever-useful Promise interface can be maintained manually.

The implementation of `makeRequest()` is now incredibly simple:

```
makeRequest = ->
    doAjax
        url: 'http://localhost:8081/'
        type: 'GET'
        dataType: 'json'
        timeout: 2000
    .done (data) ->
        setResult "Succeeded"
    .fail (data) ->
        setResult "Failed!"
```

In fact, it's basically the same as the original retry-unaware version. The only change is that the `$.ajax()` call is wrapped. Looking for opportunities like this to abstract useful functionality that can be reused in many places is crucial to keeping code DRY, and although getting it right sometimes takes a few attempts, doing so can often pay off, particularly with core functionality.

This wrapper can now be extended with a variety of logic to retry temporary failures, so that it never retries non-idempotent POST requests, or other features, and the great thing is that the logic is in a single place. Most applications will be making XHR requests in multiple places, and this type of wrapper can avoid repeating the logic or (worse) omitting it.

DEFERRING AND CANCELLING REQUESTS USING QUEUES

Generally, as a developer, you design web applications assuming they're constantly online—mostly because it's easier, but partly because dealing with different types of errors can be a little bit difficult to test and requires a reasonable knowledge of HTTP and what's actually happening "underneath."

This perspective is increasingly difficult to defend, though, because of the increasing number of mobile users who are employing online applications and finding that networks aren't reliable and actually "disappearing" for minutes if not longer.

Take the case of users trying to access applications while on a train, passing through tunnels and losing their mobile Internet for a few minutes. Your initial reaction to preparing for this kind of situation might be dismay, because in addition to possible request failures, users need to be ready if and when the network comes back on.

With a bit of thought, though, even this situation is relatively easy to communicate to the user, particularly when considering that modern browsers now make a lot more information available, especially about whether users believe they're online. For example, most people with laptops or other mobile devices are familiar with a browser's offline mode, and it's easy to trigger by turning off the WiFi device (or otherwise manually taking the machine off the network). In most cases, the browser notices instantly that the network has disappeared and can communicate that fact to scripts that are running.

STRATEGIES TO DEFER REQUESTS

As when dealing with errors, there is no correct way to decide when or how to defer requests. Indeed, whether it even makes sense to defer requests depends on the context of the application:

- Where a request is attempting to save user data back to a server, it's generally preferable to defer the request rather than throw it away completely.
- If a request is merely asking if there's "anything new" from the server, it's unlikely to be worth deferring the question in any situation—better to simply ask later when the response might come back.
- If a request is idempotent and effectively identical to one already deferred, it's unlikely to be worth deferring that request.

The difference here is policy versus mechanism. Policy is about when to defer a request until later and will vary from application to application. The mechanism is about how to defer a request, though, and like the generic retry mechanism covered earlier, there are also generic mechanisms to defer requests.

Extending the retry wrapper to handle deferring requests doesn't add much code:

```
requestCache = {}
deferQueue = []

doAjax = (options) ->
    if options.url not in requestCache
        requestCache[options.url] =
            promise: $.Deferred(),
            tries: 0
```

The request cache has been supplemented with a queue—in this instance, just a simple array—in which requests are stored if they won't be made until later. Then,

```
defer = not navigator.onLine
promise = requestCache[options.url].promise

extended_options = $.extend({
    success: (data) ->
        promise.resolve data
    error: (data) ->
        requestCache[options.url].tries++
        if requestCache[options.url].tries < 3
            $.ajax(this)
        else
            promise.reject()
}, options)

if defer
    deferQueue.push extended_options
else
    $.ajax extended_options

return promise
```

The decision to defer—the policy—is a basic one. It asks the browser if it is online, and if not, it defers the request. In practice, you can make this "smarter" for a specific application, but the mechanism to add the request options to the array instead of immediately making the request will be identical.

Note also that even if the request is deferred, the promise is still returned. In the case of a request being deferred, the promise may not be resolved for quite some time—beyond even the usual timeout that a request may have set. Whether this is correct behavior again depends on the application. You can use timers in place of request timeouts to remove deferred requests from the queue and reject the promise. For the code making the request it is as though the request had been made but then failed. This would significantly increase the logic complexity though, both of the implementation and of the testing required to make sure the implementation worked!

```
processDeferQueue = ->
    return if deferQueue.length == 0

    req = $.ajax deferQueue.shift()
    req.complete ->
        processDeferQueue()

updateOnlineStatus = ->
    status = "Offline"
    if navigator.onLine
        status = ""
```

```
        processDeferQueue()

    $('#online-status').text(status)
```

The remaining functionality required to empty the queue includes a couple of tricks. `update OnlineStatus()` is a handler that examines the online/offline status of the browser, and if the browser's online, it starts emptying the queue by calling `processDeferQueue()`.

Instead of making the deferred requests all at the same time, which would make the logic simpler but would cause the browser problems, the implementation of `processDefer-Queue()` attaches itself to the completion handler of each promise it removes from the queue. This ensures that as requests complete, whether successfully or not, the next request that has been deferred is removed from the queue and called.

Setting up and using this new wrapper is still easy:

```
makeRequest = ->
    setResult = (text) ->
        $('#result').text(text)

    doAjax
        url: 'http://localhost:8081/'
        type: 'GET'
        dataType: 'json'
        timeout: 2000
    .done (data) ->
        setResult "Succeeded"
    .fail (data) ->
        setResult "Failed!"

$ ->
    $('#start').click (e) ->
        makeRequest()

    updateOnlineStatus()
    $(window).bind "online offline", updateOnlineStatus
```

The process of making requests has barely changed. Again, the wrapper is being used, and the caller has no idea that this request might be retried on failure, or queued when the network goes away.

The only real difference is that the online and offline events of the browser are bound to the online status checker, which in turn triggers the defer queue to be emptied when the browser finds itself online again.

STRATEGIES TO CANCEL REQUESTS

In terms of mechanism, cancelling a request is surprisingly easy. If the request has been queued in any way, it can simply be removed from the queue, and any remaining promise can be rejected.

If the request is already "in flight" (it's been started but not yet completed), the jqXHR object returned by the $.ajax() call can be cancelled by calling .abort() on it, and the appropriate promises are automatically rejected.

Deciding when to cancel a request (the policy) is substantially harder, though. At the root of it, cancelling a request effectively means dropping data that had been destined for the server. In many instances, this data is valuable and dropping it is not an option.

Sometimes, the better practice is to warn a user that things are getting bad before actively starting to cancel requests. Attempting to ensure that user data isn't being lost is generally a good rule of thumb, and if data isn't at risk, not making as many requests is better than to keep making them and having them cancelled.

LOCAL STORAGE AND OFFLINE APPS

You can use a variety of different strategies to make applications resilient in the face of network failure. Deferring requests until the network is working or even cancelling them where appropriate can result in a satisfactory user experience even if it's a slightly slower one.

In some instances, though, it's better to try to go one step further and design an application that, although essentially a web application, can happily work entirely offline for long periods of time. This strategy is by far the most reliable one and doesn't result in slowdowns or other user-experience problems, but it tends to be appropriate only for applications, not websites in general.

A SHORT HISTORY OF LOCAL STORAGE

Right from the start, the earliest browsers had some form of local storage available. The feature that took off most quickly was the cookie, which is still in use today. Ostensibly designed so that browsers could retain authentication tokens and other user data, cookies are actually quite generous in terms of what they commonly offer. Up to 20 cookies for a given site, with each cookie storing at least 4K of data, is a basic requirement, with most browsers offering the ability to do much more.

Cookies have a number of downsides, though:

- Although $20 \times 4Kb$ is not an insignificant amount of data, it can be used up very quickly in practice.
- Cookies are not truly reliable. They last a set amount of time and are easily "cleaned," either accidentally or on purpose.
- Browsers send all of the cookies for a given domain as part of the request headers for each and every request (at least, without significant effort), causing each request to slow down as more data is stored.

As part of the more recent efforts to reinvigorate HTML by the Web Hypertext Application Technology Working Group (WHATWG) efforts in HTML 5, the issue of local storage came up again, and more modern, practical solutions were proposed. I'm going to examine two of the main ones; LocalStorage and IndexedDB.

LOCALSTORAGE

The first solution that was proposed, and that received considerable support in the beginning, goes by the not-entirely-imaginative name of LocalStorage. It's implemented in virtually every browser enjoying market share today (excluding Internet Explorer before version 8) and is implemented to a surprisingly consistent standard.

LocalStorage directly solves many of the local storage issues that web applications face:

- Although storage area size is not guaranteed, browsers so far have consistently allowed up to 5M of data to be stored.
- Browsers may ask users if they will allow the application to store information locally, but once received, this permission is stored for the future.
- The interface is well-supported and incredibly straightforward.

Using LocalStorage is not much more complex than accessing an object within Coffee-Script. As always, it's useful to test whether the feature exists:

```
if window?.localStorage is null
    console.log "Local storage is not supported in this browser!"
```

Given the broad support for this API, you won't often encounter a browser that doesn't have this support; however, if the code needs to work in a server-side environment, this test is still appropriate.

If the API is available, you can access it by referring to localStorage:

```
localStorage.username = "test"
```

That's literally all there is to it! Once a new piece of data is stored in the localStorage object, it will be there again in the next page request, or in the next browser tab, or the next visit to the application.

Removing data is exactly as expected:

```
delete localStorage.username
```

And looking at all the information stored locally is equally easy:

```
for key, value of localStorage
    console.log "Key is #{ key }, value is #{ value }"
```

There's also a useful event that's fired whenever the localStorage object is changed:

```
$(window).bind "storage", (event) ->
    console.log """localStorage.#{ event.key } changed from
                  #{ event.oldValue} to #{ event.newValue }"""
```

I need to mention another piece of information passed in the event: the actual URL the browser was on at the time of the change. Unfortunately, this is one piece of the implementation that isn't consistent across browsers. It's sometimes called `event.uri`, but it's usually available as `event.url`.

Avoiding Storage Problems

I implied earlier that there are other local storage solutions beyond `localStorage`, namely `IndexedDB`. Given the description of `localStorage` so far, it's difficult to see why this solution isn't sufficient. Unfortunately, it has a number of problems—problems sufficiently severe that many people advocate against using it, even though it's relatively mature at this point and enjoys broad support.

The first issue is that, although the interface looks and behaves a lot like a traditional object on its face, a number of quirks are underneath. Here is an obvious example:

```
localStorage.doesntStoreNumbers = 1
console.log typeof 1
console.log typeof localStorage.doesntStoreNumbers
```

Storing a number in local storage should be easy; however, that's not quite what happens. The output of the previous example is two lines, the first being just `number` because that's the type of the value `1`. The second line, though, is `string` because values stored in `localStorage` always come back as strings, even if that's not what they were originally.

This imposes a cost in overhead, because the option of ignoring the types isn't really available: `1 + 1 == 2`, but `"1" + "1" == "11"`—and worse, in a numeric context, it evaluates to 11, which is a potential disaster.

Given that the types cannot be ignored, some sort of scheme is required to convert the values as they come back from `localStorage`. A variety of options available are available:

- Manually remember which key had what type and convert on access (painful and error-prone!).
- Encode the type into the key name using a scheme like Hungarian notation (less error-prone but still painful).
- Store all values as a serialized JSON object (less error-prone, less painful, but still creates overhead).

None of these options are particularly enticing, and although the problem is solvable, it detracts significantly from what is a very simple API because it needs to be wrapped with a layer of extra logic rather than be accessed directly.

There's a further problem: `localStorage` doesn't take into account that the browser may have the same application open in a number of windows or tabs. This opens up the possibility that the application in one tab can read information from local storage and later write it back in response to user input, but in the meantime, the same application in another tab might have already modified the information, meaning that out-of-date information that had already been changed is being stored again.

Add to those problems that there's no way to effectively query the local storage for a specific key or a certain value—and that the performance of the implementations wasn't much to write home about in the first place—and you have many developers who feel it's simply not worth the effort.

INDEXEDDB

To cure the various maladies of `localStorage`, a variety of structured data proposals reuse the existing SQL standard in one way or another to provide the equivalent of a database and make it available as a form of local storage.

As with many standards, initially a number of competing but similar implementations were developed by different browser vendors. However, these different views eventually coalesced around a single proposal that is now called `IndexedDB`.

`IndexedDB` is not very much like databases in terms of systems used on the server-side to store massive amounts of information. There's no requirement here to create data schemas, write queries to retrieve data, and develop complex mappings to translate data from the program to the database and back. Instead, `IndexedDB` is a form of object database, which can store JavaScript (and hence CoffeeScript!) objects directly.

Although very similar to a key-value store in the same vein as `LocalStorage`, the `IndexedDB` API is almost entirely asynchronous, which means that calls into the API will return immediately, but handlers need to be set up to monitor the success (or not) of the call.

Additionally, as its name suggests, `IndexedDB` contains a concept of indexes. That is to say, it stores parts of the information stored within it such that queries on the objects contained within it can be executed very quickly. Indexes can be added in an arbitrary fashion, so if (for example) the database is storing a list of users, an index can be added on their names so that queries by name quickly find the appropriate entries.

Take a look at some quick examples, and it becomes clear that this is entirely another level of complexity:

```
$ ->
    idb = window.indexedDB ||
        window.webkitIndexedDB ||
        window.mozIndexedDB ||
        window.moz_indexedDB
```

```
idbtranstype = window.IDBTransaction ||
               window.webkitIDBTransaction ||
               {READ_WRITE: 'readwrite'}

if not idb
    console.log "IndexedDB is not supported in this browser!"
    return
```

The first thing to notice is that the actual API name isn't set in stone at this point. For most implementations, the main entry point is prefixed by the vendor to indicate that it's not generally considered entirely standards-compliant. So, job number one when using the API is to determine how to access it in the first place!

```
version = 1
db_request = idb.open "Test", version

db_request.onupgradeneeded = (event) ->
    # version of database doesn't match what we need
    db = event.target.result
    store_request = db.createObjectStore "bucket",
        keyPath: "id"
    store_request.transaction.complete = (e) -> dbReady db

db_request.onsuccess = (event) ->
    # db_request.transaction.oncomplete = (e) ->
    dbReady event.target.result
```

Once the entry point is confirmed, the local database can be opened. If this is the first time that the database has been accessed, it needs to be initialized. Each database has a version built into it, and if that version does not match the version parameter passed to the open() call an onupgradeneeded event is first.

When objects are written to the database, they're written to a specific object store. It's not too farfetched to think of object stores as directories and objects as files, although in this case, there's only one level to this hierarchy.

Before an object store can be used, it must be created, and must take place within an onupgradeneeded event handler. As a matter of good practice, then, each version needs to denote the existence of a specific set of object stores. So, in version one, there is a single store called "bucket". If you later want to add another store called "users", you need to also increment the version to 2. Databases with no version will be initialized to add both stores; databases at version 1 will simply add the new "users" store.

After a database is initialized, it's ready for use to store and retrieve objects:

```
dbReady = (db) ->
    transaction = db.transaction ["bucket"], idbtranstype.READ_WRITE
    store = transaction.objectStore "bucket"
```

```
store.add({'id': 2, 'number': 1, 'test': 'yes'}).onsuccess = ->
    console.log "The content of object with ID 2 is: ",
        store.get(2).result
```

It's not possible to access a store directly; all access must be through a transaction, which specifies which stores will be accessed and whether the access will be read-only or read-write. This allows the browser to make a number of significant performance improvements, at the cost of making the code more complex. In this manner, complete objects can be stored in the database and are retrieved in exactly the format they were stored.

The `onupgradeneeded` handler is executed within a special type of transaction that allows stores themselves to be created or removed, and which cannot be run in parallel with other queries.

COMPARING LOCAL STORAGE OPTIONS

Recommending the `IndexedDB` API for anything but the most serious uses is difficult because it's not the most broadly supported feature at this point. However, with judicious use of polyfills, it's possible to make a similar enough API available on other browsers to lessen the problem (although, if the performance of the database is critical, a polyfilled version won't likely be sufficiently quick).

Additionally, though, the API takes a lot of effort to use compared to `localStorage`, particularly in the asynchronous version, which is the API most broadly implemented so far. The standardization process between the browser vendors has taken a long time, and even where browsers support the API there is little consistency among them.

However, the effort is definitely worth it in a number of scenarios. `IndexedDB` is the future of the local storage APIs, and while in its current format it's quite complex, it does offer significant benefits, and the complexity will in time be cut down with simpler interfaces built on top of it. For those applications that need to have reliable and predictable local storage, `IndexedDB` is the best future-proofed option available.

SUMMARY

Although AJAX requests are popular and the API looks straightforward, it's actually an incredibly tough and deep subject area. Using AJAX requests on a reliable network is one thing, but dealing with needs of mobile users is quite another.

As well as digging into what AJAX requests are and how they work, I also tried to give you some insight into the problems you'll see in the real world, and how CoffeeScript can be used to write some smart logic around the basic jQuery functionality.

Technologies for storing data offline in the browser are also something of a pain point, and arguably are some of the least well-developed HTML 5 APIs. They are worth knowing about, though, and for many use cases are entirely adequate and I hope I've given you enough information about the cases where they're not!

5

OBJECT-ORIENTED DESIGN

IF EVER A FEW words could strike fear into the heart of web developers, they would be "object-oriented programming" (OOP). With online coding traditionally seen as more of a scripting endeavor, the application of OOP principles has been deemed as best applied on the server-side, where all the serious coding happens.

As AJAX-based applications have become more common, though, the client-side has become increasingly more complex, requiring more thoughtful design on the part of the developer, and OOP plays an important part there. It's too much to say that all your code should be written in an OOP style, but it's definitely true to say that

OOP should be a tool in the box, and when designing a large application, or one likely to have a substantial lifespan, it's usually the best tool.

In this chapter, I'll demonstrate the various features CoffeeScript offers for object-oriented programming, and discuss some of the best practices for designing classes. Since there is a JavaScript runtime underneath, the implementation of objects is flexible and there are opportunities to extend code with features not natively supported in the language, like mixins, and you'll take a look at those, too.

CLASSES AND INHERITANCE

Although making use of libraries such as jQuery to write code is straightforward, it becomes clear quickly to even a novice that writing procedural code—a series of bare statements on the page—doesn't get you very far. The first tool in the toolbox is the function, which allows you to write a series of statements and wrap them up so that they can be reused/recalled again and again. This principle is basic: "Don't repeat yourself."

Functions are powerful things in JavaScript, and therefore in CoffeeScript, too. Functions can contain variables and even other functions within their scope. This combination enables developers to take that wrapping one stage further and encapsulate large pieces of logic into single functions, hiding the details of the implementation from the code calling them. This is an application of another basic principle called *loose coupling*.

As useful as functions are, though, they can take you only so far on their own. The next step is to make use of a group of related principles that, taken together, are called object-oriented programming.

WHAT DOES IT MEAN TO BE OBJECT-ORIENTED?

Surprisingly, there isn't a universally agreed upon definition of what it means to be object-oriented (commonly referred to as "OO"), and perhaps even more surprising, the term generally doesn't refer to a set of features of a given language, but more to a set of capabilities. Virtually no language makes it impossible to program in an object-oriented fashion; however, programmers tend to refer to languages that provide specific syntactic constructs to manage objects as being object-oriented.

Although there is no definitive list of abilities or attributes that qualify a language as being object-oriented, there are features that are widely associated with object-oriented programming that most programmers would expect to see in such a language: encapsulation, inheritance, and "sub-type polymorphism".

- **Encapsulation:** Put simply, to *encapsulate* means to put barriers around the code you write, to hide the implementation from those using the code. This is a little like putting a case around a piece of electronics. For example, my radio is encapsulated in a box, and I'm mostly unaware of the internal implementation. It provides a series of buttons that I can push to ask it to perform certain operations, in much the same way a library provides an API.

  Both functionality and data can be encapsulated, individually or together, and an object, in a sense, is simply a reference to something that has been encapsulated: The internal behavior and data are separated from the rest of the code by an interface.

- **Inheritance:** This concept is interesting, simply because it implies a number of functions as well as a given structure, but it is also where one of the biggest syntactic differences between CoffeeScript and JavaScript occurs. To "inherit" in this context means to borrow either behavior or data, or both, from the definition of another object. Much like inheritance in other contexts, it implies a parent/child relationship, and an object that inherits from another object is often said to *descend* from it.

Now, where are these definitions of objects that are used in inheritance? In CoffeeScript, like other languages, there are classes. A template of an object, which may consist of data or functionality, and new objects are created from that class definition. However, in JavaScript, things are slightly different: There are no classes. To create an object, you simply copy an existing one. This is called *prototypical inheritance* because the object you copy is the template of the one you want to create.

■ **Subtype polymorphism:** An incredibly complex name for a very simple idea. As mentioned, inheritance effectively creates a parent/child relationship, but there can be more than one child; in fact, there could be many siblings. These are the subclasses, and in statically typed languages (for example, Java) where the class is also a type, subtype polymorphism refers to the fact that you can use an instance of the subclass (subtype) anywhere you use the main class (type).

CoffeeScript, of course, is not statically typed, so does any of this information apply here? Well, to a large extent it does because of an idea with another complex name: the *Liskov substitution principle*. (I'll come back to this principle later in the section, "Making Classes Substitutable," because though the theory is simple, it's a bit complicated in practice.)

Although your subclasses may function differently internally, through their inherited API—the interface they expose to the rest of the world because of the class from which they inherit—they should behave identically.

FUNCTIONS VERSUS OBJECTS TO ENCAPSULATE

Enough with the theory. What difference does this make to the code? Before looking at a simple class definition, consider the simple encapsulated jQuery image rotator in Chapter 2. The data and functionality were nicely grouped together and fulfilled that part of encapsulation, but there's no interface! If the programmer wants to change the rotation speed after the rotator is created, for example, there's no easy way to do so.

It's actually easy to rewrite that code as a class and demonstrate many of the important features of a class before dipping into the various technicalities:

```
class Rotator
    constructor: (slideshow) ->
        this.panels = $(slideshow).find('li')
        if this.panels.length < 2
            throw "can't rotate with fewer than 2 panels!"

        # configurable attributes
        this.active = $(slideshow).data('start') ? 0
        this.direction = $(slideshow).data('direction') ? 1
        this.speed = $(slideshow).data('speed') ? 1000

        # move panels into initial position
        $(panel).css(this.css_setting '100%') for panel in this.panels
        $(this.panels[this.active]).css(this.css_setting '0px')
```

```
    # start
    window.setInterval(this.doRotation,
                    $(slideshow).data('duration') ? 4000)

css_setting: (value) =>
    style = {}
    style[if this.direction == 1 then 'left' else 'right'] = value
    return style

set_speed: (new_speed) =>
    this.speed = new_speed

do_rotation: =>
    # which panel to show next?
    next = (this.active + this.panels.length + this.direction) %
           this.panels.length

    # move the active panel off-screen
    $(this.panels[this.active]).animate(this.css_setting '-100%',
                                    this.speed)

    # put the next panel in position, and animate on-screen
    $(this.panels[next])
        .css(this.css_setting '100%')
        .animate(this.css_setting '0px', this.speed)

    # treat the next panel as the 'active' one next loop
    this.active = next

$ ->
    for slideshow in $.find(".slideshow")
        rotator = new Rotator slideshow
```

To clarify the important differences, here's a line-by-line translation:

- An initial class name is at the start of the definition. You use this name to refer to the class so that new instances of the class can be created.
- New instances of the class are created with the convenient keyword new, and any arguments given are passed to the constructor.
- The functions and variables defined in a class are accessed within the instance by using the keyword this.
- A function wrapper is executed directly, but a class is not; rather, it has a constructor() function that runs each time an object of that type is created.
- Class functions are named with colons, and you can define functions other than constructor() with the "fat arrow" => notation.

These points will be relatively clear to anyone who has experienced an object system before, and probably to most who haven't, except for that last one. Why are there two notations, -> and =>, for function definitions?

Earlier in my description of inheritance, I mentioned the difference between CoffeeScript and JavaScript, and this difference in notation is the practical consequence. Since CoffeeScript is compiled to JavaScript, it must internally run on that prototypical system of inheritance, even though it provides a largely classful alternative. The keyword `this` is used in both systems, but unfortunately refers to different things!

Usually, CoffeeScript hides the various JavaScript foibles that a programmer doesn't need to know about, but it can't really hide this difference. Ensuring that `this` remains consistent in CoffeeScript requires a (very) small performance overhead, slightly more complex output, but more importantly, it creates a real difference among calling conventions when interoperating with JavaScript libraries and applications. So, sadly, it's a difference you need to understand.

Fortunately, the basic rules here are pretty straightforward:

- If the function is not in a class definition, use the thin arrow.
- If the function is the constructor of a class, use the thin arrow.
- If it's neither of these, and you have no overriding reason not to, use the fat arrow.

Always use the fat arrow for functions defined in classes, except the constructor, unless there's a reason not to.

EXTENDING CLASSES

Having looked at the encapsulation of objects in CoffeeScript, you're ready to look at inheritance. Inheritance is important as a form of code reuse, and it's also an issue of design and style. When programming in an object-oriented fashion, the class inheritance hierarchy is as important as any other aspect of the program architecture, and a badly thought-out structure leads to code that's very difficult to maintain.

The image rotator mentioned previously, even translated into a class-based format, suffers from a number of built-in assumptions. Primarily, the type of transition is hard-coded into the main piece of the code; later if other developers want to implement a new transition that perhaps moves the panels from the top downward, they'll have a lot of trouble. Certainly, to remove those assumptions, they'd need to reimplement much of the code already written.

This process of removing assumptions is often called *abstracting*: identifying the key things that a piece of code is doing and finding a more generalized version of the function that can form the basis of a number of more specific pieces of code.

Is it possible to teach a programmer how to abstract? Unfortunately, no. For one thing, how well an abstraction holds up over time depends heavily on how the requirements for a piece of software change over time. No matter how beautiful the design, if it doesn't fit the needs of the program, it's essentially no good, and programmers are usually not psychic. This is where experience matters a lot, but new programmers quickly learn which designs stand the test of time. (These are often referred to as *design patterns,* and they're an essential part of every programmer's toolbox.)

Here is what an abstract version of the image rotator might look like:

```
class AbstractRotator
    min_length: 1

    constructor: (slideshow) ->
        @panels = $(slideshow).find('li')
        if @panels.length < (@min_length - 1)
            throw """Can't rotate with fewer than #{ @min_length } panels,
                    only found #{ @panels.length }"""

        # configurable attributes
        @active = $(slideshow).data('start') ? 0
        @speed = $(slideshow).data('speed') ? 1000
        @duration = $(slideshow).data('duration') ? 4000

        # move panels into initial position
        @transition_off($(panel), false) for panel in @panels
        @transition_on($(@panels[@active]), false)

        # start
        window.setInterval(@do_rotation, @duration)

    transition_on: (slide, gradual) =>
        throw "Not implemented"

    transition_off: (slide, gradual) =>
        throw "Not implemented"

    choose_next: =>
        (@active + @panels.length + 1) % @panels.length

    do_rotation: =>
        # which panel to show next?
        next = @choose_next()

        # move the active panel off-screen
        @transition_off($(@panels[@active]), true)

        # put the next panel in position, and animate on-screen
        @transition_on($(@panels[next]), true)

        # treat the next panel as the 'active' one next loop
        @active = next
```

First, notice that this has seemingly disappeared; in the previous version, it was peppered everywhere. In fact, because this. (this-dot) is so common, CoffeeScript allows the use of @ instead, which makes the code noticeably more concise.

Next, notice that this code makes no CSS changes or animation calls. It knows literally nothing about the placement of slides. It implements two functions, transition_on() and `transition_off()`, which perform that task, but only as stubs that raise errors if they're called. Usually, an abstract, or *base,* class will not be a complete implementation. The extensions, the *subclasses,* fill in the gaps to provide a working solution.

A minimal implementation of an image rotator doesn't need to implement any special transition at all; it could simply show images when required, as shown here:

```
class NoAnimationRotator extends AbstractRotator
    transition_on: (slide, gradual) =>
        slide.css({'left': '0'})

    transition_off: (slide, gradual) =>
        slide.css({'left': '100%'})
```

This class is defined in the same way as any other class, except that the keyword `extends` tells CoffeeScript that this definition inherits from the one given previously. The superclass, `AbstractRotator`, also defined `transition_on()` and `transition_off()`, but the definitions given in this class override them. Every time a function with the same name is defined in the subclass, it entirely replaces the previously given definition.

Usually, an implementation this small is a sign of a poor abstraction. If a subclass is not doing very much, it's questionable whether it should be a subclass at all, but rather a small piece of logic in the superclass. In this specific case the implementation is bare-bones, but implementations of other more featureful subclasses would be significantly larger. Here's a more sophisticated implementation using animation:

```
class LeftRightRotator extends AbstractRotator
    min_length: 2

    constructor: (slideshow) ->
        super(slideshow)
        @direction = $(slideshow).data('direction') ? 1

    css_setting: (value) =>
        style = {}
        style[if this.direction == 1 then 'left' else 'right'] = value
        return style

    choose_next: () =>
        (@active + @panels.length + @direction) % @panels.length

    transition_on: (slide, gradual) =>
        @transition_off(slide, false)
        slide.animate(this.css_setting '0px', this.speed)

    transition_off: (slide, gradual) =>
        if gradual
            slide.animate(this.css_setting '-100%', this.speed)
        else
```

```
# move immediately to position ready to come on-screen,
# this simplifies the definition of transition_on()
slide.css(this.css_setting '100%')
```

Although the logic to make slides animate properly has been brought back, it's clear that the function of this class is still very much about positioning. The only piece of logic that has been reimplemented is `choose_next()`. The purpose of the gradual argument to the transition functions is clear now, too.

The constructor here is the most interesting thing to note, though, starting like this:

```
constructor: (slideshow) ->
    super(slideshow)
```

Previously, I said that functions defined in subclasses override the functions defined in the superclass. This is true, but sometimes it's not desirable. Sometimes you'll want to ensure that the original functionality still runs, but also extend it. CoffeeScript allows you to do so by using `super()`, which calls the definition of the function as the superclass has it (which, of course, could be inherited from another class above it!).

Use the ability to call the same function in the superclass very sparingly. In fact, I generally recommend not doing so at all outside the constructor, because it increases the dependency between the subclass and its parent and breaks down encapsulation.

MAKING CLASSES SUBSTITUTABLE

Earlier, I promised to revisit Liskov's substitution principle and explain it more fully, because it is important to good object-oriented design.

In the image rotators defined earlier, you'll find some dependencies between the abstract class and the implementations, notably:

- The abstract base calls `transition_on()` and `transition_off()`, expecting them to be defined in the subclass.
- The subclass can call functions defined in the parent, such as `choose_next()`.

These functions are part of the public definition of the class, and they effectively form part of the API. The substitution principle says that if you create a new subclass, it must implement the same interface as the superclass. So, for example, if I were to write a new rotator that implements `transition_off(slide, gradual)` but doesn't correctly respect `gradual=true`, the logic within the abstract class that uses that call to place the active slide into position at the start of the show would fail. The `gradual` parameter forms part of the contract, if you like, and not taking note of it is a change in behavior.

It's important to note that this doesn't mean each function must behave identically. For example, in `LeftRightRotator`, the `choose_next()` call is overridden to give the rotator the ability to count backward. That's a change in behavior, but not really a change in expectation; it's still returning a single integer.

USING THIS. IN COFFEESCRIPT

To some extent, I've glossed over precisely what `this.` is. There's some complexity with the JavaScript runtime underneath, but the CoffeeScript implementation has some details, too. Although `@` is an alias for `this.`, it often can be used in places where `this.` cannot be used.

Consider this class definition:

```
class HowThisWorks
    constructor: (@name) ->

    print_name: =>
        console.log @name
```

This is relatively standard, although a nice shortcut is used on the constructor: If an argument is referred to with `@`, the constructor automatically sets that attribute on the new instance, equivalent to this:

```
    constructor: (name) ->
        @name = name
```

Because that pattern is so common, CoffeeScript makes it easy. Then, on an instance of the class, `print_name()` does exactly what you expect: It outputs the name set on the instance. This code simply outputs `Steve`:

```
    obj = new HowThisWorks('Fred')
    obj.name = 'Steve'
    obj.print_name()
```

Within the class definition itself, though, `@` is still available but has a very different meaning. Consider this class:

```
class HowThisWorks
    @static_name: 'static'

    @print_name: =>
        console.log @static_name
```

Here, the `@` is being set on the class member names, and it doesn't refer to an instance of the class but to the class itself. These are called *static members,* because they're defined in the class, not set dynamically on an instance of the class. You use them like this:

```
    HowThisWorks.print_name()
```

No instance of the class is needed, and it can be referred to within an instance.

PRIVATE AND PROTECTED MEMBERS

Adherents of other languages may have already thought of these questions, but they're worth asking directly:

- Is it possible to hide members of CoffeeScript classes so that users of the class cannot see them at all?
- Similarly, is it possible to hide members of classes so that only subclasses can access them?

Members that are totally hidden from other parts of the code are usually referred to as *private*; members partially hidden from everything except subclasses are called *protected* (different languages may have different names for these concepts).

Again, because it's implemented on top of JavaScript, CoffeeScript is limited as to the amount of functionality it can make available, at least without significant contortions.

I should say to begin with that in dynamic languages, these types of data hiding are often not entirely necessary. They're used more often within compiled languages, because the reduced API scope of the class definition leads to faster compilation. In dynamic languages, data hiding doesn't benefit performance, so the convention is usually to prefix a `private` member name with an underscore. In this way, subclasses can access private data if they need to, negating the need for protected access, but it's clear to callers that making use of those members means tying yourself directly to its implementation.

You can create private static functions by declaring them as part of the class definition:

```
class WithPrivateMember
    priv = ->
        console.log "This is private, but static"

    constructor: ->
        priv()

obj = new WithPrivateMember()
# This does not work, as priv() is private:
# obj.priv()
```

In fact, you can also create private static variables, although they're generally not very useful. Private static functions are useful for creating helper functions that do not form part of the public API, but even here their use is questionable. If a class is to be fully extensible, such a helper function is almost always useful to a potential subclass.

Private members, and by extension protected members, are not possible to create otherwise.

MIXINS AND INTERFACES

Inheritance is one way to add functionality to objects, but another useful method is what is commonly known as a *mixin*. These are sometimes thought of as being a form of *multiple inheritance,* where a subclass inherits behavior from multiple superclasses. This leads to a number of problems and is generally frowned upon. (For example, if each superclass defines a constructor, which do you call? In what order?)

But as a form of "decoration," where additional common functionality can be added into a class without affecting the inheritance hierarchy, mixins are occasionally useful.

CoffeeScript provides no native support for mixins, but because of the underlying nature of JavaScript, adding one is easy:

```
class Mixin
    @extend = (klass, mixin) ->
        klass::[name] = method for name, method of mixin::
        klass

class Permission
    can_login: =>
        if @name == 'alex'
            return true
        return false

class Person
    constructor: (@name) ->

    Mixin.extend @, Permission
```

The `Mixin` class here is a simple helper class with a single static method, `extend()`. All `extend()` does is take two arguments, the class to be extended and the class with the methods with which to extend it. The methods are found by looping over the prototype of the donor class, accessed with the unseen-until-now `::` operator.

For example, a `Permission` class and a `Person` class are defined. Permissions are a concept that can apply to a number of different objects, objects that probably aren't substitutable for each other, so it doesn't make sense to define them in a superclass. In this example, the permission check in the mixin examines the `name` member of the class, making the mixin entirely dependent on the class definition. In practice, mixins would usually be implemented entirely separate from the definition of a given object and its implementation. Where a feature can be implemented in a stand-alone fashion and applied to a number of objects in different class hierarchies, it usually makes sense to implement the feature using mixins.

The static call to `extend()` is called at the end of the definition of `Person`, at which point, `@` still refers to the class `Person`, not an instance of it. Thus, the class definition of `Person` is extended with the methods of `Permission`.

SUMMARY

Object-orient programming is a key style for the web developer: you may not find you write everything this way, but the close support for class-based object definitions is one of the reasons many developers start learning CoffeeScript. It would be easy to write a lot more on this topic, but this chapter covered the basics:

- Defining objects using classes, and understanding the conventions used by CoffeeScript programmers to mark public and private interfaces
- The meaning of `this.` in different contexts and its incredibly useful alias: `@`
- Some tips on good class design, particularly the principle of substitutability, and looking at how to convert procedural code into classes
- Extending classes after their definition using mixins

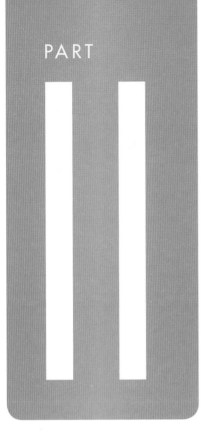

PART

II

COFFEESCRIPT PROJECTS

CHAPTER

6

USING JAVASCRIPT LIBRARIES

WHEN DEVELOPERS MOVE to a new language or to a newer version of one they were already using, they usually have to throw away much, if not all, of the code they had previously written. This can be because the syntax is too different or because its libraries use different APIs, and it's not always practical to attempt to convert code from the old style to the new. With CoffeeScript, though, things work differently: It compiles into JavaScript.

For the developer already using JavaScript, the move to CoffeeScript is much easier, because none of those problems exist. Old code is still

usable, so all of the investment in JavaScript is not lost. It's better than backward compatibility, though—CoffeeScript is also forward compatible! New code can be written in CoffeeScript and integrated into existing JavaScript projects. This chapter shows you how.

Out of necessity, you will find numerous Java-Script examples—don't let those put you off! You do need to examine some of the dustier corners. However, by the end of the chapter, you will have explored some of the deeper aspects of JavaScript and should have a renewed appreciation for the work the CoffeeScript compiler is doing for you.

EASY CALLING CONVENTIONS: DON'T THROW AWAY THAT EXISTING CODE!

Why would a developer mix CoffeeScript and JavaScript code? This is an important question. And the honest answer, from my perspective, is that in general doing so isn't a good idea. Also, developing a project in multiple languages increases the difficulty of finding and fixing bugs. However, there are many scenarios where this makes sense:

- **Making use of existing libraries:** This is probably the primary reason most developers start using CoffeeScript. It's difficult to imagine that the language would have become as popular as it is if developers had not been able to continue to use jQuery—arguably, it has become popular precisely because it's easier to use!

- **Transitioning existing projects:** This isn't as common as the preceding reason, but developers who want to use CoffeeScript but have existing (potentially large) codebases in JavaScript may have a period during which they're developing new functionality in CoffeeScript alongside the existing code. Without the ability to transition, it's much harder to choose to start using CoffeeScript.

- **Creating new libraries:** CoffeeScript provides a number of programming-in-the-large features that make it easy to write clean APIs that other developers can use, and it makes sense to start new code in CoffeeScript.

These three scenarios neatly cover the three key possibilities: calling JavaScript from a CoffeeScript application, calling CoffeeScript from a JavaScript application, and writing applications that are a mix of both.

Like many features of development systems, the fact that something is possible doesn't imply in any way that it's a good idea! I've listed these three possibilities in order of complexity. Calling JavaScript from CoffeeScript is easy, reliable, and throughout this book it happens constantly (for example, using jQuery). Going the other direction is equally reliable, but it's slightly more complex because of the increased protections CoffeeScript offers. Lastly, mixing code can be a recipe for extreme complexity (I demonstrate some potential pitfalls later in the section on mixing JavaScript directly in CoffeeScript source), but you can follow some simple rules to gain most of the benefits without running into trouble.

CALLING JAVASCRIPT FROM COFFEESCRIPT

When I say "calling conventions," what exactly am I referring to? For the most part, what I'm talking about is actually "naming conventions."

The following is a piece of simple, and not very good, JavaScript that's intended to be called on page load to hide a number of elements:

```
no_elements = 5;

function clearDisplay() {
  for (i = 0; i < no_elements; i++) {
```

```
    $('#text-' + i).hide();
  }
}
```

There's a variable, `no_elements`, and a function, `clearDisplay()`. They have obvious and clear names in JavaScript. Do they translate simply to CoffeeScript?

For functions, things are actually quite clear. By defining a function in JavaScript, you're creating a block of code that can be called using a name. The name is created in a global scope and cannot be changed, although it can be redefined later on. That global name is also available in CoffeeScript and refers to the same block of code, so life is simple.

Variables, though, are a totally different matter. Variables always have scope to the extent that it's usually not true to say that a particular variable is "global" in any sense—although there often is an outermost scope that behaves very globally. In browsers, that scope is usually `window`, so in fact, a global variable such as the preceding one will be `window.no_elements`. On the server side, though, it might be `global.no_elements`, depending on which server is executing the code.

Thankfully, the number of times access to a variable defined elsewhere in JavaScript is actually needed is very, very few, and when using third-party libraries, it's almost unheard of. Functions and objects, as far as APIs are concerned, rule.

Constructing Objects

In general, in the JavaScript world, there are two ways of creating new objects, and although they're more or less equivalent, there are minor differences between the two.

The first form uses the `new` keyword and takes full advantage of the prototypical system that JavaScript uses:

```
    user = new User();
```

Aside from the trailing semicolon, this form translates directly into CoffeeScript, `new` keyword and all. Because CoffeeScript objects are based on their JavaScript counterparts, there should be no noticeable difference between using an object defined within JavaScript versus one defined within CoffeeScript.

The second form eschews the `new` keyword, preferring instead to provide a function that returns a new object:

```
    user = User();
```

When translating this usage into CoffeeScript, it's tempting to reinsert the `new` keyword to make the call look like any other object construction. Although this tends to work in most instances, it can generate insidious bugs—particularly if the JavaScript function is implementing something like a Singleton pattern and attempting to return the same object instance for each call, for example.

So the rule here is actually easy to remember: When using an object constructor defined in JavaScript, use a direct translation in CoffeeScript, and don't insert new where it wouldn't be used natively.

CALLING COFFEESCRIPT FROM JAVASCRIPT

Going in the other direction, writing new code in CoffeeScript but calling it from JavaScript, is actually relatively easy—although there are a couple of tricks to be aware of.

Classes and objects transfer easily and natively. In fact, their usage is so similar, you only need to know the appropriate JavaScript syntax. Look again at a simple class:

```
class User
    constructor: (@name) ->

    getName: =>
        @name
```

This construct in JavaScript is almost identical to the CoffeeScript version:

```
var user = new User('test');
console.log("The user's name is " + user.getName());
```

Although many JavaScript libraries no longer require the use of the new keyword to create new instances of objects, when using code created in CoffeeScript, it's pretty much mandatory: often things will work without it, but when things go wrong the errors will be very strange and difficult to debug.

Making Functions Available

Defining classes in CoffeeScript and then using them from JavaScript code is easy. Doing the same with functions is a lot more difficult because CoffeeScript generally does not name functions.

Without names, the calling JavaScript cannot access the function directly; it needs some kind of reference to the function in order to call it. Later in the section on CommonJS, I cover a way of getting a reference to the function, but for now, assume that this is virtually impossible. After all, the usual way of getting access to data needed is by calling a function, which introduces a chicken-and-egg problem.

So the easiest course is to make the name available, and since the CoffeeScript compiler doesn't do that, you must do so manually. Here's an example for node.js:

```
global?.Test = ->
    console.log "I can be called from JavaScript now"
```

The JavaScript code is now free to call Test(), and things work as expected.

As discussed earlier, though, `global` is often used by server-side JavaScript implementations. On the browser, the uppermost scope is usually `window`. Perhaps you are happy coding for a specific implementation, or if not, perhaps you're happy doing a little bit of extra coding to cope with that difference—for example:

```
test = ->
    console.log "I can be called from JavaScript now"

window?.Test = test
global?.Test = test
```

Note that a small amount of duplication occurs, but in general, this works reasonably well, and there are ways of making this extra code a bit simpler if there's a need to export many functions.

Lastly, in many environments, `this` (used outside of class definitions) refers to whichever object is acting as the *global scope,* which means that as a final piece of simplification, the function can be written as

```
@Test = ->
    console.log "I can be called from JavaScript now"
```

USING COMMONJS MODULES

It's clear at this point that you can write libraries a number of different ways, and as expected, different developers make use of all of them, sometimes simultaneously. This problem has extended across different projects, but thankfully, solutions are now at hand to mitigate it, and one of the most useful solutions comes from CommonJS.

At its heart, CommonJS is simply a group of developers with the goal of making the broad JavaScript ecosystem more consistent and cohesive. They have defined approaches and practices in many areas, and module loading is one that they are best known for.

With any JavaScript project of significant size, early on the code gets broken up into a number of different files. The files are usually sewn back together for deployment purposes, but quickly problems with that approach arise: Do they need to be sewn back together in a specific order? How is it determined which files are needed? CommonJS module loading is the answer to these problems and more.

The module loading is based on a simple idea: expressing dependencies. If a piece of code uses a certain class or function, it needs a way of saying, "I need this." If a piece of a code provides a certain class or function, it needs a way of saying, "I provide this."

Those two pieces of information can then be used to determine which files are needed, in what order, and to some degree, the module loading system also ensures that the authors of the code use standard methods of exposing the functionality in their libraries.

Making the API Visible

Exposing functionality is simple:

```
class UserModel
    constructor: (@name) ->

module?.exports =
    User: UserModel
```

That's the full definition for a simple class, and the export statement required so that it can be used elsewhere. By now, the class definition won't be problematic for you, but the export statement does look a bit weird.

The first thing to understand is that usually the information exported will be an object. It's possible to export single values, but quite often that's too restrictive—for internal use exporting a single class may make sense, but when making available an API, usually there are a number of classes or functions to make visible.

Take a look at how that works in practice at the coffee shell. The function to find the exported information is simply called `require()`:

```
$ coffee
coffee> require('./user-model')
{ User: [Function: UserModel] }
```

The interface is simple. Pass the name of the file to `require()`, and it passes back the exported information. Although I've defined a class `User`, underneath JavaScript implements classes as functions, so the structure has come back as an object with the names given as attributes and functions as the values.

Look back at the export:

```
module?.exports =
    User: UserModel
```

The object is defined on the second line, and you can put in there as many classes or functions as you want to export. Often, the name given matches the class name, but that doesn't have to be the case (as just shown).

You could also have simply written `module.exports`; however, adding the question mark is a good practice. In environments without module loaders, `module` generally doesn't exist, so attempting to reference `module.exports` directly will cause an error.

Accessing the API

You've already been introduced to `require()`, so you know how to use it in code:

```
api = require('./user-model')
user = new api.User('alex')
console.log user.name
```

This code works as expected, and large libraries with extensive functionality are often used like this. However, if only a single piece of functionality is needed, CoffeeScript's *destructuring assignment* can make the process of getting the function references slightly simpler:

```
{User} = require('./user-model')
user = new User('alex')
console.log user.name
```

This code is functionally equivalent, but now there's no intermediate variable acting as a namespace. Destructuring assignment is really useful. It allows the developer to call a function that returns an array or an object, and immediately assign the results to separate variables.

Lastly, a useful thing to point out about the CommonJS module loader is that, as the name implies, it was originally designed for JavaScript, which means that the same `require()` will work in JavaScript and that the problem of making CoffeeScript-defined functions available in JavaScript code effectively goes away. The module export system can be used to pass the reference to a function through to the calling JavaScript, and the developer doesn't need to play tricks with the global scope.

USING EXTENDS ON EXISTING CLASSES

As we've seen, calling CoffeeScript from JavaScript, and vice versa, presents a few small problems that are easily overcome with just a bit of extra understanding. But things can get more complicated than that!

Classes can be defined in CoffeeScript, and JavaScript has an equivalent based on objects, but CoffeeScript's classful inheritance is a big addition to standard JavaScript functionality. Is it possible for a CoffeeScript class to inherit from a JavaScript object and vice versa?

The answer here is yes—but this is where things can get very complicated, very quickly.

NOT ALL OBJECTS ARE CREATED EQUAL

In CoffeeScript, the `new` keyword is used to create new instances of classes. However, in JavaScript, that's not always used—some developers prefer to ignore the prototypical inheritance.

One common pattern in the JavaScript world is to use factory functions to create new objects of a specific type, rather than using prototype objects:

```
function User(name) {
    var user = {
        name: name
    };

    user.getName = function () {
        return user.name;
    };

    return user;
}
```

Such an API is quite common because it doesn't require the caller to use new to create a new object. You simply call the function. However, this pattern ignores the prototype completely. If you want to extend an object created in that fashion within CoffeeScript you might try this as a first attempt:

```
class CoffeeUser extends User
    getName: =>
        return "Coffee user '#{ @name }'"
```

Unfortunately, this doesn't work. When one class extends another, what's really happening under the covers is that the JavaScript prototype is being copied over to create that basic inheritance. With a factory function like the preceding one, the prototype of the factory has no relation to the prototype of the objects it creates—the objects returned by new CoffeeUser() are therefore no different than standard User() objects, and the new functionality doesn't exist.

When the prototypical system has been sidestepped, relatively little can be done directly to bring objects defined in code elsewhere into line.

WRITING JAVASCRIPT LIBRARIES IN COFFEESCRIPT

CoffeeScript offers an ideal environment in which to create libraries for later use from native JavaScript. There is some degree of obfuscation here. Although readable, the JavaScript output tends to be a lot more verbose than the hand-crafted equivalent—but that's mostly because CoffeeScript is protecting developers from worse practices.

Indeed, CoffeeScript goes to great lengths to ensure that code is not accidentally polluting the global scope or doing other things that would tread on the toes of coexisting code.

PROVIDING A NATURAL INTERFACE

CoffeeScript naturally takes a relatively object-oriented view of the world, and it can be tempting to define a library API as a series of objects in the same way a developer might write a series of components for a Java application. However, it's often worth thinking about how the code is going to be used within the JavaScript and what might be the most natural interface.

One popular method is to create an API that simply returns a single type of object whose various member functions always return the object itself. This is the *fluent* interface made popular by jQuery, and it makes sense in a variety of contexts. Although it's used for DOM manipulation primarily in jQuery, similar interfaces have been used successfully to query databases and filter data.

Another less popular but still common interface goes one step further. Instead of returning a single type of object, a single instance of a type is returned via a function call. Any time that function call is made, the exact same instance is returned, no matter where the caller is. This is technically known as the Singleton pattern.

DOCUMENTING CODE

CoffeeScript doesn't have any kind of official documentation system, but if a system were to be considered at least semi-official, it would be Docco—also written by Jeremy Ashkenas. It's used throughout the CoffeeScript site and is the tool which generates the comments-by-code style documentation that documents the CoffeeScript source code. (See Figure 6-1.)

Figure 6-1: This Docco output provides clear commentary neatly aligned with the code in question.

Source: coffeescript.org/documentation/docs/scope.html

Although the resultant output tends to be very readable and accessible, it lends itself to a prosaic form of comment. Take a look at this example from the CoffeeScript cake source:

```
# Invoke another task in the current Cakefile.
invoke: (name) ->
  missingTask name unless tasks[name]
  tasks[name].action options
```

Docco requires nothing except comments before functions and doesn't support very many fancy options. Aside from Markdown syntax to do basic formatting and hyperlinking, no structured information is here at all. Whether a particular parameter is described well is up to the author, and there's no standard way of describing parameters.

From CoffeeScript 1.5 it is also possible to use Docco "inside out." Instead of writing code and documenting it with comments, it's now possible to write a document and intersperse the code within, a style called Literate Programming. Documents are saved as a `.litcoffee` file, and the code is simply indented from the rest of the document:

```
Literate CoffeeScript can make use of various
[Markdown](http://daringfireball.net/projects/markdown)
features as a normal document would. When code is required, it is simply
 indented and it runs as usual:

    test = ->
      console.log "Markdown code blocks indented by four space"

    test()
```

Within Markdown a code block must be indented by four spaces (or a tab, which I recommend you don't use), but after that normal indentation rules apply. The code is executed as if the indentation required to mark the code block doesn't exist (the leading four spaces are stripped).

Literate programming is not for everyone, but this is a particularly useful form of writing example code or API documentation when the code serves the purpose of the documentation. Another area this style shines is test cases, where literate descriptions of test cases come in very handy for maintenance.

For developers more used to systems like JavaDoc or PHPDoc, this type of system seems strange—the point of documentation surely must be to elucidate these details? Well, in many ways, it's simply a matter of taste, but in this case, at least a choice is available.

As well as Docco, a more structured system called CoffeeDoc is available. In many ways, it functions very similarly to Docco, working with block comments before and after functions, but it does a lot more work extracting function and parameter names and preparing documentation output that follows a less discursive and more API-driven structure. CoffeeDoc turns similar comments into those shown in Figure 6-2.

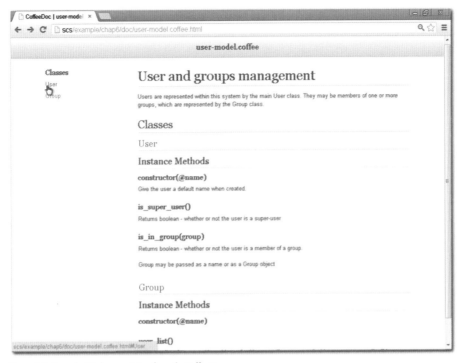

Figure 6-2: Example API documentation from the CoffeeDoc processor.

In addition, this output can be created in JSON and then can be fed into other processors, such as the popular Python documentation system, Sphinx.

MIXING JAVASCRIPT—WHEN ABSOLUTELY REQUIRED

As part of the process of compiling CoffeeScript into JavaScript, as you might imagine, the compiler makes it easy to drop specific snippets of JavaScript into the resulting output.

This feature is, of course, generally discouraged, and there's almost no good reason to ever use it. Often, developers using it in the wild have a better, more CoffeeScript-native alternative available; they just don't know it. Defining functions is a favorite. Rather than explore CoffeeScript fully and understand how it works, it's easier to simply drop in a piece of JavaScript.

In some ways, resorting on JavaScript isn't a bad thing. Even though it can be a crutch that discourages you from learning more about CoffeeScript, it's also a safety net that gives developers confidence that they're not going to end up stuck in some way attempting to interoperate their CoffeeScript with JavaScript.

Sometimes, too, it's preferable to drop in the JavaScript simply because it means not having to translate it into CoffeeScript. An example here might be reusing a snippet of JavaScript that has come from elsewhere—many services, such as web analytics or advertising servers, ask that you place a small piece of JavaScript on the page. Retaining that in the original JavaScript makes it easier for another developer to search for that piece of code, as well as ensuring that no unintentional changes in functionality are made by translating it to another language. Generally, though, I argue that such snippets should probably be in a separate file and not interspersed in the CoffeeScript.

To insert JavaScript into a program, simply surround the code with backticks (`` ` ``). Because the pass-through process isn't totally straightforward, you have to avoid a number of bear traps. Take a look at this example:

```
hide_content = ->
    `
    $.each('.panel', function (i, panel) {
        $(panel).hide();
    });
    $('.message').text("Panels hidden");
    `
    true

hide_content ()
```

I've written deliberately overcomplicated JavaScript to demonstrate the point here. The JavaScript is surrounded with backticks to mark that block as not being CoffeeScript and therefore not needing translation. Even then, though, this doesn't look terribly natural.

The content between the backticks is treated as a single expression for the purposes of CoffeeScript, even though it might be a series of expressions. This facet has some unfortunate consequences. For example, if a CoffeeScript function has only a JavaScript body, all that happens is that the first JavaScript expression is evaluated and returned—the rest of the code will not be executed!

This is because CoffeeScript functions, in the absence of explicit return statements, return the value of the last expression. The JavaScript block is such an expression, so it just returns the value of that expression, but by the time it goes through conversion to JavaScript, it's no longer a single expression but a series of statements, and the return comes before the first statement. To avoid the implicit return being inserted before the block of JavaScript being inserted, a single `true` is left as the last expression of the function, which is what ends up being automatically returned.

Also, it can be incredibly easy to think of this almost as a templating system—to put in JavaScript statements that aren't well-formed, but which in combination might be:

```
`function foo() {`
console.log "This is a CoffeeScript statement in a JavaScript function!"
`}`

foo ()
```

Sadly enough, this works—although only by chance, and if the CoffeeScript were properly indented, the compiler would throw an error. I cannot stress this enough: Don't do this! A future, smarter CoffeeScript compiler may well throw this out, and there are plenty of variations on this theme which do not, and will never, work.

To use this feature sanely, I strongly suggest sticking to these rules:

- Try to include only single statements.
- If you must have multiple statements in a block, ensure that the block is not being used in a context where it's evaluated as an expression, such as within conditionals or as the sole body of a function.
- Ensure that enclosed code is free-standing—you cannot break up JavaScript over multiple blocks and expect it to work.

SUMMARY

The main points that have been covered in this chapter are:

- Calling JavaScript functions from CoffeeScript code
- Calling CoffeeScript functions from JavaScript code
- Mixing and matching CoffeeScript and Javascript

The devil is in the detail whenever two different systems are interfaced, and bringing Java-Script and CoffeeScript directly together is no exception. There are a variety of corner-cases and errors to avoid, and I've covered the important ones. You should now be comfortable getting different pieces of code to interoperate.

You also looked at the process of developing JavaScript-native APIs in CoffeeScript and as a bonus, I demonstrated a couple of the documentation systems available to the CoffeeScript developer.

TESTING WITH JASMINE

IN MANY PROFESSIONS experts agree on a set of practices that are really good ideas, but few in the profession actively follow those conventions. In the field of web development, automated code testing is such an idea. It's not that developers think doing so is a bad idea; it's just that they rarely find the time to spend on it.

For many, the idea of automated code testing works very well for libraries with established APIs that rarely change, but in the context of peripheral application logic or, more especially, user interfaces, automated testing becomes a much more complex proposition. A variety of

tools are now available that can be brought to bear in these different situations and make automatic testing truly straightforward.

The key tool introduced in this chapter is Jasmine, which is a system for writing and running test suites. Jasmine tests describe simple observable behaviors about a piece of code, and then run the code to see if the behavior occurs. As a fundamental description of how your code should behave, these types of tests can also be viewed as a specification of the problem and can lead you to think about your code in different ways.

INTRODUCING JASMINE

Jasmine, one of the libraries originally designed for use in JavaScript, is a behavior-driven test suite. There are a variety of different ideas about how to design tests and how they should be integrated into projects. The key idea with behavior-driven development (BDD) testing is that the tests are simple and descriptive; reading them is similar to reading English.

As well as making the process of writing tests quite easy, Jasmine provides a range of interfaces by which the tests can be run and evaluated. It offers a command-line interface as you might expect, but you can also run tests within the browser or via a library API. This enables you to call and use tests in a number of contexts, maximizing the value of the test suite for a given project.

SETTING UP A SPEC AREA TO RUN JASMINE TESTS

You can run Jasmine tests a number of different ways, but the simplest and most straightforward is to begin with a command-line test runner. A test runner is the harness that actually locates and executes the tests, and it usually reports on the results. To begin with, the `jasmine-node` package from the usual `npm` sources is enough for these needs. Installing that package is easy:

```
npm install jasmine-node
```

As the name suggests, this runner uses Jasmine and node to run the tests. By convention, tests are stored in a directory called `spec/` (although it could have another name), and sometimes tests are categorized beneath that by putting different tests in different subdirectories.

A test need not be very complicated. Here is a simple spec that tests the functionality of a very bare-bones CoffeeScript class:

```coffee
class SimpleClass
    constructor: (@name) ->


describe 'SimpleClass', ->

    it 'takes the name we give it', ->
        obj = new SimpleClass('foo')
        expect(obj.name).toEqual('foo')
```

It's unusual to test the code in the same file as the test itself. Rather, in the real world, `SimpleClass` would be accessed by the test by using `require()`, but for these purposes, it helps illustrate the point. Save this file as `spec/simple.spec.coffee`. (Having `spec` in the filename is important because it lets the test runner know which files contain Jasmine tests.) You can then execute the test runner:

```
jasmine-node --coffee spec/
.
```

```
Finished in 0.01 seconds
1 test, 1 assertion, 0 failures
```

This is an example of successful output. Jasmine is saying that it completed one test, within that test was one assertion (the `expect()` call), and none of the tests failed. Were the test to fail, the output would be more like this:

```
jasmine-node --coffee spec/
F

Failures:

  1) SimpleClass takes the name we give it
   Message:
     Expected undefined to equal 'foo'.
   Stacktrace:
     Error: Expected undefined to equal 'foo'.
    at new jasmine.ExpectationResult    (jasmine-2.0.0.rc1.js:102:32)
   at null.toEqual (jasmine-2.0.0.rc1.js:1171:29)
   at null.<anonymous> (spec/simple.spec.coffee:16:31)
   at jasmine.Block.execute (jasmine-2.0.0.rc1.js:1001:15)
   at jasmine.Queue.next_ (jasmine-2.0.0.rc1.js:1790:31)
   at jasmine.Queue.start (jasmine-2.0.0.rc1.js:1743:8)
   at jasmine.Spec.execute (jasmine-2.0.0.rc1.js:2070:14)
   at jasmine.Queue.next_ (jasmine-2.0.0.rc1.js:1790:31)
   at jasmine.Queue.start (jasmine-2.0.0.rc1.js:1743:8)
   at jasmine.Suite.execute (jasmine-2.0.0.rc1.js:2215:14)

Finished in 0.013 seconds
1 test, 1 assertion, 1 failure
```

As well as noting the failure, the test runner provides information about the failure: which test failed, which expectation was not met, and a backtrace from the code at that point so that the thread of execution can be seen. (In this case, including the stack frames from the test runner isn't so useful; every backtrace will contain those, so the lines after `jasmine.Block.execute` are not that informative.)

WRITING JASMINE TESTS

"Behavioral" is an odd adjective to use when talking about tests—surely all systems of testing code are testing the behavior of the code? Well, that's true, but in this instance, the adjective is referring to the way the tests themselves are written. Each test attempts to check some specific behavior of the code, and it is structured in three parts:

- A description of what is being tested
- A statement about a behavior that the thing being tested should exhibit
- Some operations on the thing being tested and a series of expectations about the results

Look again at the simple test executed earlier:

```
describe 'SimpleClass', ->

    it 'takes the name we give it', ->
        obj = new SimpleClass('foo')
        expect(obj.name).toBe('foo')
```

The `describe()` call is giving Jasmine a good description of the artifact being tested. Quite often this will be a class name or some specific aspect of a class. The statements about behaviors expected come after that: `it()` takes two arguments, a description of the behavior and a function that tests that behavior.

Within each test come the expectations, which can also be referred to as assertions. `expect()` generally takes a single value, which is the data being tested, and the subsequent function call tests the value for a specific outcome. `toBe()` is what Jasmine refers to as a *matcher* and is one of the most commonly used, but there are plenty of others:

- `toBe` and `toNotBe` test whether a value is equal to or not equal to another. In CoffeeScript, values a and b are equal to each other if a==b, which is strict equality. `"1"==1` is `false`, and different object instances are also unlikely to be equal to each other.
- `toBeEqual` and `toNotBeEqual` test equality in the looser JavaScript sense; for example `expect("1").toBeEqual(1)` is `true`.
- `toBeDefined`, `toBeUndefined`, and `toBeNull` test against various stages of definedness.
- `toMatch` and `toNotMatch` test against a regular expression, allowing a particularly powerful range of assertions.

It's worth reading through the Jasmine API documentation in full, where you'll find a number of other tests you can perform. Those discussed here are the meat and potatoes, though, and will make up the bulk of most specs.

SPYING WITH JASMINE

Before moving on, I want to delve into one of the more advanced features of Jasmine that makes it particularly useful: *spies*. The concept of a spy is quite simple: It's a piece of code that is inserted into part of the software being tested at runtime to override references to functions that would otherwise be there, giving the test suite more insight into what the code is actually doing. This form of run-time injection, often referred to as "monkey patching" is generally frowned on, but it is a useful part of a test framework. The example here is a slightly extended version of the test class shown earlier:

```
class SimpleClass
    constructor: (name) ->
        @attrs =
            name: name
```

```
int_get_attr: (attr) =>
    @attrs[attr]

getName: =>
    @int_get_attr 'name'
```

The name value has been moved from an attribute on the object to an internal map. The behavior of this class is still testable with the previous test, but say that it's important to check that the internal interface to find that attribute is being used, rather than a direct look-up within that getName() method. Ordinarily, that would be quite hard to test, but spies allow tests like this:

```
describe 'SimpleClass', ->

    it 'knows its name', ->
        obj = new SimpleClass('foo')

        spyOn(obj, 'int_get_attr').andCallThrough()

        expect(obj.getName()).toBe 'foo'
        expect(obj.int_get_attr).toHaveBeenCalled()
```

The first key call is to spyOn(). This is saying that the test should spy on the int_get_attr() method of obj. That method is then replaced at runtime with a function defined by the spy so that any calls to that method actually go through to the Jasmine Spy rather than the object itself.

Adding addCallThrough() to the instruction tells the spy to intercept the call to int_get_attr(), and also to pass through the call to the original method. For all intents and purposes, then, the method patched in to the spy is going to be virtually undetectable to the calling code.

After the first test is passed and the name is retrieved correctly, another expect can be set up—that the int_get_attr() method has been called. One of the things the spy can do is register whether a method has been called; it can also count the number of calls and check the parameters that were used or the return result.

Spies have a variety of uses. One of the most powerful is as a tool to create mock objects. For those of you unfamiliar with mock objects, the idea is that where a complex object (or even just a function call) is making external requests or is otherwise highly coupled to some other piece of code, it's better to replace it with a simpler object that has behavior similar enough to be usable.

So, for example, instead of relying on an Ajax request to fetch data from a server, a mock object could be used with the same API that simply returns some known pre-computed value rather than perform the actual request. This approach results in a more reliable and more predictable test result, and using mocks to decouple pieces of code from each other makes the testing more independent.

One of the downsides of mocks is that to implement them correctly, almost inevitably you need to create a complete copy of the API being mocked, and for some objects, that's an awful lot of work. Spies can simplify this tremendously, though: Instead of mocking an entire object, you can use a spy to patch over the pieces that aren't wanted, leaving the rest intact.

Spies are also an excellent method of inducing errors. For example, you can use them to force objects or functions to return specific error codes without manually supplying the explicit path to trigger the error. This is great news for tests: The logical flow of code-handling errors is generally one of the least-used and most untested parts of an application, because generally errors occur only rarely.

BEHAVIOR-DRIVEN DEVELOPMENT: WHAT IS A GOOD TEST?

For a number of years around the turn of the century, test-driven development (TDD) was all the rage. Part of this movement was undoubtedly a visceral reaction to corporate development environments that relied heavily on manual QA teams to do the majority of the testing, but it also dovetailed neatly with the developers' excitement about Agile development methodologies.

The purpose of Agile development was to correct the fact that in many projects, there's insufficient information about what the end product should look like—particularly at the start of a project. Rather than attempt to project manage and plan the development of something that might not meet the needs of the end user, Agile developers simply assume that a project will change substantially.

Planning for change turns out to be something that can be done quite successfully. It means doing development in small units and performing regular testing with the end user to see how on track the development is. (You can use this approach to make small incremental changes that nudge the direction of development, rather than massive project resets.) The approach also means writing software that is adaptable.

Writing adaptable software sounds like a recipe for disaster. The temptation to build unnecessary features is great, leading to over-engineered solutions that take too long to deliver. But it turns out that there is another way of ensuring that software is adaptable: making it amenable to refactoring.

Refactoring is the process by which the internal workings of an application are changed from one design or architecture to another, and it sometimes implies changing some particularly critical pieces of code. This is where the story comes back to testing: By developing comprehensive test suites of the application functionality at different levels, you'll find it's much easier and more reliable to refactor the application software.

Substantial, well-engineered test suites are as much a development tool as they are a part of the application. With the ability to make radical changes and demonstrate that the application is still working to specification, you can be bolder about all aspects of your work, whether it's creating new features or performing routine maintenance and clean-up.

Unit Testing Versus Integration Testing

One of the key things to understand when writing tests is whether the test is supposed to be a unit test or an integration test. Some developers get them confused; other developers don't see the value in one or other of these types of tests.

A unit test should be a relatively stand-alone test of the functionality of a specific piece of code, usually a class or function. Unit tests should not test other pieces of code at the same time, which means that both the test and the artifact being tested are as separable and independent as possible: ideally, totally stand-alone. Where a class or function is coupled to another piece of code, you can use mock objects/functions or stubs to remove the dependency.

Integration tests are almost the total opposite. Instead of testing pieces of code singularly and individually, they test how the code works when it's brought together, and the ideal integration test is something that tests the final application as a whole. Integration tests necessarily depend on multiple pieces of code, if not the entire application, and generally don't make wide use of mocks or other "fake" testing harnesses.

When using tests to drive development, the unit tests are the most important. These are the tests that specify how a new piece of code is supposed to work, and should ideally fail first before the code is written. On the other hand, the integration tests should lend some degree of confidence to the release process so that the test suite passing is a sign that at least all the key functions of the application continue to work properly.

Although Jasmine can be used for integration testing, I think that its main strength is in unit testing and that there is a huge amount of value in testing the behaviors of the classes being written for an application, as a form of documentation if nothing else.

When considering what a good test should look like, then, take into account these factors:

- Does this test tell me, or a co-developer, something about how the application is supposed to behave?
- How thorough is the test in terms of the functionality being looked at?
- Do the tests exercise all the different code paths within the application?
- Are the tests at the right level of abstraction to ensure they are testing the functionality in general, and not the implementation details?

TESTING INSIDE THE BROWSER

Using console-based test runners is a really good start, and I highly recommend doing so for testing business logic and more "pure" pieces of application code. For testing server-side code, the environment makes a lot of sense because it runs on node as it would for the application. On the client-side, though, things are somewhat different.

An in-browser test runner is also an excellent addition to the testing arsenal for a number of reasons:

- Much of the client-side code tends to be concerned with UI. This means running in an environment that has a working DOM.
- Different browsers present different environments. Having an in-browser test runner allows the same suite of tests to be deployed against different browsers, ensuring compatibility.
- Often, the more graphical test runners are simply easier to use.

However, an in-browser test runner has a few downsides. Obviously, the code being tested needs to run in that environment also, so this approach isn't appropriate for testing pieces of server code, although specific functionality can be tested, and some browsers don't perform as well as others, leading to some test suites taking a little while to run.

To start doing some in-browser testing, first download the Jasmine stand-alone release at `https://github.com/pivotal/jasmine/downloads`.

Right now, this package is distributed as a ZIP archive containing various files and directories:

```
.
|-- lib
|    `-- jasmine-1.3.1
|        |-- jasmine.css
|        |-- jasmine-html.js
|        |-- jasmine.js
|        `-- MIT.LICENSE
|-- spec
|    |-- PlayerSpec.js
|    `-- SpecHelper.js
|-- SpecRunner.html
`-- src
     |-- Player.js
     `-- Song.js
```

You can remove the contents of `src/` and `spec/` at this point; `src/` contains the application code being tested, and `spec/` contains the various tests to be run. To begin with, I'll demonstrate the runner utilizing the specs used earlier.

By default, the runner—`SpecRunner.html`—is quite JavaScript-heavy and not terribly CoffeeScript-friendly. As a first step, rewrite the runner to make it more manageable:

```
<!doctype html>
<html>
<head>
  <title>Jasmine Spec Runner</title>

  <link rel="shortcut icon" type="image/png"
```

```
                                href="lib/jasmine-1.3.1/jasmine_favicon.png">
    <link rel="stylesheet" type="text/css" href="lib/jasmine-1.3.1/jasmine.css">
    <script type="text/javascript" src="lib/jasmine-1.3.1/jasmine.js"></script>
    <script type="text/javascript"
        src="lib/jasmine-1.3.1/jasmine-html.js"></script>

    <!-- include source files here... -->

    <!-- include spec files here... -->
    <script type="text/javascript" src="spec/simple.spec.js"></script>
    <script type="text/javascript" src="spec/spy.spec.js"></script>

    <script type="text/javascript" src="runner.js"></script>
</head>

<body>
</body>
</html>
```

Because the spec files contain the source being tested, no source links are listed, but for more crucial applications, you would find a set of source scripts and then the spec scripts as well. All of these scripts have been compiled from CoffeeScript to JavaScript, and the test runner code has been separated out and translated into CoffeeScript:

```
jasmineEnv = jasmine.getEnv()
jasmineEnv.updateInterval = 1000

htmlReporter = new jasmine.HtmlReporter
jasmineEnv.addReporter htmlReporter

jasmineEnv.specFilter = (spec) ->
    htmlReporter.specFilter spec

currentWindowOnload = window.onload
window.onload = ->
    currentWindowOnload?()
    jasmineEnv.execute()
```

Once it is up and running, you can open the test runner in the browser. It doesn't need to be served via a web server, either. Loading up the file directly from disk will work. The screen will look something like the one in Figure 7-1.

There are a few annoyances here, though:

- Every time a new spec is written, it needs to be manually added to the runner.
- Each new piece of code written for the application also needs to be manually added.
- There's no automatic compilation step to translate the CoffeeScript source to JavaScript.

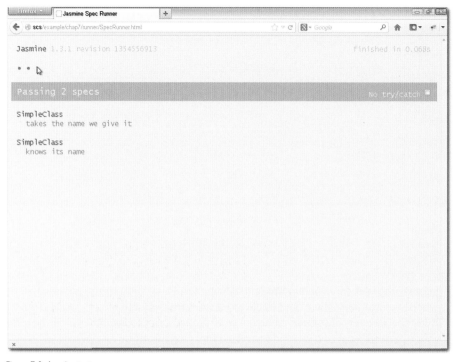

Figure 7-1: Jasmine test runners.

Later, I provide some solutions to these problems using the hem system for compiling the source and helping host the Jasmine system in general, and making it a much more integrated tool. The better Jasmine is integrated into the development environment, the more likely it will be properly used, and therefore offer the most to the developer.

When tests fail—as indeed they will, at one time or another—the test runner in the browser also adopts a rather angry color scheme. (See Figure 7-2.)

The backtrace is again quite heavy with Jasmine-specific lines, but one of the key benefits of using the browser to access this information is that it's not all in the console text buffer. It's possible to scroll up and down the page to look at what's working and what isn't and to investigate more deeply by drilling into the specific specs that are failing and the tests within. It's a more usable environment.

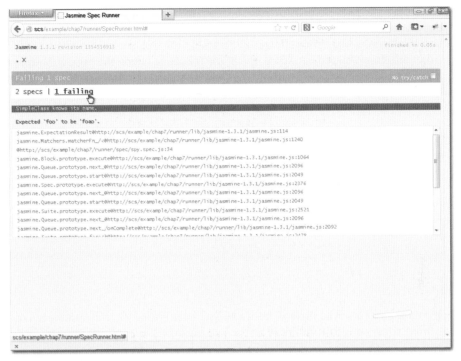

Figure 7-2: This test fails.

CONVENTIONS FOR TESTING THE UI

So far, most of the tests that have been discussed have been relatively "pure": testing pieces of class logic and other methods, where the goal is to ensure that an algorithm has been correctly implemented. That side of testing is actually relatively easy; checking functions whose inputs and outputs are fundamental data types like strings or numbers is straightforward, and in fact most developers would be entirely capable of writing a test suite for those sorts of checks without the need for any overarching framework.

Testing user interface components, though, is an entirely different practice. A number of systems are available to do this kind of work. One that springs to mind immediately is Selenium, which is a browser-hosted system that can either play back prerecorded tests (which are relatively easy to create, although quite brittle in practice) or drive the web browser through a specific API that allows you to write tests that act much as a user would when interacting with the web application.

Jasmine is an entirely adequate system for doing user interface testing, but it does require a different frame of mind. A number of differences in the environment can make things interesting. The most common stumbling blocks are the types of optimizations that browsers make to pages to speed the rendering process.

As an example, you can set up invisible sections of DOM to do testing, and for the most part this works. By setting a DOM subtree to be invisible, though, some browsers get somewhat lazy about computing various things. For example, the size of a given element might be 0 in either direction. An element that is not visible is not laid out on the page, and without the layout step the browser can't sensibly work out what dimensions it has. If the widget in question is backed by logic that attempts to respond to screen dimensions (as an example), the behavior of the widget when hidden will be very different than when it is onscreen.

There are other foibles, too. Although the test runner can run from a local `file:///` URL, some browsers will prevent certain features from working; an example might be Google Chrome's unwillingness to load local content.

All that said, testing parts of the user interface of an application is one of the most valuable things you can do. I tend to prefer these types of tests as a way of writing integration tests against an entire application, but it's also entirely possible and valid to write unit-*esque* tests against widgets and smaller pieces of functionality and ensure that they're working properly.

DRIVING JQUERY

The most popular way to perform front-end user interface testing with Jasmine is to use the Jasmine jQuery project, available at `https://github.com/velesin/jasmine-jquery`.

It's also available via `npm` as the `jasmine-jquery` package. Either way of obtaining it is fine; to use it is a minimal change to the test runner HTML to include the line:

```
<script type="text/javascript" src="path/to/jasmine-jquery.js"></script>
```

There are two key features that this provides:

- A series of jQuery-relevant matchers so that specs can be easily written making assertions about the behavior of the front-end UI
- The ability to load fixture data for the tests, including fragments of HTML and CSS, and a system for mocking AJAX queries

Some of the existing matchers available in Jasmine are simply enhanced; for example, it's possible to write `expect(DOM nodes).toBe(jQuery selector)` to set expectations about the structure of the document. If the expectation is that every element having the class `"active"` will actually be a button, the test might be

```
expect($(".active")).toBe("button")
```

jQuery is used to find the DOM nodes in question in this example, but any reference to DOM nodes can be used; the `toBe()` matcher then uses jQuery again to see if the nodes do indeed match the requirement.

As well as extending some of the existing matchers, the Jasmine jQuery suite provides a slew of new ones. Some of the most important ones are listed here:

- `toBeVisible`
- `toBeEmpty`
- `toHaveCSS`
- `toHaveAttr`
- `toHaveClass`
- `toBeFocused`

The Jasmine Spy network also receives something of an upgrade, gaining the ability to spy on events. These could be "normal" browser events, such as mouse clicks or form submissions, or other synthetic jQuery events:

```
spyEvent = spyOnEvent("form.main", "submit")
// fill in form invalidly, trigger enter key - this should be captured
expect(spyEvent).not.toHaveBeenTriggered()
```

As well as checking whether events are triggered, spies can even test whether the event was triggered and then later prevented, and whether it was triggered on a specific element on the page:

```
$("button.login").click()
expect("app:login:show").toHaveBeenTriggeredOn("body")

// submit login without filling in details
$(".login_form button").click()

expect("click").toHaveBeenPreventedOn(".login_form button")
expect("app:login:success").not.toHaveBeenTriggered()
```

FIXTURES

Most tests cannot run on their own; although it's possible to test some functions by passing in small amounts of data, most non-trivial functions need a larger amount of data to be available. In most instances, if this data is relevant to only the test suite, it's called a *fixture*.

Fixtures don't need to be absolutely authentic. They can be scaled-down versions of the real thing, and the key point is that they are predictable, although having as much variety in the data as might be encountered in real life is always a bonus.

Jasmine jQuery has the ability to load a few different types of fixtures. HTML fixtures, for example, can be loaded from a small snippet like this:

```
<div id="testform">
  <form method="POST">
    <input type="text" name="username">
```

```
      <input type="submit">
    </form>
</div>
```

By default, the fixture loader will look in `spec/javascript/fixtures/` (although this is configurable), and loading the content is straightforward: The test makes a call to `loadFixtures("testform.html")`, and the runner automatically loads the fragment into the page.

One of the benefits of this is that in addition to the snippet being available in the page, the runner also ensures that it's loaded in a container that is cleaned up between tests, ensuring that the tests don't affect each other. Fixtures are cached during runs, too, so the same fixture can be loaded again and again with very little performance penalty.

More than one fixture can be loaded at a time by giving `loadFixtures()` a list of fixtures, or by calling `appendLoadFixtures()`. There is also a `readFixtures()` function to return the contents of a fixture as a string; it's useful for testing templates, for example.

You can load stylesheets and JSON data in much the same way; each has its own global function, and each is sandboxed independently so that the data is properly cleared off the page before the next test is run:

- `loadStyleFixtures()` and `appendLoadStyleFixtures()` work similarly to their HTML counterparts.
- `getJSONFixture()` returns the JSON data contained in the fixture file, as a structure, not a string.

JSON fixtures can be incredibly useful: By combining the ability of Jasmine to spy on functions with the ability to load JSON data from a file, you can easily create mock AJAX requests. Doing so is useful in a number of ways, primarily of course, testing the application with a framework like Jasmine. However, you can use a good mock framework in other ways, too. For example, if the AJAX queries to the server are all mocked out, you can develop the front end without having to contact an actual server for the AJAX information.

SUMMARY

Testing code can be tedious work at times, but with CoffeeScript there are tools and libraries take a lot of the drudgery out of the job. It's difficult to overstate the importance of good tests, particularly for developers working on projects with an agile methodology.

In this chapter, you looked at:

- Using Jasmine to define behavior-based tests
- How spies can be used to perform sophisticated run-time checking and to stub out or mock functionality before testing
- How to run tests from both the command line and web browser environments
- Testing web-based UIs using jQuery, and loading test fixtures

8

DEBUGGING COFFEESCRIPT

NO MATTER HOW expert the programmer, some system debugging is always necessary. Developers just learning often fall back onto "printing" output to the console. Although this works and gives insight into the inner workings of the code, it doesn't scale very far or last very long.

As the sophistication of the code grows, so does the sophistication of the bugs; in fact, they tend to stay one or two steps ahead. What you need are better tools, and with the browser environment currently being one of the most popular development platforms, the tools are in abundance. Most developers will be in the enviable position of choosing those things that meet their needs best, feel most comfortable, and allow them to be their most productive.

This chapter covers a variety of tools that can be used to inspect a CoffeeScript program when it's running. There are a number of ways of attempting to detect and prevent bugs, but sometimes the easiest way forward is to watch what a program does and whether or not it is behaving in the way expected. This is a slightly more involved process with CoffeeScript because it's a compiled language, which is unusual for the web. You'll be pleased to see, though, that many familiar tools can be used, and we'll also explore some of the new features browsers support to make debugging even more efficient.

WRITING RELIABLE SOFTWARE

There are many tools available to developers who want to create reliable software. Using test frameworks, for example, demonstrates that the code works to some degree and can provide an assurance that its behavior has not changed over time. Using known patterns helps you avoid well-known design flaws and architectural mistakes. Debuggers are another important tool, allowing you to inspect the workings of the program as it executes and verify that it does what you intended.

Most developers, including me, consider debugging a necessary evil. Software exhibits a variety of problems that are referred to as *bugs,* and for the most part, there's no silver bullet. Software can go wrong in so many ways that programmers use lots of different types of debuggers to uncover what's going wrong. Traditionally, though, the web hasn't provided excellent support for debugging. Although many developers use JavaScript and basic support for inspecting JavaScript programs is built into browsers, non-web application developers rarely have access to such tools. The state of the art on the desktop includes debuggers that can change code while running, and not just stop programs but also run them backward to understand how they ended up in a specific state.

With excellent debuggers, there is little stopping you from writing an application in any language you please, but on the web, things are not so easy. Indeed, one of the main reasons people can be put off by CoffeeScript is that when their code goes wrong (and that's pretty much inevitable), they will be dropped into a JavaScript console.

Now, there's nothing wrong with JavaScript, but for many programmers—particularly those just learning CoffeeScript—it's a trifle off-putting. Developers may feel as though it provides less information and that debugging will be harder, and if they have to go through the JavaScript code anyway, why not simply write in JavaScript?

Fortunately, a number of tools make CoffeeScript not only bearable within a browser but also actually quite productive to use. You can debug CoffeeScript directly within the usual developer tools a browser offers, as well as use CoffeeScript within the console—technically, another form of Read, Evaluate, Print, Loop (REPL) interface.

As well as demonstrating these various tools, though, it also makes sense to look more deeply at how CoffeeScript is compiled into JavaScript. In previous chapters, I held off comparing CoffeeScript to JavaScript because idiomatic CoffeeScript doesn't necessarily look like it. However, at this point, it's time to find out more about what's actually happening under the covers and how this system really works.

READING AND DEBUGGING COFFEESCRIPT AND JAVASCRIPT

Interestingly, one of the key goals of the original CoffeeScript compilation process was to make the transformation as easy to understand as possible. A developer who knows JavaScript well needs to understand only a few key rules in order to make a good guess at how Coffee-Script will compile something into JavaScript:

- Variables are always defined within functions, and global variables are never used; indeed, the code output is generally wrapped within a function.
- Functions are not named; they are created as anonymous functions and references held to them using variables.
- Blocks created with indentation translate directly to bracketed structures; ditto data structures such as arrays, objects, and so on.

The output of the `coffee` compiler will generally be very readable JavaScript; less readable code is generally more indicative of developers cutting corners, such as not declaring variables or not checking that a variable has a defined value. But code that is Crockford JSLint-clean tends to look very similar. Take for example this function:

```
ellipsize = (input) ->
    if input?.length < 30 then input else "#{input[0..27]}..."

test = ellipsize "The cat sat on the very long mat."
```

This function trims sentences that are too long. The conversion to JavaScript is clear:

```
// Generated by CoffeeScript 1.4.0
(function() {
  var ellipsize, test;

  ellipsize = function(input) {
    if ((input != null ? input.length : void 0) < 30) {
      return input;
    } else {
      return "" + input.slice(0, 28) + "...";
    }
  };

  test = ellipsize("The cat sat on the mat");

}).call(this);
```

There is a great deal of sanity-checking in the output JavaScript, and the compiler goes to some lengths to ensure that the code generated won't conflict with other code by wrapping it in an anonymous function. The core logic, though, is the same. Even though the `if` statement is more verbose and the `return` in CoffeeScript is implicit, it's quite easy to see where various parts of JavaScript originated.

In some instances, the output JavaScript is a lot less concise than the input CoffeeScript. After all, CoffeeScript makes some things incredibly convenient. If it didn't, there wouldn't be as much point to using it. Comprehensions are an excellent example of this:

```
double = (x) -> x*2

evens = [double x for x in [1..10]]
```

This is wonderfully concise code, but the resultant JavaScript is anything but:

```
// Generated by CoffeeScript 1.4.0
(function() {
  var double, evens, x;

  double = function(x) {
    return x * 2;
  };

  evens = [
    (function() {
      var _i, _results;
      _results = [];
      for (x = _i = 1; _i <= 10; x = ++_i) {
        _results.push(double(x));
      }
      return _results;
    })()
  ];

}).call(this);
```

Again, a lot of the intent is clear, but while a comprehension is little more than a dressed-up loop, it's not totally clear why this loop is so large. The CoffeeScript compiler is again using anonymous functions to wrap code and ensure that it isn't causing side effects elsewhere, and it's also generating a number of internal variables that don't actually appear in the original CoffeeScript source.

Variables with names that begin with an underscore, such as _i or _results in the previous example, are generally those that have been automatically created. For this reason, it is often useful to steer clear of using variables with such names in CoffeeScript so that it's obvious which variables refer back to the original source, with the exception of naming class attributes or methods (where a leading underscore denotes a private part of the class).

So far I have suggested that it's better not to look too hard at the JavaScript output, but to attempt to learn CoffeeScript on its own merits. However, as you write more complex software, you will inevitably find yourself looking more and more at the compiled output.

Familiarizing yourself with the output is not a bad thing at all. In fact, although it will look quite complex to begin with, before long, you will be able to recognize the various structures that CoffeeScript outputs and understand where they've come from.

One other aspect I've found is that reading the output occasionally surprises me; the JavaScript construct is not what I expected, and I would have coded it by hand differently. Within the CoffeeScript issue tracker there is an awful lot of debate about exactly what code the compiler should be emitting. What is being output is the end result of those debates: the collective JavaScript knowledge of the CoffeeScript community. I often say to people that one of the best ways to really learn JavaScript is to study the output of the CoffeeScript compiler.

USING FIREBUG

Being able to read JavaScript is half of the battle, but you can employ some other tips and tricks to make the debugging experience slightly more pleasurable. To begin with, I'll discuss the use of Firebug on the Mozilla Firefox browser. I find this is one of the better environments to use. (Firebug Lite on other browers is definitely not the same thing at all.) However, the developer tools within Google Chrome have a lot to recommend them.

If you don't have it already, Firebug is available on this web page, which you can find at `https://addons.mozilla.org/en-US/firefox/addon/firebug/`.

Simply click the Download Now link to install the Firebug plug-in. In theory, it is also available within the browser by selecting Add-Ons from the Tools menu. However, when you search for Firebug, the system throws up hundreds of entries because there are now so many Firebug extensions.

Once installed, the browser toolbar should include a button with an insect logo. When grayed out, Firebug is inactive. Clicking the button activates the tool for that specific site, bringing up a panel at the bottom of the browser that can be undocked into a separate window. The panel contains a number of tabs:

- Console is the main browser console, where errors appear. It also contains a basic JavaScript REPL prompt at the bottom.
- HTML allows exploration of the current DOM tree and applied CSS rules.
- CSS shows details of the loaded stylesheet rules.
- Script shows details of the loaded scripts and gives access to the script debugger.
- Net lists the various network connections that the browser is making.
- Resource allows inspection of all the resources that have been loaded for the page, such as scripts, images, fonts, and anything else.

When activated, the panel should look like the one in Figure 8-1, which shows the Console tab.

Figure 8-1: Here the Firebug Console tab demonstrates code being run in the REPL.

The script debugger support built into Firebug is fine (although obviously reliant on the features within the browser), and one of the features that I use a lot lets me set breakpoints within the code and then step through execution, as follows:

1. Open Firebug, click Script, and select the script source file from the drop-down list. (This will be the JavaScript file.)

2. Find the line that interests you in the source code and click in the left column by the line number to set a breakpoint. (Ignore lines with gray numbers: Breakpoints cannot be set on those lines, so pick the next line up that can be used.) Figure 8-2 shows what this procedure looks like.

3. Reload the page to reset the execution of scripts or click the Rerun button on the Script tab.

4. When the breakpoint hits, it's then possible to step over the line (so that the next line can be executed), step into the line (if the line contains a function call, the next line to be executed will be the first line of that function), or step out of the line. (If it is called from a function, the next line to be executed will be the next line of that function.)

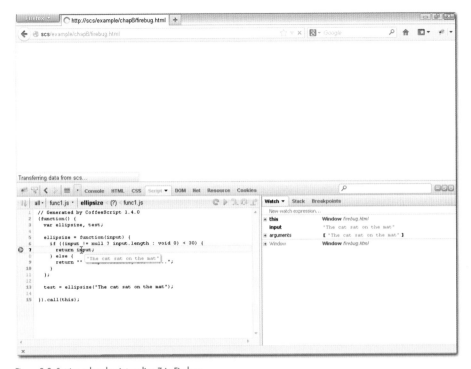

Figure 8-2: Setting a breakpoint on line 7 in Firebug

For small- to medium-size scripts, this approach is useful. The approach breaks down somewhat if the scripts become too large (it can be difficult to find the right line within the debugger) or if there are a lot of loops within the code section in question. Using the step functions around loops can be incredibly tedious and time-consuming.

One of the interesting things many web developers don't realize is that the breakpoint can be set within the code as well. Consider this short bit of code:

```
brokenFunc = ->
    debugger
    console.lg "This won't work"
```

Putting the `debugger` statement in the code triggers the browser's built-in debugging capability, which in Firebug means that it will treat the `debugger` statement as if it were a breakpoint, meaning Firebug pauses execution in the debugger. The CoffeeScript compiler also does something interesting with this code:

```
(function() {
  var brokenFunc;

  brokenFunc = function() {
    debugger;    return console.lg("This won't work");
  };
```

```
    brokenFunc();

}).call(this);
```

Generally, the output JavaScript is *pretty-printed,* which is to say that it's indented correctly and each statement appears on its own line. With the `debugger` statement, though, the line is combined with the next line in the code. This is actually really useful: When the breakpoint is triggered, it's triggering on the next line of CoffeeScript.

Using the `debugger` statement is an accurate way of pinpointing the execution of the program and which part of the original CoffeeScript is being referred to.

USING ACEBUG

Firebug is very helpful: Almost single-handedly, it turned Mozilla Firefox into a useful web development platform and has become one of the most popular plug-ins for the browser. However, it's also worth mentioning Acebug, which is effectively a plug-in for Firebug.

Like Firebug, Acebug is available from the Mozilla Add-Ons directory, which you can find at `https://addons.mozilla.org/en-US/firefox/addon/acebug`.

Acebug adds a few more features to the main Firebug UI, rather than providing something completely different. It enables the source views within Firebug to show source with syntax highlighting, for example. But the main reason for interest here is that it extends Firebug so you can evaluate CoffeeScript at runtime.

Once installed, Acebug adds little more than a simple up-arrow button to the main Firebug interface. This button is located in the far-right side of the console input. Click this button to open the more powerful Acebug console window shown in Figure 8-3.

To begin with, the console expects JavaScript. Press Shift+Return to open an Acebug command prompt, and type **lang=cf** to switch the console into CoffeeScript mode. After that, all the script typed into the console is expected to be CoffeeScript, and this can be run using the controls beneath the window. Scripts can also be loaded and saved, which can be useful when you're loading up specific code to debug.

However, as useful as the Acebug console is, there's a big difference between being able to type in CoffeeScript and test how it works and being able to directly debug the CoffeeScript source within the context of the browser. Reading the JavaScript and understanding how it's translated allows broader use of the existing JavaScript debugging tools, but a piece is still missing—source maps.

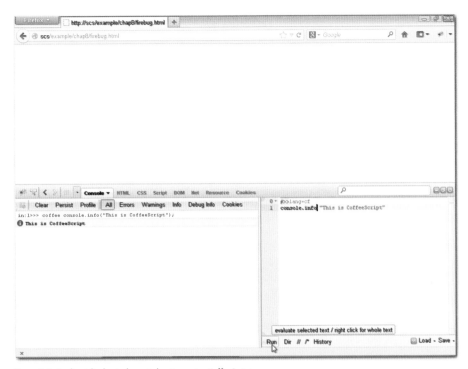

Figure 8-3: On the right the Acebug window is running CoffeeScript.

BUILDING SOURCE MAPS

There is an answer to the conundrum of how to debug CoffeeScript natively in the browser. While CoffeeScript itself is becoming rather popular, it's actually one of a set of languages that compiles into JavaScript. Other projects, such as Google's Dart project, seek to reach similar goals, and some projects, such as emscripten, have goals that are fundamentally different.

All of these languages and compilers use the JavaScript runtime as a platform for executing code. It's a tribute to the speed of modern JavaScript engines, particularly in browsers, that this is even thinkable. And as it becomes a more popular choice, more and more developers run into the problem of how to debug the native code.

Source maps are a solution to this problem, and some others, too. Originally proposed by Google, the source map's technical specification has been worked on collaboratively with other browser makers and so far enjoys support in most of the leading browsers (with the exception of Internet Explorer).

The single goal of the source map is to tie an executable statement—in this case, JavaScript—back to a line in the original source code. This is useful in a couple of different contexts:

- If CoffeeScript has been transformed into JavaScript, any JavaScript errors that occur at runtime can be traced back to the original CoffeeScript source.
- If the JavaScript has been through a preprocessor, minified, or otherwise compressed, a source map can trace the error from the compacted production source code back to the original, uncompressed version.

As a technical feature, source maps are conceptually quite simple. Modern debuggers in browsers can already give reasonable output when an error occurs, making clear which column of which line of which file triggered the error. The source map simply translates the (file, line, column) tuple back to the original source, and the browser then displays that information instead.

Now, there is some bad news: At the time of this writing, the current version of CoffeeScript (1.4) does not support the generation of source maps. While source maps are conceptually quite simple, they are actually a bit of a devil to implement. Compilers do an awful lot of work with the source code, transforming it into internal data structures before beginning the actual compilation process: It's tempting to think that they process source line-by-line, but they simply don't work like that. The information about the source needs to be carried through the entire compilation process in order for it to be available at the end to generate the source map.

INTRODUCING COFFEESCRIPT REDUX

Although the current production version of CoffeeScript doesn't support the generation of source maps, a version of CoffeeScript does: CoffeeScript Redux, available on GitHub at `https://github.com/michaelficarra/CoffeeScriptRedux`.

CoffeeScript was originally written as a Ruby program and then later rewritten in CoffeeScript to become self-hosting: The compiler could compile itself. Becoming self-hosting is a milestone for a compiler, indicating that it's quite feature complete and also predicable in its output. However, in compiler theory, things can become more sophisticated than that.

Michael Ficarra, an extremely active member of the CoffeeScript community, also happens to be a Masters student at Worcester Polytechnic Institute (WPI—pronounced, I am reliably informed, "Whoopee!"). Recognizing the various limitations in the existing CoffeeScript compiler, he put forward a project plan to write a new compiler based on well-known, more advanced compiler techniques. Being both academic and a CoffeeScript enthusiast stood him in good stead. When he publicized the plan on the crowd-funding website Kickstarter, it took less than two months to achieve $13,785 for his plan, more than the requested amount.

Named "CoffeeScript Redux," this compiler is entirely compatible with Ashkenas' CoffeeScript but brings to the table some exciting features:

- It parses source code to abstract syntax trees, working in phases; this allows the compiler to optimize the code, for example.
- Original source information is passed through the compilation process by these AST nodes, giving much better error messages on malformed input.
- Source information also allows the compiler to build source maps accurately without hacking in the feature.
- Internally defined JavaScript variables are guaranteed not to clash with the variables defined in a program. Unfortunately, this can happen with the current compiler; for example, defining _this can lead to very strange things happening.

Redux is turning into an excellent compiler. Although there are some rough edges and it hasn't yet had a formal release, the majority of code I've tested with it compiles without a problem. Internally, Redux fashions itself as CoffeeScript 2.0. Although not officially blessed, it's looking increasingly likely that it will end up being the next major version of CoffeeScript.

USING COFFEESCRIPT REDUX

Now, although I said earlier that Redux was compatible with CoffeeScript, that's only half true. It's compatible in all the ways that matter, such as language syntax, output style, and the ability for generated code from the two systems to interoperate. However, the compiler does have the same features and the same binary name, but sadly takes different arguments (albeit for good reasons), making it impossible to use as a drop-in replacement.

When trying Redux, I recommend installing it in a separate area from other npm modules. Then, if you decide to switch, you can switch out the usual version of CoffeeScript. The easiest way to get a copy is to install directly from GitHub at npm install git: //github.com/ michaelficarra/CoffeeScriptRedux.git.

Once installed, Redux provides a new coffee binary to use, and checking the version of this binary confirms the right compiler is available:

```
$ coffee -v
CoffeeScript version 2.0.0-dev
```

Compiling CoffeeScript is an entirely different exercise with Redux, which prefers to take source input via STDIN and produce output via STDOUT, as shown in this simple example:

```
class ExampleClass

    constructor: ->
        console.log "Hello world"

test = new ExampleClass
```

If this were saved as `example.coffee`, then the correct invocation to compile it into JavaScript would be

```
coffee --js <hello.coffee >hello.js
```

As noted before, the command options with Redux are entirely different from those of the traditional compiler. The command just shown is equivalent to `coffee -c hello`. Where the traditional compiler can compile only to JavaScript, Redux has a few more options, making things slightly more complicated. Look at how the compiler reacts to various errors in the source. For example, if part of the line defining the constructor is missing a character, you see the following:

```
Syntax error on line 3, column 18: unexpected '>' (\u003E)
1 : class ExampleClass
2 :
3 :     constructor: >
^ :~~~~~~~~~~~~~~~~~^
4 :          console.log "Hello world"
5 :
6 : test = new ExampleClass
```

This compares extremely well to the normal output of the traditional compiler, which would have started parsing that line as a "is greater than" comparison and found itself totally confused.

The Redux compiler can also execute code directly, and runtime errors generate similarly useful responses:

```
hello.coffee:6
      console.lg('Hello world');
                ^
TypeError: Object #<Object> has no method 'lg'
```

USING SOURCE MAPS

After all the preceding work, you're finally in a position to build a source map. To demonstrate this, the version of `'Hello world'` just shown with the runtime error calling `console.lg()` is compiled along with this bit of HTML:

```
<html>
<head>
<title>Source Map test</title>
</head>
<body>
<script src="/example.js" type="text/javascript"></script>
</body>
</html>
```

There's literally nothing else on the page. For this test, I'm using the Google Chrome browser because it's had the longest support for source maps and the feature is solid. With the browser open, press F12 to bring up the developer tools window on the page. In the bottom-right corner, you see a gear icon, which you click to bring up the Developer Tools Settings window. (See Figure 8-4.)

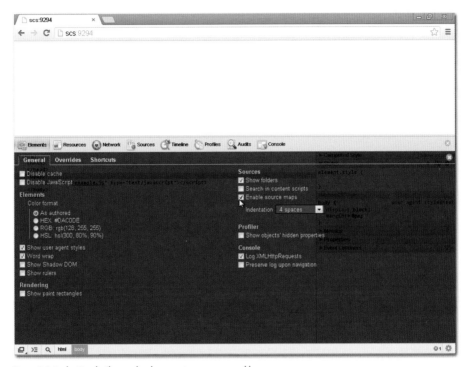

Figure 8-4: In the Google Chrome developer settings you can enable source maps.

Select the Enable Source Maps option under the Scripts heading. (This is the direction for Google Chrome version 20; with a later version, you may find that this step becomes unnecessary, but it's worth checking.) At this point, loading the page simply causes a runtime error to be visible in the console, and note that the browser complains about line 6 in example.js, as shown in Figure 8-5.

Clearly, this isn't the desired result. What you want to see is an error in this pane pointing back to the original CoffeeScript. The first step to achieve this is to build the source map. This happens as a step separate from compilation, and rather than give the compiler the code via STDIN, it's better to let it know the actual file it should read. The filename is built into the source map and is part of the information that the browser displays:

```
coffee --js -i example.coffee >example.js
coffee --source-map -i example.coffee >example.js.map
```

Figure 8-5: The Google Chrome JavaScript console shows an error.

By convention, the source map is given a `.map` file extension in addition to the existing extension. That's not entirely necessary, because the browser won't go hunting for it based on the name. The browser actually needs to be told specifically where the source map lives. This information is then added to the `example.js` file as the last line:

```
// Generated by CoffeeScript 2.0.0-dev
void function () {
  var ExampleClass, test;
  ExampleClass = function () {
    function ExampleClass() {
      console.lg('Hello world');
    }
    return ExampleClass;
  }();
  test = new ExampleClass;
}.call(this);
//@ sourceMappingURL=/example.js.map
```

The rest of this file is output by the compiler.

Although it would be convenient if the compiler had included that information automatically, this isn't really feasible for a few reasons. First, the compiler generates the source map with a different command. It doesn't know when it is outputting the JavaScript that it will later be asked to generate a source map. Second, the mapping is actually a URL—the URL that the browser will later retrieve the map from. Without an understanding of the context in which the page is being loaded, it's difficult or impossible to know what the actual URL ought to be. The source map may live in the same place, or it might live somewhere totally different.

All that said, this shouldn't be a manual process. If source maps are used in an application, they should be part of the build process. This can become increasingly hairy if the JavaScript output gets munged in various ways (concatenating source files, minifying, and so on). But tools are available to manipulate source maps as part of those processes. Again, they are incredibly application-dependent, though.

Once loaded in the browser, the error that comes up points correctly at the line in the original code, using the map. (See Figure 8-6.)

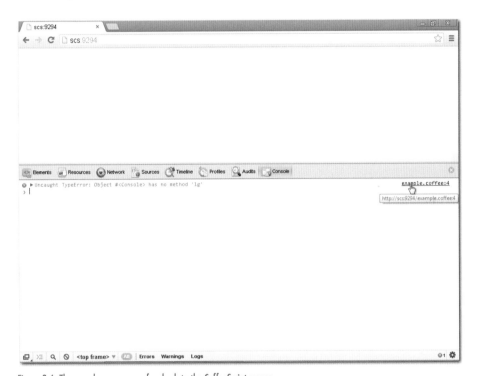

Figure 8-6: The console error now refers back to the CoffeeScript source.

Additionally, if the name of the original source file is set and the web server is able to serve a copy of the file, it's possible to click through the logged error on the console to the exact position in the source file. (See Figure 8-7.)

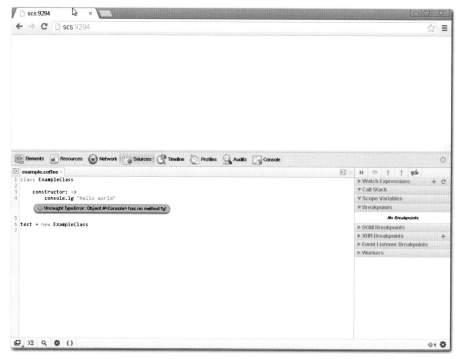

Figure 8-7: Click through to the script's original source.

SUMMARY

Debugging CoffeeScript is slightly harder than debugging JavaScript because browsers don't offer native support for the language. The tools available are very good though, once you get to know them. This chapter covered these key topics:

- Understanding the JavaScript output of the CoffeeScript compiler
- Using Firebug to set breakpoints in the JavaScript source and debug a CoffeeScript application
- Using Acebug to give the browser console a CoffeeScript REPL
- Generating CoffeeScript source maps and debugging the code more or less natively in the browser

You also took a look at using the CoffeeScript Redux compiler during the source map process. This compiler may well end up as the next major version of CoffeeScript.

CHAPTER

BUILDING RESOURCES WITH CAKE AND HEM

AS A COMPILED language, CoffeeScript source files are not the sort of thing that can be deployed directly, though actually, in all but the simplest JavaScript applications, the source is never deployed directly. To provide end users with the best performance, multiple processes are generally run over source files, which at least merges them into fewer, larger files. These processes often "minify" the files, too, by removing as much redundant information as possible.

This chapter explores a few basic, useful tools: cake, stitch, and hem. As well as covering the processes as they apply to CoffeeScript source files, the chapter explains how you can use these tools to build other resources within a project, making the whole thing ready for production deployment.

TASKS AND THE CAKEFILE

Not long after CoffeeScript was initially developed, there was a recognized need for some kind of build tool. Build tools, such as make and ant, are commonplace on other platforms. In general, build tools provide a few key features:

- The ability to express a dependency among different source files so that they can be included together
- An awareness of when source files were last modified so that they're not recompiled without reason
- Options to compile part of a project rather than the whole thing

The build tool for CoffeeScript took many cues from the popular make tool, and indeed was named after it—it's called *cake*. And, by general consensus, although cake is a powerful tool, it's an incredibly simple one.

STARTING WITH CAKE

Although cake is the tool, the most important part of the tool is actually the configuration— the *Cakefile*. This is the file that defines the various tasks needed within a project, and it's these tasks that cake executes. Without a Cakefile, cake literally does not know how to do anything.

The definitions for tasks are written directly in CoffeeScript, which gives you both enormous flexibility and a degree of responsibility to make sure that they behave themselves. Tasks can depend on other tasks, which is to say that a task can request that another task be done first.

A basic task definition can look very simple. Right now, take a look at an actual working Cakefile that does something useful (you'd need to name the file, literally, Cakefile, usually in the root directory of a project):

```coffeescript
fs = require 'fs'

option '-o', '--output [DIR]', 'directory for compiled code'

task 'watch', 'Watch current directory for changes', (options) ->
    {spawn} = require 'child_process'
    args = ['-w', '-c']
    if options.output
        args = args.concat ['-o', options.output]
    args = args.concat ['./']

    process.chdir __originalDirname

    coffee = spawn 'coffee', args
    coffee.stderr.on 'data', (data) ->
      process.stderr.write data.toString()
    coffee.stdout.on 'data', (data) ->
      console.log data.toString()
```

The task is the key part of the Cakefile. This is one of the units of work that a Cakefile defines. Essentially, a task is simply a function that takes a set of options and is given a command name and a command description—what goes on within the task is flexible, because after all, this is just CoffeeScript. The `watch` task described in the preceding code is using the coffee compiler to recompile source code in the given area into JavaScript.

`fs` and `child_process` are two node.js libraries used to read from the filesystem and execute programs (this is an oversimplification, but it will do for now!), so this task is simply executing the coffee compiler with the appropriate arguments.

If cake is called from the command line, without any arguments, it will use the task definitions to describe what tasks are available:

```
$ cake
Cakefile defines the following tasks:

cake watch                  # Watch current directory for change

  -o, --output       directory for compiled code
```

One of the key features of cake is that it will search parent directories for the presence of a Cakefile. This means that usually only one Cakefile is needed in a project, even if the source is split across a number of directories several levels deep. When the Cakefile is located in a different directory, the variable `__originalDirname` identifies the directory it was called from.

The `watch` task just defined is written in such a way that the CoffeeScript compiler is invoked in the current directory, which may be a few levels down from where the Cakefile is located. Usually, a task within a Cakefile will operate within the directory the Cakefile that defines the task is located in. This allows you to call `cake watch` in any subdirectory, and only code in that subdirectory is watched for changes and potentially recompiled.

THINKING ABOUT PROJECT DIRECTORY LAYOUT

At this point, you need to begin developing a consistent way of laying out the project directories and keeping conventions about the location of code. Doing so helps simplify the definitions of tasks and allows Cakefiles to be standardized among projects or even other users.

When developing larger applications using frameworks later on in the book, you will find some suggestions on how a web application project might be laid out; however, in general, the people working on a project and its objectives are the primary guides for a project's layout.

For example, I tend to keep my source files within a single `src/` directory, but if I were working on a project that included source written in both CoffeeScript and JavaScript, or other languages, I would probably split again by language rather than have both sets of files in the same directory.

Just keep in mind that consistency and good structure are crucial components to a project's layout.

TESTS FROM CAKE

Including tests within a project is a good idea, but unless you can easily run the tests, view the results, and make changes, their value diminishes, perhaps to the point that if they're run too infrequently, their output is never used.

For that reason, building a testing infrastructure and a set of test tasks into a project Cakefile is a priority for both new and existing CoffeeScript projects.

Jasmine, helpfully, comes with an API that you can use to build the tests into a cake task:

```
task 'test', 'Run jasmine tests', (options) ->
    {executeSpecsInFolder} = require 'jasmine-node'

    dir = __originalDirname
    executeSpecsInFolder dir + '/spec', (runner, log) ->
        if runner.results().failedCount == 0
            process.exit 0
        else
            process.exit 1
```

Again, directory layout is important. My personal preference is for a spec/ directory located immediately beneath a given source directory, to contain the tests relevant to that source code. Other people prefer a "global" spec/ or test/ directory located in the project root, containing tests for the whole project, in which case, the task wouldn't need to be defined in terms of __originalDirname.

For this example, a simple test file with a failing test is saved in spec/simple-test.coffee:

```
class SimpleClass
    constructor: (@name) ->


describe 'SimpleClass', ->
    it 'takes the name we give it', ->
        obj = new SimpleClass('foo')
        expect(obj.name).toEqual('foo')

    it 'fails an obvious error', ->
        obj = new SimpleClass('foo')
        expect(obj.name).toEqual('')
```

Running the test is now as easy as a single task call on the command line:

```
$ cake test
.F

Failures:

  1) fails an obvious error
```

```
    Message:
      Expected 'foo' to equal ''.
    Stacktrace:
      Error: Expected 'foo' to equal ''.
     at [stack trace removed]

Finished in 0.021 seconds
2 tests, 2 assertions, 1 failure
```

Further examples on using Cakefiles to build CoffeeScript projects are available on the CoffeeScript project website: `https://github.com/jashkenas/coffee-script/ wiki/%5BHowTo%5D-Compiling-and-Setting-Up-Build-Tools`.

As the tasks are defined using CoffeeScript code, there is literally very little they cannot do, and the more automation that can be built into tools the better, as a rule. So I suggest you always keep an eye out for jobs that can be defined as cake tasks, whether it's testing code, transforming data, or compiling CoffeeScript.

COMPILE SOURCE INTO SINGLE FILES FOR PRODUCTION DEPLOYMENT

Eventually, the task of identifying the various source files needed for a given page and making sure that they're correctly included becomes dull—typical of a task that really should be automated. You can solve this problem a number of different ways, but the easiest and most obvious way is to merge the various source files into a single file at the same time as they're compiled into JavaScript.

You can quickly write this by hand in a cake task:

```
source = [
  'src/users.coffee',
  'src/groups.coffee',
]

task 'build', 'Build merged file for production', (options) ->
    {exec} = require 'child_process'
    content = []

    for file, index in source then do (file, index) ->
        fs.readFile file, 'utf8', (err, fileContents) ->
            throw err if err
            content[index] = fileContents
            if index == source.length - 1
                coffee = content.join('\n')
                fs.writeFile 'output.coffee', coffee, 'utf8', (err) ->
                    throw err if err
                    command = 'coffee --compile output.coffee'
                    exec command, (err, stdout, stderr) ->
                        throw err if err
                        console.log stdout + stderr
```

This process has a couple of notable stages. First, the source files must be defined within an array, giving the build task a list of files and—crucially—the correct order in which they should be joined. For some code, the order in which the files are merged won't matter, but in some situations it will, particularly where objects or other structures are initialized as part of the process of parsing the code.

Second, the source is joined before being converted into JavaScript by the coffee compiler. Doing so isn't absolutely necessary, but it reduces the overhead of the various tweaks coffee performs, such as the surrounding closure that it adds to code being output.

HEM FOR FURTHER MINIFICATION

The higher-level tool hem brings together many of the features of the build process already discussed and more so that you don't have to write the various tasks manually and directly.

At this point, hem is probably not on your system, but like all the other packages being used here, you can easily install it by calling `npm install hem` at the command line.

hem has slightly stronger expectations about how a project's directory structure is laid out, and while these are configurable, the defaults are sensible:

- `./app/`—Contains the source code to the application.
- `./css/`—Contains any stylesheets used by the project.
- `./public/`—Contains any external resources, such as images.
- `./test/specs/`—Contains any test files included.

A sister command, `Spine.app`, will create a project with this layout already in place. Again, easily installed by calling `npm install spine.app`, Spine offers a variety of functionality that I'll cover when you look at Spine in depth in Chapter 10; but the command of interest right now is

```
$ spine app ./new-path
```

This creates the standard file layout under the directory `new-path` as well as a number of files describing the project. Once you've created these, you have some minor setup to do to bring in various library dependencies of the build system:

```
$ cd ./new-path
$ npm install .
```

Although this installs a number of different libraries, none of these become part of the project; they're simply there for the use of the various hem functions.

USING STANDARDIZED LOCATIONS

To begin, you create a standard `index.coffee` file to represent the application being written:

```
require('lib/setup')

Spine = require('spine')

class App extends Spine.Controller
  constructor: ->
    super

module.exports = App
```

At first glance, this really isn't very much use, but it is using the CommonJS module loader, which is familiar. Now, replace this `index.coffee` with new content:

```
require 'lib/setup'
User = require 'lib/user'

class App
  constructor: ->
    u = new User('alex')
    console.log u.name

module.exports = App
```

And in `app/lib/user.coffee`, save this content:

```
class User
    constructor: (@name) ->

module.exports = User
```

This is where hem starts to get quite clever. With the CommonJS module loading system in place, the code making up the application is already explicitly defining the dependencies among the different files. Using the single entry point of `index.coffee` as the main application file, hem can follow the various module dependency declarations to build a list of source files required for the application and the order in which they should be joined together.

Now, you have two ways to get hem to do the full build work. The first, and most straightforward, way is to ask it to build directly:

```
$ hem build
Built application
```

Without being very explicit, hem is letting the world know that it has done something. In fact, here's what happened:

- hem follows the dependencies among the modules, as described earlier.
- The module sources required are joined together and compiled into JavaScript, using a tool called stitch.
- Additional requirements, potentially in JavaScript, are identified from the `slug.json` configuration file and included in the source.
- The resultant JavaScript is put through a minification process that strips out as much extraneous content as possible and is saved as a single file.

After this process is complete, the file `public/application.js` contains all the application code that has been written, plus any dependencies required by the application—including jQuery if required, or any other third-party library. Literally, the whole project is reduced to a single file.

hem also contains a built-in server, which can be used to access these resources. By default, it serves the file `./public/index.html` on the root that contains references to the Spine startup guide. Starting the server is easy:

```
$ hem server
>> Strata web server version 0.15.1 running on node 0.6.18
>> Listening on 0.0.0.0:9294, CTRL+C to stop
```

It's now serving pages and can be accessed via the browser by going to `http://127.0.0.1:9294/`.

The default reference to the startup guide can be removed, leaving little except the references to `/application.js` and `/application.css`. After the content included is updated, the hem server, on request, will construct this content automatically, behind the scenes. This environment is a useful one for testing because the code being delivered to the browser is as it would be in production.

SUMMARY

Most projects end up requiring a build system of some sort. It's unlikely that you would want to deliver resources to the end user in exactly the same form as you develop them.

In this chapter you examined some of the tools that can be used to build deployment-ready files for a CoffeeScript application:

- Designing a sensible application layout for a CoffeeScript project
- Using cake to define and run build tasks as part of the development process
- Using hem to bring together the various source files and other project resources into bundles that can be deployed

PART

III

COFFEESCRIPT APPLICATION DEVELOPMENT

10

WRITING APPLICATIONS WITH SPINE

WRITING LARGE WEB applications is as much of an art as it is a skill. Many techniques can be applied to supply consistency and structure to an application, but at the end of the day, experience, taste, and common sense also play a role. Even for the accomplished developer, much of the experience of writing code from other domains doesn't readily apply to writing code with web technologies.

Using a previously written framework such as Spine.js helps in this regard. As the combined thinking of a number of developers who have built large web applications, Spine.js represents the wisdom and experience of web development boiled down into a set of best-practice designs. Even if you never use this framework, you'll find value in learning these patterns and how you can apply them to projects.

This chapter introduces Spine.js, or simply "Spine," as a framework for building applications. As a framework, Spine is incredibly lightweight, and is written in CoffeeScript. It integrates well with other web development tools such as hem, Stylus, and Jasmine, and is useful for architecting large application projects in a way that will ensure they are maintainable in the future.

INTRODUCING SPINE

Choosing a web framework is the sort of topic that gets many developers hot under the collar. Since the framework encodes or (worse!) enforces specific practices, people's attitudes toward frameworks are often closely related to whether they think those practices are good or bad and whether they offer value to the developer.

For me, two key things make Spine worth investigating: First, it's built around the most popular application structure pattern, Model-View-Controller (MVC); second, it's a relatively minimal implementation.

The MVC pattern has been around some 40 years and is certainly a concept that predates the use of asynchronous web applications. The key points of the design are enumerated here:

- Data and associated logic are stored in models.
- Data is presented to the user through views.
- The user interacts with controllers to manipulate the models.
- Changes in the model data are reflected in the associated views.

This feedback loop—the user interacting with the controller modifies models, which in turn updates the views that the user sees—is the fundamental principle and was used early in desktop application programming to ensure that business logic wasn't tied too closely to the logic presenting the user interface.

One of the key benefits of this arrangement is that the *state*—the part of the software that has to remember things—is confined to the models. Other parts of the code are, or should be, effectively stateless, making things much easier to test.

Some implementations of the MVC pattern with online applications haven't been true to the original pattern but are more like interpretations of the spirit of the pattern. HTTP is not an ideal fit for this pattern. Although the browser making HTTP requests to the server is an ideal conduit with which the user can interact with the application controller, there's no equivalent in the opposite direction. If the view needs to change, it can do so only in response to a user request.

Spine, on the other hand, is entirely a client-side application framework. All of the application—the models, views, and controllers—reside on the client, and it suffers no such disadvantage. (Although obviously, without some compensating system such as web sockets, getting data to and from the server is still a per-request operation.)

The minimalist nature of Spine is also a useful feature. Although it cuts down the amount of code in the application—laudable, but not a killer feature—the core of Spine is readable, concise CoffeeScript. It's easy to get under the hood to see how a specific feature works, but more than that, it's a great example of native CoffeeScript coding, with a number of conventions and idioms that are well worth adopting.

Alternatives to Spine

I'd like to talk about what's available other than Spine. As I've mentioned, other frameworks are available, and I thought long and hard about covering the Backbone framework (which was written by Jeremy Ashkenas, author of CoffeeScript) instead of Spine in this chapter. However, the relationship between the two frameworks is a close one. Backbone was created first and is written in JavaScript (relying as well on the Underscore.js library, which provides a number of useful additional features, many of which are now built into CoffeeScript).

Both frameworks implement the MVC pattern, although Backbone also includes the concept of collections, which are sets of model-based data that usually represent something on the server-side, such as a collection of search results, a page from a data table, or a similar subset of data. Spine has no such concept and uses methods on model classes to retrieve the data rather than going through a collection. This is more a matter of taste than of ideology, but some developers seize on it as a matter of great import.

Beyond that, the frameworks are very, very similar; in a sense, you can speak of Spine as being a CoffeeScript implementation of the Backbone.js design. Most of the developmental knowledge on one framework transfers easily to the other. CoffeeScript developers gain some useful conveniences, such as the ability to refer to the CoffeeScript source, easy integration with the hem server, and the use of the native class system. These last few points were what convinced me to cover Spine in this book; however, if you wish to explore Backbone.js instead, doing so is only a small leap.

Some other frameworks are worth mentioning, too. Angular.js has built up a large following, largely on the back of its comprehensive approach to data binding, making it immensely suitable for building large applications heavy on data. As a framework it has strong "opinions" on how features should be implemented which makes it inflexible, and has a substantial amount of code in it; it's very much the total solution, though.

Knockout.js also deserves a special mention as a declarative system based on a different pattern called Model-View-View-Model, or MVVM. Again, it relies on using two-way data binding to do a lot of the heavy lifting that people value most, but it frees you from writing views and controllers in the same style you would in MVC: A view in this instance is just an HTML page, albeit with additional special attributes that make it look more like a template. As the developer, you write models (effectively, standard JavaScript objects, with some slight enhancements), and Knockout.js binds the view and the model together tightly so that changes in one are reflected immediately in the other.

I've personally used Knockout.js with great success in a number of projects, although a point comes where the complexity of the view begins to weigh quite heavily. Although a page using Knockout.js bindings looks a lot like an HTML template, there tends to be more logic than I'm happy with, making simple interface changes more complicated to achieve.

CREATING A NEW SPINE APPLICATION

Spine comes with a few tools that make it really easy not only to start creating the application but also to add new pieces to it, and to actually set it running as well. The first step, as usual, is to ensure that the correct pieces are installed and available for use with npm:

```
npm install -g spine.app hem
```

This installs a copy of the Spine framework, the tools needed to work with projects, and the hem server, which can be used for running the application or creating deployment-suitable versions of it.

The spine tool has a number of different options:

```
usage: spine [options]

Generates a spine app using the specified command-line options

options:
 app path           Generates a new Spine application
 mobile path        Generates a new Spine Mobile application
 controller name    Generates a Spine Controller
 model name         Generates a Spine Model
```

For now, ignore the mobile option, which I cover in detail in the Chapter 12, and it's easy to see the way that this tool will be used. The first step is to create the new application. You then add controllers and models to the application as required.

Throughout the course of this chapter, I use the example of a calendar-based event booking application, demonstrating the various facilities built into Spine and showing how they can be used in the real world. Like any other Spine application, this one starts with the bare-bones template:

```
spine app booking_app
cd booking_app/
npm install .
```

These first steps are the same for each application you're starting: Create the application in a specific directory; then from within that directory, install local copies of the dependencies needed to run the application. Be particularly careful to include the trailing dot on that last line!

Spine has few dependencies, and the default application has some as well, which is why another npm install invocation is required. However, once that's done, the application is ready to run. Fortunately, hem can do this easily. Just run hem server, and it will give you this output:

```
>> Strata web server version 0.15.1 running on node 0.8.9
>> Listening on 0.0.0.0:9294, CTRL+C to stop
```

Once you run this code, you don't go back to the command prompt. The server is running, ready and waiting to serve up requests. There is a lingering question: What URL should be accessed? The short answer is http://localhost:9294/, but the slightly more involved and more correct answer is, "it depends."

You probably noticed that it has quoted an IP address of 0.0.0.0. This is computer-speak for "I will listen on any address given the chance," and it means that the server is externally available as well, if your firewall rules allow it. For most people, the local address (referred to as localhost—usually 127.0.0.1 or ::1) is the one to go for. However, if you're running hem on another machine, then you need the hostname or IP address of that server.

Attempting to run two default hem servers at the same time is bound to end in tears, and produces a long and quite angry-looking error message, the key line of which reads:

```
Error: listen EADDRINUSE
```

It's not possible for two servers to share the same port on the same IP addresses. You can specify a different port by adding the -p option to the command, for example:

```
hem server -p 8080
```

Although note that not all ports will be available, and ports beneath 1024 often require administrator privileges to use.

Once the server is up and running and you have the right URL in the browser, you'll see the default Spine page if you have access to the Internet. (See Figure 10-1.)

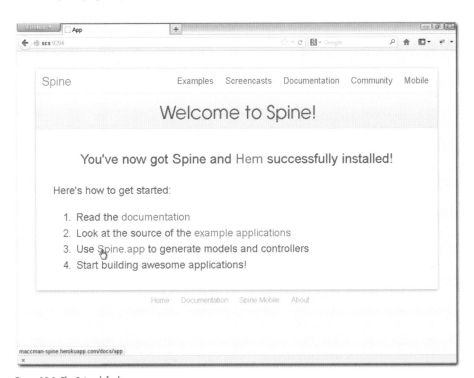

Figure 10-1: The Spine default page opens.

None of these links, or even the default page itself, is built into the application that has been created. They're gathered externally. If you don't have an Internet connection, this page will look blank, and that's okay, too.

Anatomy of a Spine Application

Before going too much further with the application just created, take a look at what's actually on the disk:

```
|-- app
|   |-- controllers
|   |-- index.coffee
|   |-- lib
|   |    `-- setup.coffee
|   |-- models
|   `-- views
|-- css
|   |-- index.styl
|   `-- mixin.styl
|-- .npmignore
|-- package.json
|-- Procfile
|-- public
|   |-- favicon.ico
|   `-- index.html
|-- slug.json
`-- test
    |-- public
    |   |-- index.html
    |   `-- lib
    |        |-- jasmine.css
    |        |-- jasmine.html.js
    |        `-- jasmine.js
    `-- specs
```

In broad terms, the top-most directories are the most interesting: app/ is where the main application code is going to live, css/ is used to create stylesheets, public/ contains any static content that may be needed, and test/ contains the various test suites for the application, which, being Jasmine-based, should be relatively familiar.

The two most interesting top-most files are package.json and slug.json, which hold some configuration for npm and hem, respectively. On the face of it, their contents are quite similar: They mainly contain dependency information for the application. slug.json, being the hem file, is concerned with the front-end code. It asks, "What are the other libraries that need to be sent to the browser for the client-side portions to function correctly?" package.json, on the other hand, is concerned with the back-end code, asking "What are the other libraries needed to build or run this application?"

Of the remaining files, Procfile is of interest only if you use the Heroku web platform, and .npmignore just lets npm know that the modules directory (created when npm install. is run) is not part of the package and shouldn't be included in any deployment.

Removing the Default Page

One of the first steps with a new application is to remove the default page. This is also a good point to look at the basic HTML structure provided and to understand what's happening when hem is delivering the application. The `public/index.html` file (not the similar file contained the in `test/` directory) by default looks something like this:

```
<!DOCTYPE html>
<html>
<head>
  <meta charset=utf-8>
  <title>App</title>
  <link rel="stylesheet" href="/application.css" type="text/css"
    charset="utf-8">
  <script src="/application.js" type="text/javascript"
    charset="utf-8"></script>
  <script type="text/javascript" charset="utf-8">
    var jQuery  = require("jqueryify");
    var exports = this;
    jQuery(function(){
      var App = require("index");
      exports.app = new App({el: $("body")});
    });
  </script>

  <!-- Getting started script - should be removed -->
  <script src=http://maccman-spine.herokuapp.com/start.js
   type="text/javascript" charset="utf-8"></script>
</head>
<body></body>
</html>
```

A few things are immediately noticeable. First, the "getting started" content is brought in with a simple script, and that script (and the associated comment) can simply be removed.

The page is HTML5, which is great. However, it's missing a useful title (easily corrected), but more oddly, it references two files that don't exist, `/application.js` and `/application.css`. Neither of these files are in the file tree, nor is there an obvious template for them.

The solution to these problems is somewhat simple, and hopefully pleasing: hem is generating those pages for the application, based on the configuration of the application. In the case of `application.js`, here's what is happening behind the scenes:

- hem examines `slug.json`, looking for dependencies and application code paths.
- Any CoffeeScript sources are converted into JavaScript.
- The resulting JavaScript files are merged, and the result is compressed.

All of the application code, including the various libraries and other pieces that might be required, are then delivered as a single file—`application.js`. This removes all need to manually compile the CoffeeScript or to write involved Cakefiles, and as a bonus, allows you to specify the versions of the libraries required.

The stylesheet system works in a very similar way, except that as well as supporting plain CSS files, it also supports the excellent Stylus library. It's possible to think of Stylus as a CSS-specific templating system, although it's slightly more powerful than that.

Bootstrapping the Application

The last step to examine is the process of actually starting the application, which happens in this piece of code:

```
<script type="text/javascript" charset="utf-8">
  var jQuery  = require("jqueryify");
  var exports = this;
  jQuery(function(){
    var App = require("index");
    exports.app = new App({el: $("body")});
  });
</script>
```

A few things are worthy of note here, too. The main thing that may be very different from your previous experience is that although this code uses jQuery, the jQuery library hasn't actually been included in the page. Instead, there's this slightly weird reference to `"jqueryify"`.

It so happens that `jqueryify` is a default dependency of the application, listed in `slug.json`, and thus is included in the main `application.js` file when that's rebuilt. However, although `jqueryify` is a Node.js module, it contains entirely client-side code a copy of jQuery, with a wrapper around it so that it can be imported with a call to `require()`.

So, by the time the browser comes to execute the on-page-ready script, the application code is already fully loaded with all its dependencies, and all that remains is to create the main class and to start the application.

This neatly illustrates one of the nice things about this approach: With a single application file, compressed and client-side cacheable, the footprint of the application can be quite low on the first HTTP request but subsequently drop to zero, and once the browser has downloaded the content, it can keep reusing it. One of the notable things about web clients today is that they tend to be on fast Internet connections, but they issue only a couple of requests at a time to a specific server—they're bandwidth-rich, but latency sensitive. Adding more requests to the page slows down the process much more than adding a few kilobytes of code. Spine apps delivered in this manner tend to be snappy and pleasing to the end user.

One last thing: Because the application ends up being delivered as a set of static media, a single script and a stylesheet, in principle, there's no reason why these files can't be generated ahead of time rather than served by a running instance of hem. This turns out to be really easy to achieve:

```
hem build
```

That's literally all there is to it. `application.js` and `application.css` are then built and placed in `public/` with the rest of the static media, ready for deployment as a web root, to be served up by your favorite web server.

BUILDING THE APPLICATION

With a skeleton application ready and waiting, it's now possible to get into the meat of the subject: building the application functionality. So far, the Model-View-Controller pattern has been discussed in the abstract. Now, it's time to review the components that actually need to be implemented. Most applications have at least one of the following:

- **Models:** These are the classes that manage data and provide state for the application.
- **Views:** These present data to the user and are essentially just HTML templates with pieces of logic in them to display the data correctly.
- **Controllers:** In Spine, these perform a couple of different functions, but are used to modify models and pass them into the views to be rendered.

Spine also provides

- **Stacks:** One of the most common tasks within web applications is to control what is onscreen at any given time, and Spine provides stacks to group controllers together to control which ones are currently active. Stacks are actually just specialized controllers, having an additional *manager* component that controls which one is active at any given time.
- **Modules:** As well as using CoffeeScript's native inheritance, Spine provides the ability to mix in additional class or instance functionality, using `Spine.Module`. This class actually forms the basis of all Spine classes.
- **Events:** Because binding DOM events to logic is an incredibly common pattern, Spine provides this as a specific module. It can be mixed into other classes, and both models and controllers have it mixed in by default.
- **Routes:** Used by controllers to map URLs (either virtual internal ones, or real ones as supported by HTML5 local history) to views, routes allow the user to navigate around the application in a controlled manner. The routes module is mixed into controllers by default.

Although this doesn't look like an awful lot, most useful tasks can be accomplished using one or more of these classes. Additional functionality is quite easy to write and build on top of these basics; indeed, the chapter examines in depth how strong mobile device support can be built on this framework as well.

As a reminder, the complete sources to the examples given in this book are available from wiley.com/go/smashingcoffeescript. *Since the application examples in this chapter are particularly involved, I recommend downloading them and using them alongside the text.*

PREPARING THE GROUND

For the calendar booking application, I've used a prewritten widget for the actual presentation of the calendar: Adam Shaw's excellent "FullCalendar" jQuery plug-in, available at http:// arshaw.com/fullcalendar.

Quite often an application will start like this: There are already pieces of library code for either the client or the server portion, and the first job is bringing the library or libraries into the project and making them available so that you can begin building the application.

Now, it's possible to download the FullCalendar plug-in and use it according to the instructions, which involves putting the various scripts into the public/ folder, altering the public/index.html file to add the scripts to the page, and then writing the code that will make use of the scripts. This isn't really the Spine way, though.

What is preferable is for the various pieces of code to be included in the system in such a way that hem can pick them up and work with them in the same way as other parts of the system, so that's the next job.

Upon downloading and unpacking the FullCalendar plug-in, you'll find a number of files. This list shows the ones you need, followed by where they should be placed:

- fullcalendar/fullcalendar.js is the main script file; copy this to ./lib/.
- jquery/jquery-ui-X.X.X.custom.min.js includes some jQuery UI routines; copy this to ./lib/ as well.
- jquery/jquery-X.X.X.min.js is a copy of jQuery; copy this to ./lib/ too.
- fullcalendar/fullcalendar.css is the main stylesheet; copy this to ./css/.

Actually, the situation with the jQuery UI file is slightly more complex. FullCalendar uses some specific interactions from jQuery UI—drag and drop behavior, mostly—to offer specific features. It provides a custom version of the code including only those behaviors. However, if it's likely that other features may be needed in the application, you may as well include the full version of jQuery UI (or, at least, a version customized for the application). FullCalendar won't mind; it just needs those behaviours.

Including the JavaScript is straightforward: Once the file is in the project, hem needs to be told that it's a dependency by editing the slug.json. However, there is a slight additional wrinkle: As a relatively standard jQuery plug-in, FullCalendar expects to be able to attach itself to the jQuery object, which doesn't lend itself naturally to jqueryify.

You have two options here. The first more complex one is to wrap FullCalendar in the same way that `jqueryify` wraps jQuery so that FullCalendar can be brought into the project as a standard Node module. There is a lot to recommend about that process, but it's a bit complex for now. So this is the second option: Remove `jquerify` and include the standard jQuery script. While quicker to start with, this method doesn't throw away many of the benefits of the first process; it just doesn't provide the ability to reference the library with `require()`.

So, in addition to the other scripts downloaded, grab a copy of jQuery (and, remember, it doesn't need to be the minimized version—hem will do that work) and save it in the `./lib/` directory.

REMOVING JQUERYIFY

Removing `jqueryify` is not hard. The first stop is `app/lib/setup.coffee`. This is the runtime list of dependencies of the application. Simply remove the `require('jqueryify')` reference.

Next, remove the reference to `jqueryify` from `slug.json` and add the new external libraries. It will now look something like this:

```
{
  "dependencies": [
    "es5-shimify",
    "json2ify",
    "spine",
    "spine/lib/local",
    "spine/lib/ajax",
    "spine/lib/route",
    "spine/lib/manager"
  ],
  "libs": [
    "./lib/jquery-1.8.3.js",
    "./lib/jquery-ui-1.8.23.custom.min.js",
    "./lib/fullcalendar.js"
  ]
}
```

There is a final runtime reference to `jqueryify` in `public/index.html` as part of the application bootstrap. Since jQuery is included in the main application, this is no longer needed, and it can be simplified:

```
<script type="text/javascript" charset="utf-8">
  var exports = this;
  jQuery(function(){
    var App = require("index");
    exports.app = new App({el: $("body")});
  });
</script>
```

Lastly—for good taste—update the `package.json` to reflect the new application dependencies, again removing the reference to `jqueryify`. This doesn't affect much unless you intend to package the application as an `npm` module, but it's always good to keep the information within a project consistent. The unneeded module can then be removed with `npm uninstall jqueryify`.

With that, the JavaScript side is finished, but recall that earlier the CSS stylesheet required by the calendar was also copied into place. This hasn't yet been included in the CSS build, so any use of the widget is going to look slightly odd. Now is an excellent time to look slightly deeper at Stylus—the system used to generate the output styles—and see how that side of the system fits together.

STYLING AN APPLICATION WITH STYLUS

Stylus is a library in its own right—a system separate from Spine in the same way that hem and other parts of the default framework are usable in their own right. It's not far wrong to think of Stylus as a templating system, but as well as being designed specifically for CSS, Stylus has a few features that make using it a bit more powerful than a more generic system of templates.

Now, consider some of the problems specific to CSS, which all web developers come up against one way or another. The list is in a sense endless, and different developers make different points, but these are the main things that spring to my mind:

- **Difficult or impossible to reuse CSS rules:** CSS has inheritance, but it applies to nodes in the DOM; classes can be used as a form of mix-in to apply common rules to different elements, but then the set of required classes needs to be set on each node.
- **Easy to write invalid CSS:** Browsers are incredibly forgiving, but it's easy to leave a quote dangling, or miss a parenthesis, and things break.
- **CSS can be very verbose:** Developers often find themselves writing the same, or similar, rules again and again; this gets even worse when vendor prefixes are thrown into the mix.
- **When compiled, CSS can be very difficult to plough through:** Finding where a rule has come from, particularly if a templating system is generating the CSS, can be a royal pain.

For some larger projects, these are extreme pain points, impacting maintainability and your ability to get work done. Stylus has answers for all these failings and more, though, and is a huge boon for serious development work.

WORKING WITH STYLUS

In a lot of ways there are huge similarities between Stylus and CoffeeScript: they share some common principles and their syntax has ended up very similar. Indentation is significant, various pieces of punctuation are optional, and the emphasis is on brevity. As tools, they make a lot of sense together.

You may also have come across tools similar to Stylus before. LESS and SASS are two obvious examples of what people tend to refer to as CSS preprocessors, tools that add features to stylesheets by way of additional grammar, which then lets you write the stylesheet more concisely. Stylus also takes a lot of inspiration from these tools, SASS in particular, so having some experience with either LESS or SASS will help you immensely.

Nothing speaks louder than a good example, so look at this slightly knotty CSS and examine the Stylus used to generate it:

```css
nav ul {
  border: 1px #3b3b3b;
  padding: 0;
  margin-top: 0;
}
nav ul li {
  list-style: none outside none;
  display: inline-block;
  color: #555;
}
nav ul li:hover {
  color: #666;
}
```

This is a relatively typical piece of CSS: A fair bit of repetition is in the selectors being used, and the colors being set are obviously related to each other, being shades of gray (although the relationship between them is not totally clear). If these rules were to become much more complicated, you would find it useful to start including comments about exactly how and why these rules should be used together.

In Stylus, though, things are a lot clearer. This is the equivalent rule:

```stylus
$theme-menu = #555

nav ul
  border 1px darken($theme-menu, 30%)
  padding 0
  margin-top 0

  li
    list-style none outside none
    display inline-block
    color $theme-menu

    &:hover
      color lighten($theme-menu, 10%)
```

This probably doesn't need much explaining, which speaks to the clarity of the system. A variable is declared to hold a reference to the main color being used, but Stylus understands the concepts of colors well and can manipulate them. So, instead of having to list separate colors where needed, it's now possible to say "that color, but 10% lighter," and that's what Stylus outputs.

> *By the way, variables don't need a $ prefix to be treated as such. That's simply my personal preference; I find it helps to highlight the terms in the stylesheet that have been set up in that way.*

The relationship between the different nodes is indicated by the significant whitespace, so it's no longer necessary to keep repeating selector information. Also, the various braces and other pieces of punctuation in the CSS have disappeared. You can still use them, but they're optional, and it's often clearer without them.

One piece of punctuation has appeared, though: &. This is the parent reference always refers to the parent selector. In the last example, writing `& :hover` is equivalent to writing `li :hover` as the selector above it is just `li`. Using the parent reference reduces the amount of repetitive code even further, allows rules to be moved around more easily and in fact becomes even more useful with Stylus mix-ins that I discuss in the next section.

TAKING A DEEPER LOOK AT STYLUS FEATURES

With that introduction out of the way, it's time to call out some of the most useful Stylus features. The full documentation on the system is available at `http://learnboost. github.com/stylus`.

However, the following are the key facilities that I use again and again.

Mix-Ins and Functions

One thing all template languages tend to have is a concept of *macros*—pieces of code that are reusable in a number of different places. Mix-ins and functions have that role in Stylus, and although they end up being defined similarly, they have quite different roles: A mix-in essentially imports CSS rules into the current declaration, and a function is used to calculate a value:

```
fs(a)
  min(a, 10)

fw(w)
  font-weight w

div.title
  font-size fs(11)
  fw(bold)
```

In this example, `fw()` is a mix-in and `fs()` is a function. (I don't recommend this as a naming strategy, by the way!) The call to `fs()` is used to calculate the font size for the title, and the call to `fw()` is used to set the font-weight, resulting in:

```
div.title {
  font-size: 10;
  font-weight: bold;
}
```

The result of a function is one or more values, which are the last things evaluated in the function—in that respect, they're entirely like CoffeeScript functions. Both mix-ins and functions can make use of conditions—if and else statements, and additionally if and unless as postfix conditionals—again, entirely like CoffeeScript:

```
boxify(width)
  display block
  width width > 300 ? width : 300px
  if width > 400
    height 200px
  margin 10 unless width <= 400

div.content
  boxify 800px
```

This illustrates Stylus's ability to handle units properly, as well as the kind of logic that can be set up as part of a mix-in (or a function, for that matter). These rules produce the following results:

```
div.content {
  display: block;
  width: 800px;
  height: 200px;
  margin: 10;
}
```

This is an incredibly powerful tool, and it takes Stylus a fair way along the track to becoming a programming language in its own right, which is as much a negative thing as a positive thing, though. Putting too much logic and calculation into a stylesheet is a recipe for future disaster, and having the restraint to use it only where it makes sense takes practice.

Variables and Property Lookup

Variables shouldn't be new to you at this point, and again similarly to CoffeeScript, but with different syntax, it's possible to interpolate variables into strings. The most obvious reason for doing so is to generate vendor prefixes more easily:

```
prefix(property, args...)
  -{moz- + property} args
  -{webkit- + property} args
  -{o- + property} args
  {property} args

div.boxy
  prefix(border-radius, 5px)
```

Here's the result:

```
div.boxy {
  -moz-border-radius: 5px;
  -webkit-border-radius: 5px;
  -o-border-radius: 5px;
  border-radius: 5px;
}
```

Variables (whether function parameters or variables set explicitly) are very useful tools, but in many instances, the information that you may want in the variable is already somewhere in a rule:

```
square()
  min-height @width

img.photo
  width 100px
  square()
```

This `@-notation` is a property lookup, again quite CoffeeScript-like, and is wonderfully useful with mix-ins, because the same mix-in can be used in a number of different places and operate correctly for the context it's been called in:

```
img.photo {
  width: 100px;
  min-height: 100px;
}
```

Built-In Functions

Stylus has a variety of built-in functions, largely with rich support for manipulating the key data types within stylesheets: colors, units of length, and files on disk.

Mathematical abilities include the ability to work out the minimum and maximum of two numbers with `min()` and `max()`, as well as rounding up with `ceil()` and rounding down with `floor()`. These functions, combined with the various expressions that can be used (once again, virtually identical to CoffeeScript), end up being some of the most commonly used features because of their ability to calculate relative dimensions easily.

It also has great support for arrays and pairs, with the ability to push (`push()`) values onto the end of an array, use `unshift()` to move them onto the start of an array, and find the `keys()` and `values()` in a list of pairs of values. There is even a `join()` function to turn arrays into a single string value, although no matching `split()` at the time of this writing. Additionally, arrays can be iterated over to create multiple rules at once.

Lastly, there are a few slightly more esoteric functions, which are nonetheless very powerful and worth mentioning just as an example of the breadth of functionality. You can use `match()` to test whether a given string matches a specific regular expression pattern, which is a feature that should definitely be used quite sparingly but that could one day be a lifesaver. `image-size()` is also interesting: It takes the path to an image, and it creates the correct `width` and `height` declarations for that image.

I suggest reading through the full documentation just to get a complete picture of Stylus's repertoire. I also caution that like most things, the 80/20 rule applies strongly: Probably a core of about 20 percent of the feature set will become the mainstay of what may get used, and for most people, it will be a similar set. You may be tempted to try to use ever-smarter features within the system, but it's usually best to avoid doing so unless you have a really good reason not to. What you gain by reducing the size of the stylesheet can end up being lost when the next poor developer comes along and has to spend time figuring out what's actually going on.

The last thing I suggest having a look at is a project called nib. This is a library of mix-ins designed for Stylus users to get the maximum out of CSS 3. It's available at `http://visionmedia.github.com/nib`.

If there is a CSS 3 feature that you'd like to use, the chances are that nib already has a mix-in that makes the feature much easier to use and that is cross-browser compatible by default.

SPINE'S DEFAULT STYLS

Now, look at the default files provided by the skeleton Spine application: `./css/index.styl` and `./css/mixin.styl`. The key file is the first one, and in its untouched state, it's incredibly straightforward:

```
@import './mixin'
```

Notice that `@import` is a valid declaration in a CSS file, usually asking the browser to go and fetch another stylesheet. However, in this case, it isn't giving a full URL, and in fact, even the filename appears to be missing the file extension!

What's happening here is that the Stylus system is taking over this specific declaration and in-lining the content of `mixin.styl`. If the reference is to a file with a `.css` file extension, the content is in-lined without processing, effectively just a nice way of saving the browser some work and giving it the content it would have to go and get anyway. Without an extension, though, Stylus treats the file as another Stylus stylesheet: The content is pulled in, as though the rules had been written directly in the file, before the stylesheet is further processed.

The `mixin.styl` file is far more interesting. As the name suggests, this is a series of mix-ins provided to make life a bit more straightforward for you, and to give some hints at the kinds of things that are possible. Here are some examples of these functions:

```
border-radius()
  -moz-border-radius: arguments
  -webkit-border-radius: arguments
  border-radius: arguments
```

When browsers first began to implement parts of the CSS3 standard, the ability to add corners to boxes was one of the first things developers jumped on. Before this, achieving those rounded corners required careful placement of four images within the box, being careful to place them pixel-perfect against the border edge so that they covered the corner but also lined up with the sides. However, although the CSS was a much more robust solution, it required vendor prefixes for wide compatibility, and when many boxes needed round corners, this ended up bloating CSS stylesheets unnecessarily.

The `border-radius()` mix-in solves this problem nicely. A simple Stylus rule like

```
.title
  border-radius 8px
```

generates a complete CSS rule like this:

```
.title {
  -moz-border-radius: 8px;
  -webkit-border-radius: 8px;
  border-radius: 8px;
}
```

Over the course of a large stylesheet, it's easy to see how the use of mix-ins is a powerful tool: It keeps the code concise, but it's also keeping it DRY. (Remember: don't repeat yourself!) If a new vendor prefix is needed on the border-radius rules, one line of code adds that, and when the CSS is rebuilt, it will flow into all the rules using the mix-in.

This example is even better:

```
vbg-gradient(fc = #FFF, tc = #FFF)
  background: fc
  background: -webkit-gradient(linear, left top, left bottom, from(fc), to(tc))
  background: -moz-linear-gradient(top, fc, tc)
  background: linear-gradient(top, fc, tc)
```

Putting a vertical background gradient on an element is a common enough task, and yes, again this takes care of some vendor prefixes. But actually, some more value is being added here: The WebKit version of this rule is not much like the Mozilla implementation, or the vanilla CSS3 version.

In my experience, when vendor prefixes require slightly different syntax or—worse—they take the same arguments but in a different order, it's a recipe for bugs. You won't notice there is an error in the CSS; in fact, the CSS looks more correct because the rule blends into its surroundings. Only testing the CSS on the relevant browser will reveal the problem.

You can use mix-ins to ease that pain dramatically. Where CSS declarations are inconsistent among browsers, you can use a mix-in to effectively standardize the syntax or calling convention throughout the stylesheet.

In the example of the vertical background gradient used earlier, you need only to mix it into your rule like this:

```
div.content
  vbg-gradient tc=#ddd
```

Notice that only the color being mixed to is given; the color being mixed from is a default parameter. It generates this CSS rule:

```
div.content {
  background: #ddd;
  background: -webkit-gradient(linear, left top, left bottom, from(#ddd),
to(#fff));
  background: -moz-linear-gradient(top, #ddd, #fff);
  background: linear-gradient(top, #ddd, #fff);
}
```

With a simple mix-in like that, it becomes much harder to get the rule wrong, and that in turn, means the output CSS is much more likely to be correct.

Now that you've been through the default files, it's easy to see how the CSS for the Full Calendar plug-in can be included. My rule is to use `index.styl` as a place to import styles, because it then gives a reasonable overview of the order in which they're defined:

```
@import './mixin'

// external styles
@import './fullcalendar.css'
```

Using `@import` with other Stylus templates has been covered before; using it with CSS files deserves a bit more discussion. By default, Stylus passes through declarations that are references to CSS files. That is to say, `.styl` references are processed, `.css` references are left as-is, and the browser has to sort them out. For some purposes, that's okay, but there's no real point to doing that. The browser has to download the rules anyway, and they can still conflict even if they're in separate files.

Stylus also treats the two types of files the same way if asked, though, and will import the raw CSS content as it would another Stylus file. This is a recent feature, enabled by giving hem the option `--includeCss` at the command line. If the version of hem you are using does not have this feature, the `@import` line containing the reference to a CSS file will be output as-is. An easy work-around if that is the case is to leave a copy of the CSS file in the `public/` directory in the same path, where the browser will load it.

Beyond that, exactly how this file should be laid out is up to you. CSS resets that exhaustively define the default CSS rules so that they are consistent between all browsers are relatively popular, and should come first. I tend to include basic pieces of layout, perhaps the grid definitions and things like that, with any external stylesheets that may be needed. Only after including all those things, do I think about adding application stylesheets, and again, I structure those into different files (separating out typography, layout, user interface, color schemes, and so on).

STARTING WITH CONTROLLERS

Now that the various libraries are set up in the system, it would be nice to see them working; the most straightforward way to do this is to hack the call into the main application file `app/index.coffee`:

```
require('lib/setup')

Spine = require('spine')

class App extends Spine.Controller
  constructor: ->
    super

module.exports = App
```

This is the heart of the application class and it's interesting that the application itself is just another instance of the normal controller, doing nothing special other than including the `setup.coffee` with the run-time dependencies.

A calendar can be added to the page by adjusting the constructor:

```
@cal = $('<div>')
$('body').append(@cal)
@cal.fullCalendar()
```

However, this is not really good style. Although you have a controller here in the form of the App class, it's usually better to create specific controllers for pieces of user interface, no matter how "global" they might end up being. The application object itself can be used to instantiate the various controllers needed, but it's usually better not to write the logic directly into that top-level class.

Creating a new controller in the first instance is simple: the spine app can do this. Since the calendar is going to be the main piece of this application, you create that controller first by using `spine controller calendar`:

```
create    app/controllers/calendar.coffee
create    test/specs/controllers/calendar.coffee
```

As expected, this command creates a new controller, but at the same time it creates a specification for the controller in the `test` folder. As mentioned previously, the test framework uses the familiar Jasmine behavior-driven tests. Take a quick look at the calendar test first:

```
require = window.require

describe 'Calendar', ->
```

```
Calendar = require('controllers/calendar')

it 'can noop', ->
```

By default this isn't doing much: it's importing the correct library, but nothing is being tested. However, you can take a look at the test runner and confirm that it's coming up correctly. By default, hem automatically serves up the test suite under the /test/ URL, which will usually be http://localhost:9294/test/.

TESTING CONTROLLERS

A best practice for most developers is to attempt to drive development using tests, where the test is developed before the feature it is testing. This first test should fail because the artifact it is testing hasn't been written yet. Then the developer starts writing the feature so that the tests pass. A minimum first set of tests for the calendar controller might look like this:

```
describe 'Calendar', ->
  Calendar = require('controllers/calendar')

  it 'exists', ->
    expect(Calendar).toBeDefined()
    calendar = new Calendar()
    expect(calendar).toBeDefined()

  it 'creates a DOM element with a calendar', ->
    dom = new Calendar()
    expect(dom.el).toBeDefined()
    expect($(dom.el).hasClass('fc')).toBe(true)
```

Most of these tests actually pass because even an empty controller should be exported correctly and create a DOM node to add to the page (the el attribute of the Controller object). As it stands this is testing Spine functionality rather than application functionality, but it's always a good idea to test some of the pre-requisites for later tests to ensure that they are starting from a known working set of conditions. The final test—looking for the class fc on the DOM element—fails though, since that class is added by the FullCalendar plug-in when it first runs, and the controller code that isn't yet written.

Now it's time to focus on the controller. The controller itself has been created and from the test so far you can tell that it is functioning, but it isn't doing anything yet. The empty controller is basically a blank canvas:

```
Spine = require('spine')

class Calendar extends Spine.Controller
  constructor: ->
    super

module.exports = Calendar
```

As bare as this code is, the constructor is simply calling the inherited constructor, so those two lines are extraneous too. This is the absolute bare minimum of a controller.

To get the tests to pass, the code needs to define a controller that creates a FullCalendar widget:

```
class Calendar extends Spine.Controller

    tag: "div"

    constructor: ->
        super
        @el.fullCalendar
            height: 600
            width: 600
            defaultView: "month"

    render: =>
        @el.fullCalendar "render"
```

The root tag @el is specified as a <div>, and then the constructor calls the FullCalendar plug-in on that element itself. This isn't always the right way to add functionality to the page, because most of the time @el is a container for other elements. In this case it makes sense because the controller is really just a widget, but the usual pattern creates new DOM nodes that are then appended to the container @el.

Creation of the calendar itself is done as part of the constructor. Although there is a render() method defined in the controller, this isn't called as part of the standard process and it would probably be better named refresh(). It's a conventional name rather than part of the Spine API.

CONTROLLING THE PAGE

It's worth talking through what the vanilla Spine.Controller is doing in the background. One of the first things it does is create the DOM node for this controller; by default this controller is a <div> node, but you can override that with the @tag attribute. Quite often I include tag—as shown in the earlier example—even with the default, just so that it's explicit.

There are some additional useful default attributes:

- className: Since the controller is creating the DOM node, it looks at this to see if there is a specific CSS class that should be set on the node.
- attributes: Similar to className but more general; this allows other attributes to be set on the node by default. It's even possible to set the class attribute and that will override the className. (I strongly recommend not using that "feature", though!)
- events: One of the most common operations developers perform with front-end code is listen for events with handlers. Spine makes this easy by building the functionality into

the controller itself, using a dictionary in the format `{"event selector": "method name"}`.

- `elements`: Similar to the `events` use case, object attributes can be quickly set to DOM nodes by listing selectors in this dictionary, in the format `{"selector": "attribute name"}`.

These last two items are so important it's worth going through a specific example:

```
Spine = require('spine')

class Example extends Spine.Controller

  events:
    "click .button": "buttonClick"

  elements:
    ".button": "button"
    ".text": "label"

  constructor: ->
    super

    @html """
      <p><button class="button">Click me</button></p>
      <p class="text"></p>
    """

  buttonClick: (e) =>
    e.preventDefault()
    $(@label).text "Button clicked!"

module.exports = Example
```

The `@html()` method is a neat short-hand for "replace the contents of `@el` with this." In this example, the method is being used in the constructor to set the output; ordinarily this would be separated into a template, which will be clearer later in this chapter when I cover views in more detail.

`buttonClick()` is the click handler being attached to the button on the page, and note that it's not being attached manually: `Spine.Controller` is handling that work, by looking through `@events`. In this example, `Spine.Controller` sees it needs to deliver click events to any node matching `.button` to the `buttonClick()` method. Everything is referred to via the use of strings, so a direct function reference is not needed.

Within the click handler is a reference to `@label`, and again this isn't something that has been set up manually. `@elements` is used to find parts of the page based on the selectors, so both `@label` and `@button` are set up automatically.

In addition to the `html()` method on the controller, several other utility functions are automatically provided:

- `append(elements…)`, to add new DOM nodes to `@el`
- `prepend(elements…)`, which also adds new DOM nodes to `@el`, but does so by inserting it before the existing content
- `appendTo(element)`, which appends `@el` to either `element.el` or `element` itself (making it very convenient to use this to attach controllers to other controllers)
- `replace(element)`, which removes the existing node `@el` itself and replaces it with a new one given

These utility functions probably feel familiar because they're similar to the node manipulation jQuery provides. The interesting side-effect of using this approach rather than assigning attributes manually, though, is that the information in `@elements` is used to update the automatically set attributes on the object, ensuring that the references are always the correct and latest ones!

The same goes for the handlers set up in `@events`: if content of `@el` changes at a later date, the correct event handlers still fire. It wouldn't matter in the previous example if the button were added after `@events` had been processed, making it not only simple to use this infrastructure, but also beneficial. The days of manual event handling should be over.

A couple of non-DOM related methods are available as well. The most useful is the `log()` call that comes from the Spine.Log mix-in. (By default it's only mixed into controllers, but it can be mixed in elsewhere too.) If the attribute `@trace` is `true` on an object, then a call to `@log()` results in a `console.log()` call with the same arguments, but prefixed by the contents of the `@logPrefix` attribute:

```
class Example extends Spine.Controller

  logPrefix: '[controllers.example.Example]'
  trace: true

  constructor:
    @log "Ready"
```

When this controller is instantiated, the browser console shows the message `[controllers.example.Example] Ready`. With the use of `@trace`, the logging functionality can be turned on or off on a per-class basis. I highly recommend using this functionality rather than manual calls to `console.log()`. I tend to set a prefix that includes the local path to the file and then the class name (since a file could contain multiple class definitions). I also recommend leaving in logging statements that are potentially useful and simply turning them off, rather than removing them from the code.

As a final neat touch, Spine offers a controller method called $. This is the jQuery API (or Zepto, if you prefer a lighter-weight version) but scoped to @el. In simple terms, it means that this type of query is unnecessary:

```
$(@el).find('.button')
```

This version is more concise and does the same thing:

```
@$('.button')
```

As you might imagine, the selectors used in @events and @elements are scoped in exactly the same way. You might have asked yourself why I used class-based selectors in the example earlier: because of this scoping effect, there is no need to use lots of IDs on elements. In fact, since element identifiers are required to be unique in a given HTML document (very strange results can occur if this rule is violated) it's actually much nicer to use classes.

Developers tend to be wary of different ways of selecting things. The benefit of IDs is that the element returned is exactly what you want, but the downside is that they can clash. Classes don't clash, but you need to keep in mind that the same class names might be used elsewhere. With this built-in scoping system, you get the best of both worlds: certainty that the selectors are operating only over the template, and the security that the template won't disrupt other parts of the page.

I strongly recommend sticking to these built-in class methods for manipulating the DOM and setting up events. The usual jQuery interface can be made available, but it can be trivially easy for code in one controller to inspect or modify DOM nodes "owned" by another controller. Doing that accidentally is problematic; doing it deliberately is really poor design. It should never be necessary to do the latter, and by using @$ consistently rather than $ it's impossible to do the former.

ADDING CONTROLLERS

Having come this far—writing a controller for the calendar that runs the plug-in on the correct DOM element, and passes the basic suite of tests—is good, but the application itself isn't really doing anything interesting yet. The controller is ready, but it isn't being used.

Spine applications can be thought of as trees of controllers, really. The main application class is a controller itself, and its main job is to instantiate the other controllers that are needed and mediate between them. A simple application may have only a couple of controllers, but by using controllers for UI elements as well, it's possible to quickly generate tens of the things without realizing it.

A simple way of adding the calendar controller into the application is to modify the root controller in `app/index.coffee`:

```
class App extends Spine.Controller

  constructor: ->
    super
    @calendar = new (require "controllers/calendar")()
    @calendar.appendTo @
```

All that has been added here are two lines. The first creates the calendar controller object: since there is only one controller exported from the `app/controllers/calendar.coffee` file, there isn't a need to refer to the class name of the controller directly. This pattern is quite common in Spine applications, particularly with view templates. It's concise and also contains the file name reference right where the call is being made.

The alternative would be to do something like `Calendar = require "controllers/calendar"` at the top of the file, and call new `Calendar ()` later. This alternative is less concise, but that isn't a problem unless the controller is accessing a large number of templates.

STACKING CONTROLLERS

Most applications developed under a framework like Spine are intended to be single-page applications, sometimes referred to as Rich Internet Applications or RIAs. There are two key Spine features that you architect the application easily from the start: stacks, which ensure that only one controller in a group is active at any one time, and routes, which map URLs to controllers.

These two features can be used separately, but I think they're most valuable when used together. For example, a stack for a basic content management system looks like this:

```
Stack = require('spine/lib/manager').Stack
{PageView, PagePrint, PageEdit} = require 'controllers/pages'

class Pages extends Spine.Stack

  controllers:
    view: PageView
    printable: PagePrint
    edit: PageEdit

  routes:
    '/pages/:id':        'view'
    '/pages/:id/print':  'printable'
    '/pages/:id/edit':   'edit'

  default: 'view'
```

At its heart a stack is just another type of controller, although its role is basically to manage groups of controllers. The stack ensures that only one controller is active at a time, and when this stack is created it first activates the controller labeled "view" (which is `PageView` as defined by the `default` attribute.

The controllers are individually labeled under the `controllers` attribute, and then referred to by label in the routes. The role of a route is to identify which controller should be active based on the URL currently set in the browser. The routes configured in this example identify three different URL formats, each having an identifier as a variable component. The path `/pages/123/edit` routes to the PageEdit controller by this rule set.

Navigation to a URL can be caused a number of different ways. The application can trigger this itself by calling `@navigate(path)` but equally navigation can be triggered by the user clicking a link. Virtually all browsers support hash fragment based navigation, resulting in paths that look like `example.com/#/internal/path`. For the purposes of the application, everything before and including the # symbol is ignored. The browser, on the other hand, mainly cares about the part of the URL before the # symbol and ignores any changes after it. This convention ensures that the browser remains on the page, while the application is able to identify different locations based on the changes to URL.

Modern browsers also have the option of using HTML 5's History API, which provides the same facility but without using in-page anchors (appending a # and extra information to the URL) to ensure that the browser doesn't actually navigate away from the page. Enable the History API by calling `Spine.Route.setup(history: true)` early in the application start up. Unfortunately, it's more or less impossible to turn this feature on for just those browsers that support it.

When navigation to a specific URL is triggered the routing rules are consulted to work out which controller to activate. The chosen controller's `active()` method is then called, passing in any potential variable parameters identified in the route:

```
class PageEdit extends Spine.Controller

    active: (params) =>
        super

        @page = Page.find params.id
        @render()
```

In this example, the route has a variable identifier component—named `id` in the route—and therefore is available in `active()` as `params.id`.

In addition to managing which controller is active the stack modifies the DOM nodes assigned as controller containers. Each time `active()` is called on a controller, the CSS class active is set on its container node and removed from any other controllers in the stack. This ensures that inactive controllers can be hidden from view with a simple CSS rule:

```
.stack > *:not(.active) {
  display: none
}
```

VIEWING THE RESULTS

It might feel slightly odd that I've managed to come this far by only writing a few scraps of HTML. The view is where the "output" happens, and is therefore one of the key parts of the application. With a good understanding of what the controller is doing it's now possible to look at where the view fits in and in all honesty, views in Spine are simple.

There are a number of different ways of generating the HTML needed for an application. Frameworks like Spine are aimed squarely at the "single page application" where the application runs entirely on the client-side. The user doesn't visit other pages and the browser doesn't refresh pages from the server. Using hem (and stitch, underneath) to compile and deliver JavaScript and CSS works well, but it doesn't really address the problem of how or when to deliver HTML markup to the browser.

There are a few different approaches you can take:

- **Write all the HTML required into a single page, hiding everything to begin with:** This approach has the advantage of being quick and simple, but isn't maintainable and causes the initial page load to be quite slow.
- **Write the HTML in different files and use a compiler to generate a single page:** This approach is more maintainable than the first approach, but doesn't address any of the other shortcomings.
- **Load the HTML as required, perhaps through AJAX calls:** This approach is much more lightweight, but requires a running server doing work for the application. This application could never work offline.
- **Generate the HTML on-the-fly in the controller, using strings or jQuery calls:** This approach is definitely lightweight but mixes the view into the controller, creating coupling where it isn't wanted.

None of these solutions are ideal, and thankfully Spine provides an alternative: HTML can be written into different files and then compiled into JavaScript functions. This allows the controller to access the view without requiring everything to be built into the page, and keeps the view structurally separate from the controller.

Spine provides this feature by fully integrating a template engine called Eco. Like the other libraries used by Spine, Eco is a natural fit, allowing CoffeeScript expressions in the template code. Eco can also be extended using functions called "helpers" to allow specialized template handling code to be re-used throughout the application. It's also written in CoffeeScript and is easy code to follow. I would recommend having a read through to try to follow what's going on internally.

USING (J)ECO TEMPLATES

Although I just said that Spine provides a single template engine, there are actually two slightly different forms that can be used: the standard Eco template, and the hem-specific "jEco" template. The difference will be fully explored later in this chapter, but suffice to say for now that the template syntax and expressions are identical. The key difference is simply that jEco templates come wrapped with some extra logic.

Eco is comparable to common server-side templating systems: The concepts are the same, and the syntax looks incredibly similar to other systems you might be familiar with.

The most fundamental part of Eco is the use of expressions. Each template is "rendered" by feeding the template into Eco with some data (the data is the "context"). Eco evaluates the various expressions within the template and outputs a string. The expressions are more or less plain CoffeeScript expressions, so a template may look like this:

```
<% if @categories.length: %>
    <ul>
    <% for category in @categories: %>
        <li>
            <a href="<%= category.url %>">
                <%= category.name %>
            </a>
        </li>
    <% end %>
    </ul>
<% else: %>
    <p>No categories to list.</p>
<% end %>
```

There are some minor differences apparent: for example, in CoffeeScript, code is easily delimited into blocks just by using indentation. That's not really possible within the context of HTML, so blocks are created by the use of a colon on loops or conditionals within the Eco tags. It is good style to indent the tags to separate the blocks visually, but the indentation itself is not used.

Eco has two main tag types: <% for evaluating expressions without generating output, and <%= to output the value of an expression. A template is called on a set of data that is provided by the controller; a minimal example to run the previous template looks like this:

```
render: =>
  data =
    categories: [
      { url: '/', name: 'Home' },
      { url: '/contact', name: 'Contacts' },
      { url: '/tags', name: '<tags & attributes>' }
    ]
  @html require('views/demo')(data)
```

With this data, the resultant HTML output would be this:

```
<ul>
  <li>
```

```
    <a href="/"> Home </a>
  </li>
  <li>
    <a href="/contact"> Contacts </a>
  </li>
  <li>
    <a href="/tags"> &lt;tags &amp; attributes&gt; </a>
  </li>
</ul>
```

One of the advantages of using a system like this is the built-in escaping: on the last item being rendered the various special HTML characters have been changed into entities to prevent them from being misinterpreted. The <%= tag does this to all data, so there is no need to escape data before output. As well as making the code more straightforward this tag makes the application more secure, because there are fewer possibilities to attack the application using cross-site scripting flaws or similar methods.

Eco is neatly integrated into the hem build system, so neatly in fact it may not have been entirely clear how the template is being accessed. This is the key line:

```
@html require('views/demo')(data)
```

The @html method call is on the controller, and is replacing the content of the element associated with the controller, so it's clear that the require() method is where the HTML content is actually coming from. How this works is quite clever, though.

As part of the build process, hem looks through the project to find templates with an extension of either .eco (as in this case) or .jeco. It then compiles the templates using Eco, turning them into JavaScript functions that accept the context data as an argument. These are placed in modules named after the template, so views/demo refers to the file app/views/demo.eco. Each module exports this single compiled function, so the template can be run directly from the require() call by simply passing in the data.

DATA BINDING

hem recognizes two types of Eco template files: The .eco variety is pretty straightforward. The .jeco variety is quite different.

Generating HTML from templates on the client-side is an easy process. A common problem developers have is the next step after that: responding to events that are triggered on the generated DOM nodes. It's usually necessary to have the data that was used to create the template available in the event handler. For example, if there is a list of files in the user interface each with a Delete button, using the same click handler for each button makes sense. The handler needs to be able to identify which specific file the user is requesting to delete.

.jeco templates provide a convenient solution to this problem. When compiled .jeco templates act the same as regular templates with some important differences:

- Instead of exporting a function that returns HTML, they export a function that returns a DOM tree.
- Data used to "render" the template output is saved as $.data('item') on the top-level DOM node.
- As a special case, the template function can be passed an array of data. The template is run once for each item in the array—effectively running the template multiple times—and each data item is associated with the relevant DOM node. This is ideal for producing lists of items using a single template.

Although little more than a crude form of data binding, this system is really useful when data is being used to output a list of items and generic event handlers are processing events on that list. It leads to a natural two-controller pattern that is common in Spine applications:

```
class Files extends Spine.Controller
  constructor: ->
    super
    @list = new FilesList()
    @render()

  render: =>
    @html "<ul></ul>"
    @list.appendTo @el.find('ul')
```

This is the "master" controller whose sole job is to act as a container for the list that is going to be embedded. For ease, I've embedded the HTML directly into the render function, but I recommend against this in practice. Embedding HTML mixes the view and controller together, and they should be separate. It's much better to have that content as an .eco template. @list is the controller for the individual items and is using a .jeco template, producing some UI for each item:

```
class FilesList extends Spine.Controller
  events:
    "click .action-delete": "deleteFile"

  constructor: ->
    super
    @render()

  render: =>
    data = [
      { name: 'README.md' },
      { name: 'index.html' },
      { name: 'index.css' }
    ]
```

```
@html require('views/files')(data)

deleteFile: (e) =>
  e.preventDefault()
  item = $(e.target).parents('li').data('item')
  confirm "Do you want to delete #{ item.name} ?"
```

The `render()` function here passes an array into the template as context rather than an object. Since `app/views/files.jeco` is a `.jeco` template, there is an implicit loop, binding each data item in the array to the "rendered" DOM nodes.

`deleteFile()` is set up as a click handler by the `@events` table and receives click events from the simple `files.jeco` template:

```
<li>
  <%= @name %> <button class="action-delete">Delete</button>
</li>
```

When the event is triggered, the click handler finds the parent `<li>` node and examines the data associated with that node. The `<li>` node is the root node in the template fragment and is where the object in the `data` array has been bound.

Finding the root node for the template is crucial to find the associated data. Searching the DOM tree from `e.target` upwards can be slow and potentially error prone. Another approach is to listen for the events on the root node itself and dispatch them appropriately:

```
class FilesList extends Spine.Controller

  events:
    "click li": "click"

  click: (e) =>
    item = $(e.currentTarget).data('item')

    if $(e.target).hasClass('action-delete')
      e.preventDefault()
      @deleteFile item

  deleteFile: (item) =>
    confirm "Do you want to delete #{ item.name} ?"
```

This style has the advantage of finding the right item information immediately and works by using event bubbling. The handler is attached to the root template node, which is also a parent of the target of the event. The data item can then be fetched from `e.currentTarget` since that will always be the root node.

If multiple events are being handled (for example, a number of buttons on each item) then they must be distinguished somehow. `e.target` can be examined to determine which interface element caused the event to trigger. In the last example the class on the button being clicked is checked to determine the user's action. This kind of approach is usually very reliable, although if the template becomes too complex the logic within the handlers can become a bit tortured.

MODELLING CLIENT-SIDE DATA

The most crucial parts of any application are the algorithms and structures that represent the core data the application is dealing with. In some applications the core data is about people, in others the core data is about physical objects. This process of relating the data to the domain in which the application operates is generally referred to as "modeling."

Among the original proponents of object-oriented programming techniques, there was extensive debate about whether developers should seek to model the real world directly. Some felt that the power of objects was that they allow the programmer to relate their internal processes to things happening for real: as an example, in a financial accounts handling system, each transaction might be represented by a separate object.

Others felt that attempting to develop solutions that closely matched the real world in their internal architecture was missing the point. Their argument was that the developer should use the structures and algorithms that best suit the problem, which might be quite different than the way the problem is structured in the real world. Search engines, for example, don't model their database as a series of documents but instead extract keywords and form statistical models of data. It would be too slow to perform searches on individual documents.

This argument has never really gone away: This is a classic problem that doesn't have a "right answer." Using models based on real-world objects is a useful metaphor that helps programmers understand a problem and write code that correctly solves it. However, real-world models are usually not the most efficient structures for solving a problem and in some instances can be disastrously inefficient. Choosing the correct data structures for an application may be the most important decision you can make when writing a program.

CREATING A SPINE MODEL

For the calendar application I'm going to take a real-world approach to defining the model. The calendar is going to contain events, and each event will have a defined start and end. Events need to be named somehow for display on the calendar and an extended description of what they are about would be useful.

The plug-in I'm using to display this information, FullCalendar, has similar ideas about what events look like. So I'm going to write an event model that is very close to what the plug-in expects to reduce the need for any "translation" of data.

To begin with, a model needs some defined attributes, but not much else. By convention these attributes are saved in the application's models directory. Create the model for an event by calling `spine model event`:

```
create    app/models/event.coffee
create    test/specs/models/event.coffee
```

As before, Spine creates the file for the code as well as a test. This is a simple model that represents only data to begin with, so there is nothing useful to test at this stage. Add some extra fields to the model in app/models/event.coffee so that it looks like this:

```
Spine = require 'spine'

class Event extends Spine.Model
    @configure "Event", "title", "allDay", "description", "start", "end"

module.exports = Event
```

Models are based on normal CoffeeScript classes but with a few differences. The attributes that a model has need to be predeclared before anything else happens in the class, which is what the call to @configure() does. The name of the class is passed in followed by the list of attributes the model will have.

In this example, I've given the model the same attributes expected by FullCalendar. After @configure() is called, the rest of the class can be defined as usual.

After a model is defined it can be used anywhere in the application in the usual way. Creating a new event for the calendar looks like this:

```
Event = require 'models/event'
now = new Date()

event = Event.create
    title: "New event"
    start: now
    end: new Date(now.getTime() + (60 * 60 * 1000))
```

create() is a static method on all Spine models and allows the caller to create the object but also "save" it:

```
event = new Event
    title: "New event"
    start: now
    end: new Date(now.getTime() + (60 * 60 * 1000))
event.save()
```

What saving actually does will become gradually clearer when you look at model events and server-side persistence. The most important change to understand at this point is that save() gives the object a unique identifier that can be used to find the object again later:

```
event.save()
event_id = event.id

retrieved_event = Event.find(event_id)
```

Under the covers Spine uses a system called "dynamic records." What this means is that when you ask for a reference to an object that already exists in a model, you get back exactly the same reference each time. In the previous example, it's true that `event` and `retrieved_event` contain the same information, but also they are precisely the same object. If I change `event.title` to some new value, `retrieved_event.title` immediately reflects that new value, whether `event` has been saved or not. This is an extremely important point to understand and remember!

WORKING WITH MODELS

You've seen how model objects can be created, saved, and retrieved by their unique identifiers. There are some other important static methods to know:

- `exists(id)`: Determines whether an object with that unique identifier exists
- `destroy(id)`: Removes an object with a given unique identifier
- `destroyAll()`: Removes all objects of that model
- `all()`: Fetches all objects of that model
- `count()`: Counts the objects of that model that exist

These are relatively simple methods to understand but the most useful static method is more difficult to explain. `select()` is used to "search" the objects for a given model, and return only those that meet certain criteria. To do this a callback function that discriminates between wanted and unwanted objects is passed.

As an example, imagine that you want to search for all events currently taking place. This requires a search for any event that had already started but not yet finished:

```
current_events = Event.select (event) ->
    now = new Date()
    event.start < now < event.end
```

`Event.select()` is being passed an anonymous function that takes an event as an argument and returns an expression that evaluates to `true` if the event it was given is currently taking place. Internally `select()` passes each object of that model to the anonymous function it was given, and if the function evaluates to `true` it includes that object in its return list. To put it another way, it's returning all the objects for that model except those for which the function returns `false`.

This is a tremendously flexible system. The filtering or search process can be as simple or as complex as the function given to `select()`.

In addition to the static methods you saw earlier, there are some useful instance methods:

- `load(attrs)`: Updates the attributes of the model object from the attributes of the object passed in
- `destroy()`: Removes a specific model object
- `toJson()`: Turns the model object into a plain JavaScript object containing only the keys and values of the configured model attributes.

I highly recommend working through the detailed Spine API documentation at a later point, but particularly with regard to models. There are other less-common methods available, that in certain circumstances are highly useful. For example, it is possible to create new model objects directly from forms. In practice this isn't useful for all developers, but for some applications it may be a real time-saver.

TRIGGERING MODEL EVENTS

Spine models have a sort of "life cycle" associated with them, and emit events in response to various changes. Four key events are associated with individual records in a model:

- `create` is emitted when the instance is first created.
- `update` is emitted when the data in the instance is changed.
- `destroy` is emitted when the instance is destroyed.
- `error` is emitted when the data in the instance fails validation. (You look at the validation process later in this chapter.)

These additional three events are slightly less specific:

- `save` is emitted when an instance is either created or updated.
- `change` is emitted when an instance is created, updated, or destroyed.
- `refresh` is emitted when all the records have been replaced by new data from the server.

It's possible to bind to any of these events through the model and react to the changes in the data. These events can be used to drive updates to the user interface by setting up handlers that listen for changes in model data and call `render()` (or an equivalent function) when changes occur.

With a model for events defined, it's possible to demonstrate how the user interface can be made to react to data events. The process I want to create looks like this:

1. The user clicks on an appropriate date in the calendar to create a new event.
2. FullCalendar receives the event and passes it through to the controller.
3. The controller receives the event and creates a new event.
4. The model fires a `create` event, triggering FullCalendar to re-load the data.

This is a clean architecture: The separate pieces of code communicate using a system of well-defined events. Now look at how this is implemented in the controller. The first change is in the controller:

```
Spine = require 'spine'
Event = require 'models/calendar'

class Calendar extends Spine.Controller
```

```
    tag: "div"

    constructor: ->
        super
        @el.fullCalendar
            height: 600
            width: 600
            defaultView: "month"
            events: @getEvents
            dayClick: @dayClick

        Event.bind "change", (event) =>
            @el.fullCalendar "refetchEvents"
```

FullCalendar is passed two handlers that are not yet defined. `getEvents()` is the data source for the calendar. FullCalendar expects to be able to call this function and receive a list of events for the calendar. `dayClick()` is a function that FullCalendar will call to indicate that it has received a click event on that calendar.

To listen for changes in the underlying data, I've bound to the `change` event on the Event model. This ensures that any new, changed, or removed events are picked up the same way. In this example, Full Calendar is asked to wipe the calendar and re-fetch the events using the `getEvents()` function passed to it earlier.

If `getEvents()` was a wrapper around an AJAX call, I wouldn't recommend this as an architecture. Throwing away good data and retrieving it all again is a wasteful approach. However, with Spine models, the data is usually already client-side. Take a look at what that function is doing:

```
    getEvents: (start, end, callback) =>
        events = Event.select (event) ->
            start <= event.start <= end or start <= event.end <= end
        callback events
```

FullCalendar is passing through a date range and a callback, requesting that all events between the start and end date be passed to the function it has provided. This is an easy filter to create using the `select()` method of the model: All events that start or finish within the date range provided are included in the selection. The result is then passed to the callback.

The remaining work is to create the event itself in response to calendar clicks:

```
    dayClick: (date, allDay, jsEvent, view) =>
        ev = new Event
            title: "New event"
            allDay: allDay
            start: date
        ev.save()
```

The arguments to this handler are again defined by FullCalendar. For these purposes only the date clicked on and whether or not the event is an all-day event are needed. A new event with no set title is created, and the act of calling `save()` triggers the event that then causes the calendar to refresh.

VALIDATING MODELS

I've demonstrated some of the features of models allowing you to save and retrieve data, but that functionality is not much use if the application cannot be sure the data is *correct*. Validating that the data meets specific criteria is an invaluable step before accepting it, and the most sensible place to do this is within the model itself.

A model validation function is extremely easy to write. This is how the Event model could be extended to include basic validation:

```
class Event extends Spine.Model
    @configure "Event", "title", "allDay", "description", "start", "end"

    validate: =>
        if @start > @end
            return "Event ends before it starts"
        if @title == ""
            return "Event has no title"
```

For any Spine model `validate()` is called immediately before the model is saved. If `validate()` returns anything at all, validation fails. By convention, a string containing a useful error message is the normal means of failing validation.

Validation occurs specifically when the methods `save()`, `create()` or `update Attributes()` are called on a model object, and these methods return `false` if validation fails. (Ordinarily the object itself would be returned, as part of a somewhat-fluid API design.)

In addition to changing the result of those method calls when validation fails the `error` event is triggered on the model. Following are several of the options that help you handle this event:

- Ignoring the event is always a possibility. This usually isn't the most user-friendly approach, though.
- The error string can be displayed to the user, in the hope that the information in it contains enough information to help them work out what went wrong.
- If the user is actively editing some model data, the specific piece of data that is "invalid" can be marked as such in the user interface; the user is then prevented from saving the new data before it is marked as valid. This is preferable from the user interface point of view, but involves much more work.

This isn't actually that different a task to form validation, which you looked at in Chapter 3, and some similar solutions can be brought to bear on the problem.

EDITING MODEL DATA

The calendar application you looked at can create basic events, but provides little ability to edit those events. To be useful the application should allow the user to change the information held against the event, such as the title or the start time. The FullCalendar plug-in also allows users to move events around using drag-and-drop, and the application should support that too.

This is conceptually simple as a process. The application will have interfaces that the user can use to manipulate the data for events. Those changes are reflected in the model, which is then saved.

Since the plug-in supports drag-and-drop as a way of changing basic information, that makes a good place to start. First, the plug-in needs to be told that the editable features should be turned on. I've changed the creation of the calendar to this:

```
@el.fullCalendar
    height: 600
    width: 600
    defaultView: "month"
    events: @getEvents
    dayClick: @dayClick
    editable: true
    eventResizeStop: @changeEvent
    eventDragStop: @changeEvent
    header:
        left: "month,agendaWeek,agendaDay"
        center: "title"
        right: "today prev,next"
```

The editable attribute is set to `true` to turn on the editable features. When the calendar allows an event to be moved, it's effectively changing the start and end time and date associated with the event.

The plug-in can communicate these changes in two ways: the `eventResizeStop` event (which indicates the user has resized the event, changing the end date) and the `eventDrag-Stop` (which indicates the event was dragged, changing both start and end date). Because I don't mind whether the start date has changed, I've set the same handler on both events.

Lastly, the header configuration has changed. This changes the user interface of the calendar to allow day and week views to be selected as well as the default month view. This is a cosmetic change, but resizing an event to make it shorter or longer works best on the day and week views.

In the case of the FullCalendar plug-in, the underlying event data it's using is the Event model created in the application. This makes the event handler incredibly simple:

```
changeEvent: (event, jsEvent, ui, view) =>
    event.save()
```

Handlers that save state from the user interface are rarely this simple, and in this case the handler works only because the model defined for events is compatible with FullCalendar's expectations. This is an example of forward-thinking API design choices on the part of Adam Shaw, the plug-in author.

In other cases, you won't be so lucky. The more usual procedure would look like this:

1. Retrieve the new data from the interface (probably from a form).
2. Find the object in the model that needs to be updated.
3. Update the object with the new data.
4. Save the object.

In a procedure like that, when the user clicks an event on the calendar a dialog should appear, to allow the editing of the textual information. jQuery UI provides a useful dialog widget for just this purpose.

A useful pattern in Spine apps is to separate new user interfaces into separate controllers, particularly if there is some degree of interactivity associated with the interface. For this task, I create a standalone controller to display the dialog.

To begin with, the calendar itself is updated to create the dialog and trigger it in response to events being clicked:

```
constructor: ->
    super
    @el.fullCalendar

        ...

        eventClick: @eventClick

    @dialog = new EventEditor()

eventClick: (event, jsEvent, view) =>
    @dialog.open(event)
```

I left out most of the FullCalendar configuration except for the new event handler. Event-Editor is the name of the controller about to be defined, leaving the handler the simple task of passing the event in question through for editing.

This demonstrates the benefit of separating functionality into controllers. Adding this new dialog is a small change, and the code is quite loosely coupled.

For the body of the dialog an Eco template is required. Save this as views/calendar/editevent.eco:

```
<form>
    <p>Title: <input name="title" type="text" value="<%= @title %>"></p>
    <p>All day?  <input name="allDay" type="checkbox" value="1" <% if
```

```
@allDay: %>checked="checked"<% end %></p>
    <hr>
    <p>Description:</p>
    <textarea name="description"><%= @description %></textarea>
</form>
```

Notice that this template is expecting to inject the information being edited directly into the form. It is possible to load the data at run-time too, for example using one of the form binding systems covered in Chapter 13. In this case, the form is simply re-rendered every time an event needs to be edited.

Even though this controller is for a specialized user interface, it's created the same way as any other controller:

```
class EventEditor extends Spine.Controller

    constructor: ->
        super
        @template = require 'views/calendar/editevent'
        @el.dialog
            autoOpen: false
            buttons:
                "Save": @save_edit
                "Cancel": @cancel_edit

    render: =>
        @html @template(@currentEvent)

    open: (event) =>
        @currentEvent = event
        @render()
        @el.dialog 'open'
```

The constructor loads the Eco template and adds the jQuery Dialog widget to the container element. By default the dialog box doesn't open when created and contains two buttons: Save and Cancel. These buttons trigger different event handlers when clicked.

To generate the form itself, the render() function passes the current event being edited through to the template function that was pre-loaded in the constructor. The design of this dialog is that the form will be re-rendered each time an event needs to be edited. The compiled Eco template is simply a regular function, and can therefore be re-used by the render() function as many times as needed.

The open() function provides the main piece of API—the function called by the calendar click event handler to open the dialog. It expects to be given a reference to the event being edited that is saved as @currentEvent so that the event can later be updated if required.

Before opening the dialog box, render() is called to ensure the form contains the latest data. The dialog is then opened and the user is able to edit the data associated with the event.

Earlier you saw the dialog buttons were connected to event handlers. If the user clicks Cancel, the dialog only needs to be closed. If the user clicks Save, the updated data needs to be stored on the model and then the model itself needs to be saved:

```
_done: (save) =>
    if save
        inputs = @$("form").serializeArray()
        @currentEvent[i.name] = i.value for i in inputs
        @currentEvent.allDay = 'allDay' in (i.name for i in inputs)
        @currentEvent.save()
    @currentEvent = null
    @el.dialog 'close'


save_edit: => @_done true


cancel_edit: => @_done false
```

For both events the dialog box needs to be closed and the current event removed. The key difference between the events is that for Cancel the data should not be saved. An easy way to perform this kind of work is to make the event handlers themselves small wrappers around a more generic function, which is what I've done in this last example.

Another benefit of the dialog box being in a separate controller is now apparent. Since there is only one form associated with this controller, the process of retrieving the data from the form is simple: @$("form") refers only to the form in the editevent.eco template.

Some special handling is given to the checkbox: In its unchecked state the checkbox would not appear in the result from serializeArray() and the allDay attribute is left as is. This could be incorrect since the user may have unchecked the box as part of their edit, so it should be set to false if there is no data for the checkbox.

Notice that after the event is saved there is no message to the parent controller to let it know that the calendar should be refreshed. This is still being taken care of by the model-level events; the save() call in the dialog controller causes a change event to be fired. The calendar is listening for those events and refreshes automatically. This example neatly demonstrates how events on models can be used to decouple user interface logic, leading to simpler and more correct application code.

STORING DATA ON THE SERVER

In many of the previous samples of code, the save() function has been called on model instances. Where exactly is this data being saved? The answer is that right now, it isn't being saved: One refresh of the browser page and the data is gone. The only meaningful effect save() is having right now is that it triggers events.

Most modern browsers have a system called LocalStorage available. (In fact, you look at this in much more depth in Chapter 12.) This system allows a web application to store data on the local disk (subject to the user's approval), allowing the data to survive the refresh of the page and remain accessible if the browser goes offline. This is a basic step up and can be added to Spine models very simply:

```
class Event extends Spine.Model
    @configure "Event", "title", "allDay", "description", "start", "end"
    @extend Spine.Model.Local
```

All you need is the additional extension. Internally, this extension hooks into the regular load and save process, ensuring that the data is retrieved from or saved to the browser.

Using `LocalStorage` might be okay for some applications, but it is quite a limited system. Even if storing the information in the browser alone were sufficient, `LocalStorage` has a relatively small 5Mb capacity in most browsers. What you really need is a process that enables Spine to retrieve information from the server using AJAX, and save data back when it is created or updated.

Surprisingly, adding an AJAX-backed persistence model into a model definition is straightforward:

```
class Event extends Spine.Model
    @configure "Event", "title", "allDay", "description", "start", "end"
    @extend Spine.Model.Ajax
```

At a basic level that is all that is required: Internal data loading and saving is again intercepted and routed to the server. This might look too good to be true, and in a way it is: Although it's simple to extend a model in this fashion, there are some quite rigid rules about how the persistence layer communicates with the server.

The Ajax persistence assumes the server-side data API is REST-based. The basic URL that it uses is derived from the class name in the first instance. The name is converted to lower-case and then pluralized, so that the Event model is expected to be available on the URL `/events`.

If the default choice of URL is not acceptable, then adding a static `@url` attribute to the class definition overrides that path. Either way, the basic load and save operations take place against the path given:

- `GET /events` is used to retrieve all the objects for a model.
- `POST /events` is used to create a new object for a model.
- `PUT /events/:id` is used to update a specific object (where the object identifier itself is appended to the URL).
- `DELETE /events/:id` is used to remove an object.

There are REST-style solutions available for node.js that make the development of the server-side counterpart to this scheme quite straightforward. Readers with Ruby experience may recognize this scheme in particular from the Ruby on Rails framework, and, indeed, Spine integrates incredibly well with Rails.

Data is passed to and from the server as JSON objects as you might expect, but you might not have expected this persistence mechanism to load all the server-side objects at once. This is done for a couple of reasons:

- It simplifies the process of retrieving the data, since the client never needs to work out which objects are available on the server-side.
- Useful model features such as `@search()` can assume that all objects are always available locally, instead of attempting to construct some kind of search that the server would understand to retrieve a subset of objects.

These reasons are entirely understandable, but come with their own set of drawbacks:

- There's no mechanism by which the server can notify the client that an object has changed, making this system less useful for applications where multiple users are accessing the same data at the same time.
- The application has to download all the available objects before it starts to execute, putting a practical limit on the amount of data it can sensibly work with.
- With this "download all" behavior the application may end up consuming large amounts of bandwidth.

These compromises are unacceptable for some applications. If that is the case, the Spine models can still be used, but a custom persistence mechanism needs to be designed.

One obvious way of reducing the load is to download lists of object identifiers in the first instance rather than the entire objects, and lazily load objects as required. Equally, the search mechanism could be restricted in functionality to enable the handling of queries on the server-side. Which approach is the best will depend on the application.

SUMMARY

In this chapter you took a speedy, but relatively deep, look at Spine. As a web application framework Spine is lightweight, but it provides a variety of crucial features that much larger and more impressive systems are still built around:

- The Model-View-Controller design pattern is a useful template for architecting code.
- Stylus—a CoffeeScript-alike solution for CSS—has a powerful, expressive syntax that can be used to solve practical development problems.
- Eco is an engine for templating HTML code, and the jEco system is useful for binding the resulting templates with the data that drives them, simplifying click handlers and view-level logic.
- Controllers can be used to decouple functionality and provide a high-level navigation and interface control mechanism.
- Lastly, Spine's data model support was to demonstrate how using model-based events can help you keep the view up to date while still keeping code loosely coupled.

11

WRITING JQUERY PLUG-INS

FOR MANY DEVELOPERS, the process of creating dynamic websites or AJAX-style applications begins and ends with jQuery. There's no doubt at all that jQuery is an incredibly useful library, but it's very easy—and tempting—to simply keep writing procedural-style jQuery calls and do without all of the things that jQuery doesn't provide the facilities to do.

There's no need to feel boxed in by jQuery, because right from the start it was designed to be easily extensible. Without touching any of the core code, you can add new API and behaviors to the library, and do so in a maintainable fashion. While this is of course possible in JavaScript, the capabilities provided by CoffeeScript actually make this even more useful.

This chapter looks at the development of jQuery plug-ins with CoffeeScript in both a procedural and object-oriented fashion and how jQuery UI widgets can be created. Either of these frameworks can be used to create new interactive interface elements, but there are some basic differences in how they work and the fundamental architecture.

ANATOMY OF A JQUERY PLUG-IN

When the jQuery library was first published, it was seen as a compatibility library—a kind of shim that developers could use to smooth over the various cracks in different browsers so that they could get on with the real work of developing web applications.

It didn't take long, though, for other developers to start adding functionality to jQuery, and in fact the first plug-in arrived at the end of January 2006—some two weeks after the main announcement of jQuery (although jQuery had, at that point, been in development for months).

As with any other system of extension, you may wonder why it should be an extension at all. As an open-source project, coding additional functionality and contributing it shouldn't be a problem—assuming, of course, that the code is good enough!

Good plug-ins tend to have one or more of the following features:

- They implement functionality that is at a higher level of abstraction than the rest of the library, and could be seen as simply a grouping of a lot of lower-level functionality.
- They implement functionality that is of narrow interest—only a small minority of the user base is likely to want to use it.
- There is no compelling reason for the plug-in to be in core because it doesn't need to access internals or make use of any other special privilege.

Indeed, in my opinion, the last reason is particularly good. For the same reason developers use object-oriented design, design by contract, or use any of the other myriad methods of decoupling code, keeping code as separate from other code as possible and making use of a small but well-understood shared API is a fundamental aspect of software development that pops up in many different ways.

Using plug-ins provides a great way of packaging self-contained functionality. With jQuery, they are particularly good at adding behavior or user-interface functionality to a page. Some words of warning though: First, plug-ins have an incredibly limited API and include serious restrictions on how they can be accessed. Second, they're not a panacea—by self-contained functionality, I mean something such as a drop-down menu or a type of animation. A whole application is no doubt self-contained; however, it is far too complicated to design within the framework of a plug-in. If a plug-in ends up being more than three or four pages of code, it's probably already too complicated and should be broken up.

CREATING A SKELETON PLUG-IN

This is another rare occasion where a JavaScript appetizer needs to come before the main course of CoffeeScript. Because this is a JavaScript library, the majority of the documentation for plug-ins (available at `http://docs.jquery.com/Plugins/Authoring`) is written with JavaScript in mind. The best-practice skeleton is particularly insightful, so it's the starting point:

```
(function($){

  var methods = {
     init: function (options) {
       return this.each(function() {
             // Initialize the plug-in here, once for each DOM node passed
       });
     },
     destroy: function () {
       return this.each(function(){
          // remove each attached node
       })
     },
     reposition: function () {},
     show: function () {},
     hide: function () {},
     update: function (content ) {}
  };

  $.fn.tooltip = function (method) {
    if (methods[method]) {
      return methods[method].apply(this,
          Array.prototype.slice.call(arguments, 1));
    } else if (typeof method === 'object' || ! method) {
      return methods.init.apply(this, arguments);
    } else {
      $.error('Method ' +  method + ' does not exist on jQuery.tooltip');
    }
  };
})(jQuery);
```

This plug-in is designed to act as a tooltip—to provide a pop-up text box when the user moves the mouse pointer over an onscreen option—although the actual functionality is missing (notice the various empty function bodies in methods).

As an API, this couldn't be simpler: The plug-in is a function that does slightly different things depending on how it is called:

- If it's passed an instance of jQuery (which will have an associated number of selected DOM nodes), it initializes the plug-in on each node passed.
- If it's passed a method name defined in methods, it calls that method.
- It causes an error if it isn't called correctly.

By defining the function on $.fn, the instance of jQuery has been extended with this new API—and it's important to remember that this is happening at runtime.

The meat of the plug-in, then, is the methods table—which has the various functions that represent the behavior of the plug-in, and it is this section that will change from plug-in to plug-in. Most plug-ins do two things, at minimum: set-up, also known as init(), and tear-down, or destroy().

I'm sure the point regarding `init()` is clear: This is where the plug-in does the initial work and sets up any ongoing functionality that is required. However, `destroy()` takes a little more explaining—after all, if the user is going to move on to another page, what is the point of deliberately destroying the instance of the plug-in?

The primary reason is to ensure that a DOM node doesn't need to be destroyed just to remove a plug-in. A plug-in may need to be removed for many reasons—for example, if a page has a large number of dynamic elements—but in theory, they can be removed when the element is removed.

For larger applications, though, there are times when a plug-in is added to a DOM node that's to be long-lived. For example, think about a plug-in used to edit part of a page within a content-management system that automatically makes parts of the page editable or not. When users finish editing, they want the page to return to the static mode, without the editor. Perhaps the relevant DOM node is simply deleted and re-created, but this approach steps on the toes of any other attached plug-in—meaning that the application must track which plug-ins are using which nodes and manage them appropriately.

Instead, using `destroy()`, the plug-in can selectively remove the parts of the node that should be removed, and the rest of the node (including any other active plug-ins) remains. This approach is much cleaner than destroy and re-create and means that plug-in management isn't required. Additionally, on pages with many elements, the browser does slightly better on the memory-management front—keeping the pages fast.

Now that the JavaScript version is covered, take a look at how that translates into CoffeeScript. I kept this relatively straightforward for side-by-side comparison:

```
(($) ->

    methods =
        init: (options) ->
            @.each ->
                # initialise the plug-in here, once for each DOM node passed

        destroy: ->
            @.each ->
                # remove each attached node

        reposition: ->
            # etc.

    $.fn.tooltip = (method) ->
        if method of methods
            methods[method].apply this, arguments[1...]
        else if typeof method == 'object' or not method
            methods.init.apply this, arguments
        else
            $.error "Method #{ method } does not exist on jQuery.tooltip"

)(jQuery)
```

A couple of the empty method bodies are left out for simplicity, but even so, it's clear that this code is tighter and more concise than the JavaScript version. Additionally, the overall wrapper—aliasing $ to jQuery on the off-chance that code calling the plug-in has turned that jQuery option off—isn't really needed; $ = jQuery at the top of the file is sufficient, because CoffeeScript already wraps the body of the code by default.

Writing a procedural plug-in using this skeleton is an exercise in filling in the blanks. The structure is straightforward, and most plug-ins will have at most three or four extra methods defined.

However, a few things still aren't right. Primarily, this code doesn't mix well with Coffee-Script's class-style object-oriented features, which means that some of the existing development patterns and practices you've looked at are difficult to apply.

WRITING A CLASSFUL PLUG-IN

Although the prototypical nature of JavaScript inheritance can provide the functionality required, within CoffeeScript it feels unnatural to use those features directly—the provided classes and inheritances are more straightforward, easier to use, and (arguably, at least) more idiomatic CoffeeScript.

jQuery's plug-in interface assumes the inverse, though, which is not entirely surprising because the library was designed for JavaScript, and for the majority of its life until this point, CoffeeScript didn't even exist. However, this does demonstrate how a CoffeeScript API can be adapted for even the most un-CoffeeScript-like codebase.

Before looking at how a CoffeeScript class-based plug-in might be integrated into jQuery, take a look at how such a plug-in might be written. To keep things simple, the same API is used, but with a few modifications:

- Instead of a plain object and manual apply, there is a standard class.
- There is an init() function—the constructor—and a destroy() function.
- API calls are methods defined in the class.

The example here will be an upgraded <select> element, allowing developers to put whatever elements within the drop-down they want, not just the plain text that most browsers are limited to.

Constructing this new select is the most difficult piece, so first think about the structure of the rest of this plug-in, which is starting from a regular class:

```coffeescript
class UpdateSelectPlugin

    defaults:
        background: "white"

    constructor: (@name, @element, options) ->
```

```
    # TODO

destroy: =>
    @select.remove()
    $(@element).show()

show: =>
    @showing = true
    @items.show()

hide: =>
    @showing = false
    @items.hide()

setval: (value) =>
    @options.value = value
    @selected_elem.text @values[value]

getval: =>
    @options.value
```

Every plug-in needs some kind of configuration, and with configuration comes a requirement for some sensible defaults—and `@defaults` will be used to set up `@options` in the constructor. As well as the constructor and `destroy()`, there is a getter/setter pair to retrieve the currently selected value, and two functions to `show()` or `hide()` the new drop-down itself. Unlike the previous plug-in, each one of these methods is defined using the fat arrow (`=>`) to refer to a specific instance of the plug-in.

Here also is a specific pattern worth discussing. For many HTML form elements, the value of the element and the visible text are one and the same: `<input>` of various types and `<textarea>` being obvious examples. For `<select>` that may or may not be true, and in some instances it's better if the displayed value and the actual value are different. This plug-in is going to use `@values` as a store of the "display" value to use, keeping the actual form value separate. The display values will be stored in `@values` on initialization.

Now, on to the constructor—this is where all the real work is done, setting up the new page elements, creating the behaviors, and joining it all up:

```
constructor: (@name, @element, options) ->
    @options = $.extend {}, @defaults, options

    jqe = $(@element)
    @showing = false

    @select = $('<div>',
        width: jqe.outerWidth()
        class: 'updateSelect')

    @selected_elem = $('<div>',
```

```
        width: jqe.outerWidth())

@items = $('<ul></ul>')
    .css
        'cursor': 'pointer'
        'background-color': @options.background
    .hide()
@values = {}
```

So far, the code is setting up the containing structures for the new drop-down: @select is the container for this new width, @items the drop-down list that will be displayed when the user clicks the widget, and @selected_elem displays the currently selected item (and, for the most part, will fill the container).

jqe is the original <select> element, wrapped in jQuery, and the outerWidth() is used to ensure that the replacement selector that is being placed on the page is the same dimension as the existing one. This is important because if the size of the element changes the browser will be forced to "reflow" the page—this element and others following it will likely end up being positioned differently, causing a jarring experience for the user.

The next step is to work through the <select> element that is being overridden to look at the options that were available—these are going to be replicated in the new element to ensure you don't need to specify that same information twice:

```
jqe.find('option').each (i, option) =>
    val = $(option).attr('value')
    label = $(option).text() ? val
    @values[val] = label

    item = $('<li>',
        'html': $(option).html(),
        'data-value': val)
    @items.append(item)

@options.value = jqe.val()
@selected_elem.text @values[@options.value]

@select.append(@selected_elem, @items)
```

HANDLING EVENTS AND BEHAVIOR

With these elements in place, you can set up the various behavioral event handlers. This is an interesting element, though, because some behavior is desired:

- Clicking the element itself—which shows the currently selected value—should show or hide the drop-down.
- Clicking a drop-down element should select that element and hide the drop-down.
- Clicking anywhere else when the drop-down is open should hide the drop-down.

Note that some problems start to become apparent. A basic implementation of handlers for this might look as follows:

```
@select.bind 'click', (e) =>
    e.preventDefault()
    if @showing then @hide() else @show()

@select.on 'click', 'li', (e) =>
    e.preventDefault()
    e.stopPropagation()
    @setval $(e.target).data('value')
    @hide()
```

The first handler is used on the main element to show or hide the drop-down. That's straight-forward enough, but then the click handler for the drop-down element has an interesting extra clause: `e.stopPropagation()`.

`preventDefault()` is used liberally and stops the browser from taking the default action on a link—such as visiting another page. `stopPropagation()` is seen much less often and is used to prevent an event from bubbling. When a node on a page receives an event, such as a click, it passes that event on to the parent in the hierarchy. This is how, for example, a hover state can work on multiple items within a DOM tree: The node that the pointer is over gets a mouseover event that then bubbles up through its parent nodes, causing each of them to move into the hover state (if they weren't already).

If the user clicks a DOM node that is beneath the main container, the container receives the click event as well—and because the behavior is already bound to that event (to show or hide the drop-down), the behavior is triggered inappropriately.

One way to prevent this situation is to use `stopPropagation()`, which ensures that the event doesn't bubble up the DOM node hierarchy. However, this is usually a sign of poor design: It's always possible to ignore an event, but it's never possible to get back an event that hasn't bubbled up.

There are performance reasons to avoid bubbling events. Although browsers take shortcuts, bubbling events further than necessary to trigger the various bound handlers can slow performance, especially when there are a lot of handlers on a page. Even then, though, preventing the bubbling should generally be a method of last resort.

A better approach is to ignore or interpret events based on the target of the event:

```
@select.on 'click', (e) =>
    e.preventDefault()
    if e.target == @selected_elem[0]
        if @showing then @hide() else @show()
    else
        @setval $(e.target).data('value')
        @hide()
```

```
$('html').on 'click', (e) =>
    if not $.contains @select[0], e.target
        @hide()
```

The first click handler is doing the job of the previous two. It's bound to the overall container, and if the target is the selected element label, then it toggles the drop-down. If the target is not the label, the handler assumes the target is a drop-down item, and records the item's value before hiding the drop-down list.

The second click handler is new and triggers the drop-down to close if there is a click somewhere else on the page while it is open, copying native behavior. Again, this type of handler is difficult to write if stopPropagation() were in use: The handler results in certain clicks not bubbling, and therefore doesn't trigger the behavior.

The only task remaining in the constructor is to hide the original element on the page:

```
jqe.after(@select).hide()
```

ATTACHING THE PLUG-IN TO JQUERY

Having written a plug-in based on a class structure, you may be thinking that it's not totally clear how this might now be used with jQuery. The absolute ideal interface would be something like this:

```
$.fn.updateSelect = UpdateSelectPlugin
```

Unfortunately, jQuery is not going to instantiate the plug-in for you, so something smarter is needed. It needs to be able to create instances of a plug-in, as well as do the mapping of (potentially chained) function calls to instance method calls. On the bright side, this is a piece of code that can be reused and need not be boilerplate:

```
attach = (klass, name) ->
    $.fn[name] = (optsOrMethod, args...) ->
        result = []

        for elem in @
            data = $(elem).data()
            obj = data["plugin_#{name}"] ?= new klass(name,
                                                        elem, optsOrMethod)
            result.push(obj)

            if obj[optsOrMethod]
                obj[optsOrMethod](args...)

        return result
```

The fundamental tool being used here is jQuery's data() functionality. You can use it to store arbitrary data against a DOM node, and to ensure that references to any objects are cleaned up if the node is removed from the document.

So, first, the element is inspected to see if there is an existing instance attached with the plug-in name, and if so it is retrieved, otherwise a new one is created. Then, if a valid method name was passed, it is called on that instance with the other arguments provided.

This functionality is then attached to jQuery, using the name provided. `klass` is simply a misspelled version of `class`—being a reserved word, you can't say `class` directly—so the API is actually simple: A class and a name are all you need:

```
$ ->
    attach(UpdateSelectPlugin, 'updateSelect')
    $('select.important').updateSelect({background: "red"})
    $('select.notimportant').updateSelect()
```

Now the functionality to create instances attached to specific nodes has been added to jQuery and can be called directly. The API is also translated, so to remove this updated selector from the .notimportant elements is as simple as this:

```
$('select.notimportant').updateSelect 'destroy'
```

Other methods such as `getval()` and `setval()` work in a similar manner. And indeed, the actual object itself can be retrieved and operated on directly:

```
sel = $('#upgrade').updateSelect()?[0]
sel.setval 'orange'
console.log sel.getval()
```

As well as using the standard jQuery API then, it's possible to make available a more advanced API that feels more natural to the CoffeeScript developer.

INHERITING FROM AN EXISTING PLUG-IN

Now that you've done all the work to define a plug-in in the form of standard CoffeeScript class, it's time to see the actual benefits of that work. The key benefit of defining a plug-in as a CoffeeScript class is the ability to inherit from it, to re-use functionality. For the most part, the public API of a plug-in is not going to change much, but internally there will be a variety of methods which could be overridden. Architecting the internal structures correctly is the most difficult part of ensuring that the code can be re-used.

With the upgraded drop-down class, the `show()` and `hide()` methods are separate, even though they aren't complicated. The separation enables you to override them in a subclass. It's now easy to write a new plug-in with a different animation to display the drop-down. For example, to make the drop-down fade in is as simple as this:

```
class FadeSelectPlugin extends UpdateSelectPlugin

    show: =>
        @showing = true
```

```
        @items.fadeIn()

    hide: =>
        @showing = false
        @items.fadeOut()
```

You could implement such a simple change as a piece of configuration rather than a sub-class. For a small number of such features, that's a reasonable approach. However, that kind of compromise tends to work out badly in the long run when many such features are implemented. The code becomes punctuated by various `if` clauses that change behavior based on different pieces of configuration.

JQUERY UI

Although the plug-in system for jQuery is very powerful, there is another way of developing the pieces of reusable user interface that applications tend to need—jQuery UI.

As one of the projects underneath the general jQuery umbrella, jQuery UI fits into the general ethos of the library as you might expect. The role of jQuery UI (or *jqUI*) is to provide a set of effects, behaviors, and pieces of UI that fit well into a jQuery-based project, and work on both a small and a large scale.

As well as providing parts of the code and the framework for putting these widgets together, jqUI includes a CSS-based system called *theme roller* that separates the styles used to create the structure of the widgets from the styles used to adapt the look and feel of the widgets.

USING WIDGETS INSTEAD OF PLUG-INS

On the face of it, jQuery plug-ins and jqUI widgets look similar. You invoke them in basically the same way—for example, to create a date picker in jqUI, you call `$('selector').datepicker()`, and the widget is created. However, although the developer API is essentially the same, that's where the similarities end.

The key underpinning of jqUI as a system is the *Widget Factory,* also known as `$.widget`, the base on which all the widgets are built. Not only does `$.widget` provide a common structure and interface, it encodes a system of inheritance that allows widgets built using it to be cleanly and easily extended.

With this structure in place, widgets tend to be a lot more sophisticated than jQuery plug-ins. In particular:

- It's usually easy to remove an effect from an element once it has been added—few plug-ins allow the developer to downgrade an element later.
- It's usually easy to change the effect applied to an element.
- Plug-ins often don't pass events up to the code that called them.

The factory includes these standard features:

- Encapsulating the functionality in a single object
- Associating the object with the DOM node it's applied to, using `$.data()`
- Namespacing the API to prevent name clashing or just to keep things tidy
- Protecting against widgets being instantiated more than once

The best-practice design for a jqUI widget is comfortable JavaScript having been designed with that language in mind, but is less than ideal for CoffeeScript. Again, take a look at the JavaScript first:

```javascript
// the jQuery.custom namespace will automatically be created if needed
$.widget("custom.widget", {
  options: {
    className : ""
  },
  _create: function() {
    // this function creates the widget
  },
  do_something: function() {
    // this is a "public" method
  },
  _widgetfunc: function() {
    // this is an uncallable "private" method
  }
  _setOption: function(key, value) {
    // this is used to respond to option changes
    switch (key) {
      case "some_option":
        break;
    }
    this._super("_setOption", key, value);
  },
  destroy: function() {
    // this un-applies the widget
    this._super("destroy");
  }
});
```

This is already a lot more compelling than the jQuery equivalent. There is much less boiler-plate code, and this looks a lot more like a standard object.

Translating the custom select object into a jqUI widget is not straightforward, so it's useful to compare this to the previous jQuery-only-efforts. The base of the widget looks similar to the plug-in:

```coffeescript
$.widget 'custom.updateselect',
    version: '0.1'
```

```
options:
    background: "white"

_setOptions: ->
    @_super arguments
    @_refresh()

_setOption: (key, value) ->
    @_super "_setOption", key, value

show: ->
    @showing = true
    @items.show()

hide: ->
    @showing = false
    @items.hide()

setval: (value) ->
    @options.value = value
    @selected_elem.text @values[value]

getval: ->
    @options.value
```

The majority of this code deals with options and values, one way or another. `@options.value` is where the selected value ends up, and the main work is done when the new piece of UI is created:

```
_create: ->
    # @element and @options already set up for us
    jqe = $(@element)
    @showing = false

    @select = $('<div>',
        width: jqe.outerWidth()
        class: 'updateSelect')

    @selected_elem = $('<div>',
        width: jqe.outerWidth())

    @items = $('<ul></ul>')
        .css
            'cursor': 'pointer'
            'background-color': @options.background
        .hide()
    @values = {}
```

So far, the process is similar to previous approaches. You look at the existing elements, and set up some replacements. However, by the time you need callbacks and click handlers, some of the drawbacks of this approach become apparent:

```coffeescript
$this = @

jqe.find('option').each (i, option) ->
    val = $(option).attr('value')
    label = $(option).text() ? val
    $this.values[val] = label

    item = $('<li>',
        html: $(option).html(),
        'data-value': val)
    $this.items.append(item)

@options.value = jqe.val()
@selected_elem.text @values[@options.value]

@select.append(@selected_elem, @items)

@select.on 'click', (e) ->
    e.preventDefault()
    if e.target == $this.selected_elem[0]
        if $this.showing then $this.hide() else $this.show()
    else
        $this.setval $(e.target).data('value')
        $this.hide()

$('html').on 'click', (e) ->
    if not $.contains $this.select[0], e.target
        $this.hide()

jqe.after(@select).hide()
```

Usually, aliasing `this` to another variable is unnecessary, which is part of the point of CoffeeScript. Unfortunately, though, it's not possible to make use of that binding feature in this instance: You aren't working with a class, so the mechanics are like they are in standard JavaScript.

This design is not entirely unlike most jqUI widgets, whether written in CoffeeScript or not—setting up the new element is usually the hardest part of the work, and the limited interaction means that a few ugly click handlers are required.

WRITING A TAGGING COMPONENT

To really look into the power of jqUI, you need a slightly more sophisticated and interactive widget. One of the things that the library does well is provide basic widgets, like types of buttons, that can be composed into more complex widgets.

As an example, take a look at a tagging component. This kind of widget is familiar to users of Facebook, Gmail, or other similar web-based systems. The widget looks like a text input box; when the user clicks in it a dropdown displays values from which the user can choose. If the user selects one of the suggested values, that value is put into the input as a kind of button. Some examples are shown in Figure 11-1.

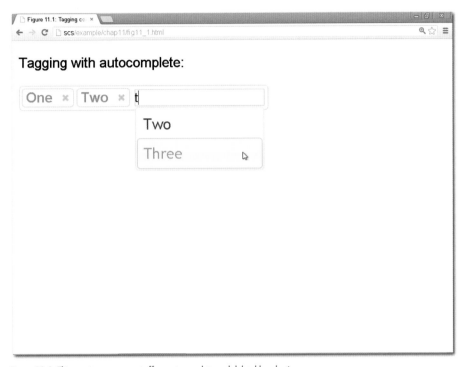

Figure 11-1: This tagging component offers autocomplete and deletable selections.

These components can be sophisticated:

- If values have been selected, users can get rid of them by clicking a Close or Delete button on each, or by back-spacing over them—mixing text and graphical inputs.
- If the user types a value that didn't appear in the suggestion box, the widget may suggest to the server that the value be created so that it is added to future suggestions.

Of course, different developers want widgets to work in different ways. This widget can be extended in numerous ways by different people. This flexibility is crucial.

You build a widget like this out of several components:

- A text box for input
- A suggestion drop-down

- A list of buttons
- A container to wrap everything together

This widget will be built as a jqUI widget, and fortunately jqUI provides a drop-down/ suggestion widget that you can use for this task.

Placing buttons within a text box input is obviously difficult (or, in fact, impossible in many instances), so that's not quite what will happen. Although this widget looks like a text box, the user types into a borderless text box inside the widget. (See Figure 11-2.)

Figure 11-2: Highlighted widget components.

To achieve this you need to use a little bit of CSS and, of course, some markup, which is easy:

```
<div>
    <ul>
        <li>Selected <a href='#'>[X]</a></li>
        <li>Another selected <a href='#'>[X]</a></li>
    </ul>
    <input />
</div>
```

This markup represents a tagging component with two items already selected. It is maintained by the widget, with the list representing an internal list of selected values.

Creating this markup is not involved, so what would be the heavyweight part of a widget is not too complicated. With some internal data defined, the work mainly involves creating DOM nodes to represent that data:

```
widget_name = "simplewidget"

$.widget "custom.#{ widget_name }",
    options:
        values: ["one", "two", "three", "four"]

    _selected: []
```

```
_create: ->
    @pieces =
        auto: $("<input>").autocomplete
            source: @options.values
            select: @_event_select
        selected: $("<ul></ul>")


    $(@pieces.selected).on 'click', 'a', @_event_remove


    @refresh()

_makeButton: (item) ->
    close = $("<a href='#'>[X]</a>")
    $("<li>#{ item.label} </li>").append close

refresh: ->
    @pieces.selected.html('')
    for obj in @_selected
        $(@pieces.selected).append @_makeButton obj


    $(@element).html('')
            .addClass(widget_name)
            .append(@pieces.selected)
            .append(@pieces.auto)
```

The widget name is defined at the start because it is needed in a couple of places to ensure that it doesn't conflict with other plug-ins potentially active on the same DOM nodes. `@options.values` represents the default values that the autocomplete system brings up. These can be overridden when the widget is created, and are simply fed into the `autocomplete()` widget.

Two event handlers are set but still need to be written: `__event_select()` is triggered when the user selects an item from the autocomplete drop-down, and `_event_remove()`, which is triggered when the user removes an item in the list.

`_makeButton()` is a helper function. The widget needs to create inline buttons when the `_event_select()` handler fires, so it makes sense to have a single function responsible for that.

The event handlers now store a lot of the complexity:

```
_event_select: (event, ui) ->
    event.preventDefault()
    self = $(event.target).parent().data(widget_name)
    self._selected.push ui.item
    $(self.pieces.auto).val('')
    self.pieces.selected.append(self._makeButton ui.item)
```

This fires when an item is selected from the drop-down. `self` is a reference to what would normally be `this`—the object is bound automatically by jqUI to the container of the widget, so that is a convenient way of picking the reference back up.

Having gotten the reference, the selected value is stored internally and the button representing that value displays in the user interface, which is less costly than rerendering the widget.

The `remove` event does the inverse. It removes the button from the user interface and removes the value from the internal list:

```
_event_remove: (event) ->
    event.preventDefault()
    self = $(event.target).parents(".#{ widget_name }").data(widget_name)
    index = $(event.target).parent().index()
    $(self.pieces.selected).find("li").slice(index, index+1).remove()
    self._selected.splice(index, 1)
```

Again, the reference to the actual instantiated widget object must be looked up via the DOM because you don't have `this` bound as it would be in a normal CoffeeScript class instance.

The hard work of the widget is now completed, and now you just have to implement the option API so that the selected value can be set or retrieved:

```
selected: ->
    item.value for item in @_selected

_setOption: (key, value) ->
    switch key
        when "selected"
            @_selected = value
            @refresh()

    @_super "_setOption", key, value
```

This is now an entirely standard jqUI widget, created through the widget factory, and it can be used to create a tagging widget on an empty `div` with a single call:

```
widget = $('#widget').simplewidget()
```

BRIDGING THE DIVIDE

Although the tagging widget is written as relatively nice CoffeeScript, and is low on boiler-plate, it's still not ideal. In particular, it's not possible to write widgets like this using the normal CoffeeScript class hierarchy.

In this instance, examining why that's a problem is a bit of work. After all, isn't CoffeeScript just JavaScript underneath? Well, the short answer is "Yes," but sadly the longer, more accurate answer is "Yes, but . . ."

Both jqUI and CoffeeScript do some of the same work. To allow one widget to extend from another, jqUI puts in place a somewhat classical-looking inheritance hierarchy in much the same way that CoffeeScript does with its class definitions.

However, although both pieces of software are trying to achieve the same thing, they go about it in a different way, which can cause problems trying to combine the two systems. As an obvious example, a method on a CoffeeScript object can have a bound version of `this`, whereas a jqUI widget generally won't. If a CoffeeScript object inherits from a jqUI one and calls the superclass from a bound method, weird things happen.

Take a step back at this point, though. What is the jqUI widget factory actually doing for you? The factory is made up of several different pieces:

- `$.widget()`: This is the main entry point to the factory, but it mainly concerns itself with the functionality for this inheritance hierarchy.
- `$.widget.extend()`: This mixes one object into another.
- `$.widget.bridge()`: This is the function that converts a single function call on the jQuery object to a series of method calls on the widget object.
- `$.Widget()`: Not to be confused with its lowercase brother, this documents the interface that widgets should conform to.

Looking at the various preceding parts, you can see that `$.widget.bridge()` is definitely interesting, and `$.Widget()` is sort of interesting, but you could probably do without the rest of it. And it turns out that this is actually true. CoffeeScript developers don't get as much out of the full widget factory as JavaScript developers do. Most of the work the factory is doing is already done by CoffeeScript, and it doesn't make sense to try to merge the two somehow.

Once the main widget factory is set aside, you're free to write a class hierarchy that makes sense and uses the CoffeeScript-native features.

One thing the widget factory does is call the `_init()` method of a new widget when it's set up so that a base class can be created to mimic that functionality:

```coffeescript
class JqueryUIWidget
    options: {}

    constructor: (options, @element) ->
        @options = $.extend(@options, options)
        if @widget_name
            $(@element).data(@widget_name, @)
        @_init()

    widget: =>
        @element

    _init: =>
    _setOption: =>
    refresh: =>
```

This base class updates the options in the class definition and provides a getter to access the DOM element associated with the widget. If a widget name is given, that name is then used to associate the instance of the widget with the DOM element.

It would be nice if you didn't have to supply a widget name. Unfortunately, this is difficult for a number of reasons. Mainly, it's difficult or impossible to determine from a given object what its class actually is—because the class is essentially a CoffeeScript invention. Without being able to determine the class, it's impossible to work out a widget name that makes sense and doesn't clash with other widgets, so you must provide one.

The start of the new version of the tagging widget now looks a lot more like standard CoffeeScript:

```
class SimpleWidget extends JqueryUIWidget

    widget_name: "simplewidget"

    options:
        values: ["One", "Two", "Three", "Four"]

    _selected: []

    _init: =>
        @pieces =
            auto: $("<input>")
            selected: $("<ul></ul>")

        @refresh()
```

Once the widget is created, the fat-arrow bound methods can be used, which immediately starts making many of the references easier and clearer. The process of refreshing the content also starts looking a lot clearer:

```
    refresh: =>
        @pieces.selected.off('click').html('')
        for obj in @_selected
            @pieces.selected.append @_makeButton obj

        $(@element).html('')
                .addClass(@widget_name)
                .append(@pieces.selected)
                .append(@pieces.auto)

        @pieces.auto.autocomplete
                source: @options.values
                select: @_event_select

        @pieces.selected.on 'click', 'span', @_event_remove
```

The event handlers are in place in the same way, although they end up being simpler:

```
_event_select: (event, ui) =>
    event.preventDefault()
    @_selected.push ui.item
    $(@pieces.auto).val('')
    @pieces.selected.append(@_makeButton ui.item)

_event_remove: (event) =>
    event.preventDefault()
    index = $(event.target).parent().index()
    @pieces.selected.find("li").slice(index, index+1).remove()
    @_selected.splice(index, 1)
```

There's now no need to look up the instance from the DOM because the reference is bound to the methods.

And the private button-making method is updated with some additional jqUI classes to make it look slightly more the part:

```
_makeButton: (item) =>
    $("""<li class="ui-state-default ui-corner-all">#{ item.label}
        <span class="ui-icon ui-icon-close"></span></li>""")
```

That's all the code required for the widget, and you can use the class without it being available via the jQuery API. However, the point is to retain the same API—and this is where `$.widget.bridge()` comes in. Functionally, this works almost identically to the `attach()` you saw earlier when looking at classful jQuery plug-ins:

```
$.widget.bridge "simplewidget", SimpleWidget

$('#widget').simplewidget()
```

And that's all there is to it!

There's nothing wrong with this avenue. It simplifies the process of writing widgets and creating hierarchies of widgets. However, on the flip side, this approach takes widgets out of the normal jqUI hierarchy, which may or may not be a problem. As a result, it's not possible to extend from a classful widget using a widget factory object or vice versa. Whether that is desirable depends on the context in which the code is to be used. My experience of jqUI widgets is that outside of the core widgets provided by the project themselves, very few of them are actually cleanly extensible anyway.

SUMMARY

Developing new user interface elements is one of the first things programmers usually do when introduced to jQuery. This chapter takes development with jQuery a few steps further:

- You learned about the basic anatomy of a jQuery plug-in, and developed skeleton frameworks for CoffeeScript in both a procedural and object-oriented style.
- You examined the skeleton used for jQuery UI widgets and explored the detail of the jQuery UI widget factory.
- You learned a system of writing object-oriented jQuery UI outside of the widget factory framework.

12

MOBILE COFFEESCRIPT APPLICATIONS

WHEN IT SEEMS like there's nowhere new for the web to go and that innovation is slowing down, something new comes along and throws a spanner in the works. Right now, that something is mobile. Although people have been able to access the Internet using various mobile systems for over 20 years, the advent of mobile broadband connections and smartphones has signaled an entirely new breed of mobile user.

Today's mobile web has come a long way, and although it's still not as rich or engaging as the traditional experience, users expect a highly functional and, above all else, fast experience. A wealth of mobile devices with broadly different functionalities has also dragged the

web developer back into the pit of browser compatibility worries and endless testing. Luckily, there are tools available to tame this beast.

This chapter takes a look at two useful frameworks for developing mobile applications. Spine.mobile extends the main Spine framework that you looked at in Chapter 10, adding various mobile-focused features. jQuery Mobile is a new project that adds mobile features and user interface to the jQuery library, similar to how jQuery UI works. Either of these is useful on its own, but you'll also see how these libraries can be combined.

UNDERSTANDING MOBILE FIRST PRINCIPLES

What is the point of using a mobile web browser? After all, as well as the bandwidth costs being significantly more expensive than the wired equivalent, the devices are smaller, less capable, and don't last very long on batteries. To say they don't provide an equivalent experience is putting it mildly.

That would be an incredibly cynical point of view, though. Over the past 20 years, mobile use has exploded across the globe, and the past ten years have been marked by the advent of the *smartphone:* a device with previously unheard of technical specifications and capabilities.

Not only have phones become smaller and more powerful, they also have sold like hot cakes all over the world and have redefined the meaning of personal computing. A mid-range phone, at the time of this writing, delivers a quad-core CPU running at 1.5 GHz, 2GB RAM, a 16GB disk, and a five-inch screen capable of playing high-definition movie content at full resolution. (I write this safe in the knowledge that such information will quickly date this book and imagine that in a few years, readers will chuckle at these specifications.)

The mobile world is hardly limited to phones. Tablet computers are quickly becoming one of the most popular hardware categories, and although they're somewhat lacking in portability, they boast technical specifications and large screens generally with a higher resolution than much more expensive laptops.

Obviously, mobile is more than a trend or fashion. In most ways that matter, the actual definition of computing is changing. The traditional "box and monitor" setup of a desktop computer now represents a small part of the overall computer market, and even the laptop is becoming less popular as people find they can make do without a keyboard in favor of a touchscreen.

Many developers have come to an inescapable conclusion: Not only is mobile important, but also it may well be *the* most important delivery mechanism. *Mobile first* is the handy catchphrase that these developers live by. In essence, this perspective accepts that mobile is important and badly served by existing desktop-focused sites. Instead of continuing to design desktop sites as developers have done, it might be better to make the site work with mobile first and then extend it gracefully for the full desktop experience.

There is a lot to be said for this point of view. Rather than mobile playing second fiddle to the desktop alternative, mobile first asks developers to create a common core of a site that works well across a broad range of devices and then tune it up when possible. In theory, this approach may mean less work for developers, and in practice, it gives users a more consistent experience.

Mobile is wonderful, but like some other wonderful things, it has a significant downside. Actually, in this case, there are quite a few:

- The mobile marketplace is technologically fractured.
- The mobile experience necessarily varies by geography.
- Mobile is a very new environment.

I want to explore these various issues one by one because each one has a direct impact on the development of mobile and touch devices.

First, the technologically fractured marketplace: In many ways, the browser market for mobile devices is very much like the "bad old days" of Netscape and Internet Explorer. Many different versions of browsers are available, and many of them have poor support for various key standards. In fact, iPhone's original versions of mobile Safari were cynically labeled "the new IE 6" by some, as they lack a number of crucial features and have spotty support for some modern web standards but have a broad base of users who are unlikely to upgrade quickly.

Although it's probably a stretch to say that the situation in the current marketplace is as bad as it was back in the "bad old days," it's certainly true that the promise of HTML 5 hasn't yet materialized and that there are a number of competing standards for even basic functionality such as touch detection. Browser compatibility in this market is difficult.

Second, remember that mobile very often means exactly that: mobile. With the advent of 3G and 4G in particular, mobile devices have access to relatively high bandwidth, allowing their users to download a large amount of data and have very rich experiences. As the bandwidth on the radio side has increased, though, the footprint of the radio masts has decreased—outside metropolitan areas, in particular, it's very easy to run out of signal.

Developers targeting mobile devices need to plan for disconnection. Lack of access to a network is not simply a transient condition or something that can be ignored in favor of waiting for the user to refresh the page; it's a technological fact of life that needs to be baked in right from the start. There are some solutions, including those discussed in previous chapters, such as the various forms of local storage support (see Chapter 4), but there are certainly no silver bullets.

Lastly, this industry is still quite young. Mobile devices are incredibly powerful, and the browsers on them are vastly better than the old desktop browsers, but mobile is still not as polished a development environment as the desktop.

For example, if you're developing an application that's broken on a mobile device and you need to break out the debugger, using Firebug on most of these devices is a no-no. Potentially, you might be able to use Firebug Lite, but that may not be a huge help. Mobile versions of Chrome can be remotely connected, but right now doing so requires a wired USB connection and is generally a bit of a pain to set up. Most mobile environments have emulators in which things can be tested, but these are even more of a pain, and the more effort it takes to bring up the testing environment, the less likely it is that you can use automated testing tools like Jasmine or Selenium.

JQUERY AND MOBILE APPLICATIONS

Single-page applications are generally a good approach to mobile development. Spine can be used to deliver this (I discuss Spine in detail in Chapter 10).

However, Spine is by no means the only game in town. jQuery is entirely usable in the mobile world, as are the jQuery UI widgets, and for many developers, using a library that they're already familiar with is a great way to gently explore this brave new world.

Additionally, though, jQuery has a specific mobile-friendly version, imaginatively entitled *jQuery mobile,* available at `http://jquerymobile.com/`. The rest of this chapter focuses on Spine and jQuery for mobile devices.

SPINE.MOBILE

Spine.mobile is the name of a flavor of Spine that is aimed squarely at mobile phone devices, and you can access it at `http://spinejs.com/mobile`.

Many of the same things that made Spine attractive apply here, too. Instead of Spine.mobile being a rewrite or a significant addition to Spine, it is actually a relatively small amount of library code that makes the development of Spine apps for the mobile device much easier to accomplish. And, as with the main portion of Spine, Spine.mobile is written in clear and documented CoffeeScript; it's a good idea to open up the source files and take a peek.

So, what does Spine.mobile bring to the table? The key additional features from your point of view as a developer are

- You can use the initial setup, which is aimed at mobile, right out of the box.
- The specialist stage and panels enable you to develop mobile-friendly UI.
- Transitions and events are tuned to mobile hardware.
- Hem integration lets you build and package up your mobile app into an easy-to-deploy bundle.

There are other benefits as well. The combination of offline support and the ability to deliver an application via PhoneGap in particular means that this framework makes it possible to write a mobile HTML 5 application that can be packaged and delivered as a native application with virtually full access to the hardware on the device. This usage is outside the scope of this book, but it's worth knowing just how far you can take Spine.mobile.

Spine.mobile is influenced by the look and feel of the various operating systems of Apple mobile devices—iOS, in particular. However, as a system, it's very easy to theme and restyle, either to provide a similarly integrated experience on other operating systems (such as Android) or, indeed, to provide an entirely different experience.

Starting a Basic Spine.mobile Application

Downloading and setting up a new project is straightforward, and if Spine is already available, then you already have all the components you need. Getting them is simply a matter of asking npm for them:

```
npm install -g spine spine.app hem
```

If you haven't yet read through the part of this book that covers Spine (Chapter 10), I recommend doing that first before going much further. The mobile framework is built upon the standard Spine framework, and you will need to feel comfortable with the basic Spine concepts before moving on to the differences in the mobile version.

Setting up a new project can be done with the `spine` command, but this time tell it that the project is a mobile one:

```
spine mobile ./application
```

Once `spine` is finished, the directory tree looks almost identical to a regular Spine app. The only difference is the addition of a `theme.styl` file in the `css` directory.

Starting the application, before any modifications, is also the same: grab any additional modules you need locally and start hem:

```
npm install .
hem server
```

hem displays the IP address and port that it's listening to, by default 0.0.0.0:9294. Ordinarily, this would translate to the URL `http://127.0.0.1:9294/`, although you may need to change the port number if hem has not been able to open the default port. Accessing the URL in the browser confirms that things are working properly, as shown in Figure 12-1.

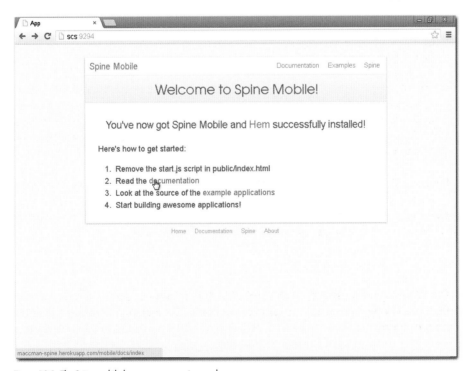

Figure 12-1: The Spine.mobile home page opens in your browser.

The key entry point to starting up the application is in `public/index.html`, and this startup page is displayed by the "Getting Started" script added to that page—one of the first steps to beginning to use the project is to remove that script.

As in a regular Spine application, everything else is bundled up by hem: the models, controllers, and other pieces of code are turned into a single `application.js` file, and the style sheets are processed and compiled similarly. However, from this point on, things begin to get a little bit different.

Setting the Stage (and Panels)

Spine makes two key facilities available in its mobile variant: the global stage and panels. Most users of mobile applications are familiar with the transitions that applications use to go from one page to another. They usually orient a user to the fact that progress forward is a transition to the right, whereas going back is a transition to the left. To facilitate these transitions, panels are used to hold the parts of the user interface so that they can be swapped on and off screen as needed.

Using panels is all very well, but they need to be tied together somehow, and the object that does so is called the *stage.* In general, an application has a single stage containing multiple panels; the application itself is an instance of the global stage.

Spine generates the markup for these elements instead of requiring you to create them manually; indeed, the main `index.html` file generally has an entirely empty <body> tag, but it's useful to take a look at what it's creating:

```
<body class="stage">
    <header></header>
    <article class="viewport">

        <div class="panel active">
            <header></header>
            <article></article>
        </div>

        <div class="panel">
            <header></header>
            <article></article>
        </div>

    </article>
    <footer></footer>
</body>
```

This markup demonstrates a single stage containing two panels, the first of which is active. The first thing to notice is the use of HTML 5 tags: The semantics of the header, article, and footer are translated directly into the interface of the phone. (See Figure 12-2.)

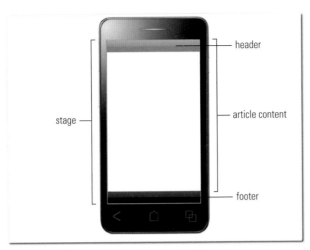

Figure 12-2: The basic Spine display, related to the HTML mark-up

The toolbars at the top and bottom of the application are not always there. Some applications may drop one or the other or, indeed, have neither. But developers use consistent conventions in a lot of mobile applications. The top toolbar is mapped to `<header>` in both the stage and the panels, and the bottom toolbar is the `<footer>` of the stage.

The part remaining, which is `<article>` in both the stage and the panels, is effectively the content area. Also, notice that the stage `<article>` ends up stretching over the stage `<header>` (via the use of the `viewport` class). This is because the stage `<header>` actually isn't all that useful; it simply serves as a standard backdrop so that the toolbars in different panels can transition smoothly.

Understanding the Stages and Panels

Before barreling into implementation, I want to take a few moments to talk about what the stages and panels actually are. Although so far I've talked about these components as though they are brand-new features of Spine.mobile, that's not entirely true: Underneath, both stages and panels within it are simply standard Spine controllers.

Although I've tended to refer to the stage and the global stage as one and the same, and for many applications they will be, you can have more than one stage. The stages are held together by a single manager, and the global stage is simply the first stage in the application.

The implementation of the stage is simple and largely concerned with providing transition support between stages. Although many applications don't directly use this support, it's there. But it's just a Spine controller and can be treated as such.

The story with the panel is similar. Again, it's just a Spine controller underneath, although it inherits from the stage rather than from `Spine.Controller` directly. Again, a large part of the code deals with transitions between panels, although at the panel level, it deals with a separate header and content area rather than an entire container. (The stage, because it contains everything including the footer, can be transitioned as a single container.)

Two utility functions at the panel level are worth mentioning:

- `setTitle(title)` is used to change the text of the title in the header of this panel.
- `addButton(text, callback)` is used to add a button to the header of the panel.

CREATING AN E-COMMERCE SHOP

To show you the power of the system, I'll walk you through some of the steps for setting up an e-commerce shop using Spine.mobile. The idea here is to do what is generally known as an *m-commerce* (mobile commerce) destination—that is, putting together an application that allows users to find the products they're looking for and taking them all the way to purchase in a mobile-friendly environment.

> *I'm covering the build of the application step by step, but there is quite a lot of code covered in this chapter. I'd like to remind you that you can download the full source to this application at* `http://wiley.com/go/smashingcoffeescript`.

Users access the application with one hand, so the interface is thumb-driven: Important buttons are near the bottom, and the user navigates through scrolling with swipes and tapping large buttons.

The first step is to put together the home page. Right now, there's a bare-bones application in `app/index.coffee`, and no models, views, or controllers. I like to put important pages, such as the home page, in their own controllers—for no other reason than that they tend to grow odd features and defy attempts to standardize them.

So the first step is to create a new controller called Home. This can be done manually, but running the command `spine controller home` will set up the basic controller for us in `controllers/home.coffee`. Update the controller so that it looks like this:

```coffee
Spine = require 'spine'
{Panel} = require 'spine.mobile'

class Home extends Panel

    title: 'Toy Shop'

    constructor: ->
        super

        @routes
            '/home': (params) -> @active(params)

        @render()
```

```
    render: =>
        @html require('views/home/index')()

module.exports = Home
```

I've made the executive decision that this e-commerce shop will sell toys. It's probably for the best that I'm not a businessman in my real life!

Along with setting the title for this panel, the constructor adds a single route that enables this panel and calls the `render()` function to generate the actual interface. As a single-page application, its panels are rendered relatively early on and tend to stick around. Be sure to bear this in mind, particularly if the application will load data in chunks, because continual rerendering on application startup is an unfortunate side effect of not paying close attention to what's going on initially.

Setting Up Your Application's Navigation

A controller for the homepage has been created, but the actual view template has not yet been created; the spine app doesn't set this up for you. Views are stored in the views directory, in a directory named after the controller. For the homepage the full path to the view should be `views/home/index.eco` and the initial contents are deliberately simple:

```
<h3>Welcome!</h3>

<p>This is the mobile website for the online toyshop. Browse
our products and if you like it, why not buy it?</p>

<ul class="nav-list">
        <li><a class="nav-item" data-navigate="/products">Latest products</a></li>
        <li><a class="nav-item" data-navigate="/cart">Your cart</a></li>
        <li><a class="nav-item" data-navigate="/login">Your account</a></li>
</ul>
```

Certainly, the promotional text is unlikely to win any awards; however, the main function of this page is to serve as a navigational launching point for the user.

Again, this layout highlights the difference between mobile and desktop apps. A desktop-oriented site is more likely to display navigation at the top or side of every page so that the user can flit from page to page with ease. On a mobile screen, every pixel counts, and every part of the screen taken up with navigation is a piece of wasted display. Also, the farther down a page you are, the more tedious it is to return to where the navigation is.

Another wrinkle is that routing is more or less invisible to the end user, which is contradictory to design principles used on desktop applications. Most of the time, the URL bar is not visible to users, and it's possible to package mobile sites like this as applications—either as HTML 5 applications or as native apps via a system such as PhoneGap—where there is no URL bar.

Calls to `navigate()` within the application don't result in changes to the URL. The slightly annoying side effect of this is that if the application attempts to navigate to an invalid route, nothing happens. There are a number of foibles of mobile development, and this happens to be one of them.

These types of launch points are more common because, although they involve an extra click, the user can get to them quickly. It doesn't have to be the case that the home page or any other page is used for navigation, either; navigation could appear in a pop-up or as a response to a swipe command, although users sometimes have trouble discovering such solutions.

Handling Events

Some links are now added to the mobile page, but they're inactive and don't work. They need to be hooked up to `navigate()`. You can achieve this by adding a click handler to the homepage panel:

```
events:
    'tap .nav-item': 'click'

click: (e) =>
    @navigate $(e.target).data('navigate'), trans: 'right'
```

The `click()` handler is nice and simple: If called, it looks to see if the event target has a `data-navigate` attribute, and if so, the handler navigates to that attribute. The object passed through asks that the transition move toward the right, which indicates progress forward rather than backward.

This handler could also look at the `href` attribute; however, because the URL doesn't actually exist on the server making this content available, doing so feels semantically wrong to me. It also requires the use of a class or some additional URL inspection logic to prevent the internal click handler from taking over links to external sites (for example). However, I wouldn't say that this approach is wrong per se; you can find plenty of examples online of apps that do just that.

Like any other Spine controller, this handler is triggered by an event table; however, something new is here: the tap event. As discussed previously, mobile browsers make slightly different events available in different ways, but Spine.mobile tries to smooth this process out in a number of ways:

- Touch start and end events are analyzed and turned into swipe events, including direction (for example `swipeUp`, `swipeDown`, `swipeLeft`, `swipeRight`).
- If the device is a touch device, click events are generally ignored.
- If the device is not touch-capable, click events are turned into tap events.

This isn't entirely ideal because swipe events are not readily synthesizable on non touch devices, but it enables you to develop a mobile site that will function effectively on a desktop device.

Emulating touchscreen devices

Recent versions of the Google Chrome browser include basic touch input emulation as a feature for developers. Press F12 to access the developer tools, and then click on the gear in the bottom-right corner to access developer settings. Under the User Agent heading is an Emulate Touch Events option.

When this option is enabled, the mouse can be used to generate touch events in the browser, including swipes. However, it does not disable mouse events, so you can still expect to receive mouseover events, for example.

Receiving both mouse and touch events sounds odd, but in practice most developers need to assume that this can happen anyway. The release of Microsoft Windows 8 has highlighted that touch-friendly operating systems are still going to be paired with desktop-class hardware, and that devices with both a touchscreen and a mouse should be expected.

I generally recommend that developers design applications that work correctly with just touch, just mouse, or the combination of touch and mouse.

Writing Extensible Panels

Although the footer is more or less a global fixture for the application, the same is not true of the header. It can be useful to keep all or part of the header the same as the user navigates through the application, though. This can be done by creating an abstract panel class as an intermediary between the panels being used and the `Spine.Panel` class.

In this instance, although I've written a navigation handler for the homepage panel, it would probably be better in the intermediate object because it's the type of functionality that should be reused on different panels again and again. This approach gives me the opportunity to change the behavior of the group in a consistent way without having to resort to patching the parent object.

I've called this intermediate controller `BasePanel`, and it can be created using `spine.app` as usual:

```
Spine = require 'spine'
{Panel} = require 'spine.mobile'

class BasePanel extends Panel

    constructor: ->
        super

    click: (e) =>
        @navigate $(e.target).data('navigate'), trans: 'right'

module.exports = BasePanel
```

The updated homepage controller then inherits from this new base:

```coffeescript
BasePanel = require 'controllers/basepanel'

class Home extends BasePanel

    events:
        'tap .nav-item': 'click'

    title: 'Toy Shop'

    constructor: ->
        super

        @routes
            '/home': (params) -> @active(params)

        @render()

    render: =>
        @html require('views/home/index')()
        @el.addClass('ui-page').find(".nav-list").listview()
        @el.removeClass('ui-page')

module.exports = Home
```

PROVIDING A PRODUCT LISTING

The first page of any note in an e-commerce site usually displays the product catalog. Sometimes it is set up to display product categories, where products are grouped into various families and the user navigates the hierarchy. More commonly now, a search facility requires the user to enter keywords and then returns an appropriate list of products to the user.

For the purpose of this example, I'm using a piece of static data on the back end to render a list of products, but nothing prevents a category-based or search-based approach from being usable. The key with mobile is to get users to the product or information they're interested in as quickly as possible.

For small lists of information, like a small product catalog, simply displaying the list is the most thumb-friendly approach. As the length of a list gets longer, breaking it into chunks such as categories makes sense. At a certain length the categories become too lengthy or large and typed keyword search is the easier interface. There is a trade-off where the interface is becoming more complex in order to find the right result for the user more quickly.

In an ideal world, the search engine is the best solution for this, but if the search results aren't great or if users aren't in a position to explain exactly what they're looking for, a browsable hierarchy can be more friendly.

The route already prescribed for this page is /products, and it needs a controller and a view, but before you can add those, you need a model to represent the data:

```
Spine = require('spine')

class Product extends Spine.Model
  @configure 'Product', 'name', 'price', 'description', 'image'

  @extend Spine.Model.Ajax

  @url: "/productlist.json"

module.exports = Product
```

Making use of the standard Spine AJAX-backed model means that much of the work of creating, loading, and saving products is unnecessary, so although a static file is in use for this example, it's easy to have this model talk to a back-end web service that is retrieving data from a database or search engine. The JSON format closely follows the model definition:

```
[
    {
        "id": 1,
        "name": "Toy bear",
        "price": 1499,
        "description": "A lovely cuddly bear, perfect for small children",
        "image": "",
        "new": true
    },
    {
        "id": 2,
        "name": "Fire engine",
        "price": 2999,
        "description": "Fight fires with this chunky red fire engine!",
        "image": "",
        "new": false
    }
]
```

This productlist.json can be placed in the public/ folder of the project, and the hem server will automatically make it available. This kind of approach is handy for all sorts of static data and is useful for prototyping different user interface ideas quickly without requiring a working server to respond to data requests.

Controlling Related Panels

With a (very simple) product database in place, the controllers and views for the various product-oriented application pages can now be set up:

```
class ProductPanel extends Panel

    constructor: ->
        super

        @show = new ProductView
        @list = new ProductList

        @routes
            '/products/:id': (params) -> @show.active(params)
            '/products':     (params) -> @list.active(params)

        Product.fetch()

module.exports = ProductPanel
```

The `ProductPanel` controller is the main controller for all product-related activities. Two routes are set up—one to list all products, one to show an individual product page—and these are assigned to two yet-to-be-created controllers. In addition, the product information is loaded as part of the constructor.

At this point, it may not seem terribly wise to be loading up the product information right at the start. After all, you hope your shop will be successful enough that there will be too many products to hold in memory at once! This doesn't need to be a direct model, though. A smarter model that's doing search or pagination behind the scenes would be equally useful.

No view is associated with this controller; it's more like an umbrella that serves only to instantiate the other panels that will be needed. This pattern is relatively common: Panels rarely share the screen with each other. (It's possible to have a sufficiently complex pop-up dialog, for example, that needs its own controller, but it doesn't make much sense to have that in a pop-up panel.) Here, there is a state binding them together (in this case, the product data), so it makes sense to group them by panel. Since this panel isn't actually going to display anything directly, it doesn't need to inherit from the `BasePanel` class set up earlier.

Listing the products available in the shop requires a `ProductList` panel:

```
class ProductList extends BasePanel

    title: 'Products'

    className: 'products list listView'

    constructor: ->
        super
        Product.bind 'refresh change', @render

    render: =>
        items = Product.all()
        @html require('views/product/list')(items)
```

So far, all of this is familiar. This panel is behaving as the other panels, although it's the first one passing data into the template. This is an opportune moment to start using the `.jeco` template format. Recall that as well as compiling the template into the application, the `.jeco` format provides an additional piece of jQuery that binds the original data into the template output. As in normal Spine, this works brilliantly for list handling within `Spine.model`.

The view is placed in `views/product/list.jeco` and is just a template for a single item:

```
<div class="item">
  <%= @name %>
</div>
```

Since a series of items is being passed through to the template, the output will be a series of `<div class="item">`, but now the event handling becomes really straightforward:

```
    events:
        'tap .item': 'click'

    click: (e) =>
        item = $(e.target).data('item')
        @navigate '/products', item.id, trans: 'right'
```

Any time a node with the class `item` is clicked, the handler above it is triggered. Since the `.jeco` template is outputting those nodes, the original data item can be retrieved straight from the click target, and `navigate` can be called immediately with the item ID. This listing isn't a lot to write home about at this point, but it looks like the one in Figure 12-3.

Figure 12-3: Produce a basic list of products.

Developing the Product Page

The next stage of the process is to get the user to the product page. This is where the interesting work happens. Users get the opportunity to add the product to their baskets and start the purchasing process.

Look at the panel for the product page; the route for this has already been set up:

```
class ProductView extends BasePanel

    title: 'Product page'

    className: 'products show'

    constructor: ->
        super
        @active (params) ->
            @change params

    render: =>
        return unless @item
        @html require('views/product/view')(@item)
        @setTitle @item.name

    change: (params) =>
        @item = Product.find(params.id)
        @render()
```

This is a great example to help explain how the rendering system is working. Rendering should happen as early as possible so that by the time the panel is active and has transitioned onto the screen, it's already set up. If this isn't the case, the display changes oddly partway through, or worse, the browser is so busy drawing the panel that the transition effect stutters and the site loses that feeling of smoothness.

The product page is not a static page, though. It has to be able to display a number of different products, and rendering one time is simply not enough. So rather than calling render() as part of the constructor, this panel registers a handler that is called anytime the panel is activated through the navigation system.

The handler is an anonymous function that calls change() whenever the panel is activated and is installed by passing the function to active() on the controller. In this example, active() is defined in the Spine Manager, and has two roles: calling it without an argument activates the panel, but passing a function as an argument ensures that function is called every time the panel is activated.

When the panel is activated, the ID of the product to be shown is passed through; this is part of the route specified. This information is then used to look up the product, and render() is called so that the product can be run through the template and displayed on the page.

The view does little more than display the relevant product information:

```
<div class="productview">
    <img src="<%= @image %>" />

    <h3><%= @name %></h3>

    <p><%= @description %></p>

    <p>$ <%= @price / 100 %></p>

    <button class="addToBasket" data-icon="plus">Add to basket</button>
</div>
```

An add to basket action enables the user to place this item into his shopping cart. (See Figure 12-4.)

Figure 12-4: The product page has minimal formatting.

BRINGING IN JQUERY MOBILE

Although Spine.mobile does an excellent job of making the mobile environment much more accessible and usable, this simple system is little more than an excellent framework for a single-page application.

Clearly, though, to present the user with a normal mobile experience, a user interface layer is needed. For desktop applications, jQuery UI is an example of a library that plays this role nicely, not just putting together various usable widgets and a sensible theme but also providing some of the building blocks to create custom widgets that behave predictably within the browser environment.

Luckily, such a library is available for the touch environment, too, and it is called *jQuery Mobile*. It's available at `http://jquerymobile.com/`.

jQuery Mobile, or jQM, provides numerous features, with the most important of those listed here:

- A flexible theme and layout system that has been bench-tested in a variety of mobile browsers, not just the "A-grade" variety
- A progressive enhancement system to make use of additional functionality where the browser supports it
- Built-in navigation, transition, and event support
- A broad range of mobile- and touch-friendly widgets for a variety of uses

You likely noticed some overlap with Spine.mobile here. Although Spine doesn't delve into the world of widgets, or even that far into the world of layout, it definitely does a lot of work in the transition and event department and has its own system of navigation.

Moreover, for jQM's progressive enhancement to work really well, pages must have some declarative content built into them, which doesn't work amazingly well with Spine.mobile's render infrastructure. The progressive enhancement tends to get lost if a panel ever needs to be rerendered, if the automatic system runs at the right time to enhance the page at all.

However, these two systems are not incompatible, and in fact some substantial benefits occur when running the two of them together. Primarily, you are able to start using the wide variety of jQM widgets, which are well designed and blend well into sites that have a native feel (the sort that Spine.mobile provides out of the box). It just takes a little extra effort.

The first step to making this work is to bring in jQM's stylesheet and code, which requires some edits to `public/index.html`:

```
<link rel="stylesheet" href="/application.css"
                            type="text/css" charset="utf-8">
<link rel="stylesheet" href="/jqm/jquery.mobile-1.2.0.min.css" />

<script src="/application.js"
                   type="text/javascript" charset="utf-8"></script>
<script type="text/javascript" charset="utf-8">
  var jQuery  = require("jqueryify");
  var exports = this;
  jQuery(function(){
    var App = require("index");
    exports.app = new App({el: jQuery("body")});
  });

  jQuery(document).bind("mobileinit", function(){
    jQuery.extend(jQuery.mobile, {
      ajaxEnabled: false,
      autoInitializePage: false,
```

```
      activePageClass: 'active',
      hashListeningEnabled: false,
      linkBindingEnabled: false,
      pushStateEnabled: false
    });
  });
</script>
<script src="/jqm/jquery.mobile-1.2.0.js"></script>
```

The `application.css` and `application.js` files are already listed; these are the main bundles for the application being written. And although it's possible to bundle the jQM stylesheet into the existing bundle, that's a step too far at this point.

It's also technically plausible to bundle in the jQM JavaScript file, but that would cause problems at this point. To ensure that jQM and Spine.mobile play well together, many of jQM's automatic features need to be turned off first.

You achieve this by configuring the jQM library by adjusting the settings on `jQuery. mobile`, which is done when the `mobileinit` event is received. It's tempting to think that order doesn't matter and that this configuration can be done at any point, but that's not the case!

To make the mobile experience as slick as possible, jQM starts many of its features early in the browser's page lifecycle. It doesn't wait for the DOM-ready event to start doing things, and in fact if the `<script>` block with the event handler is placed after the reference to the jQM script, it's highly probable that if the jQM script was cached locally, the `mobileinit` event may have been triggered even before the event handler could be set up.

Here are the key automatic features being disabled:

- **AJAX links:** By default, jQM intercepts links and attempts to load them via AJAX so that pages can be transitioned on and off, which interferes with the Spine `navigate()` system.
- **Hash listening, link binding, push support:** Again, part of jQM's navigation support, this interferes with Spine.
- **Page initialization:** jQM can interrogate a page for widgets and automatically create them; this doesn't work well with Spine's render support. The alternative is to instantiate manually, which is fine.

It's not absolutely the case that this is the right line to draw. For example, jQM's AJAX link support can coexist with Spine.mobile. It wouldn't even be that hard to use jQM's system of navigation in preference to Spine.mobile's own and to rely on the system of transitions provided by jQM.

However, if the core mobile support is to be provided by jQM, the better approach is to write a standard Spine application with jQM, rather than attempt to meld it into Spine.mobile, and indeed you can find a few examples online of people who have done just that.

Activating jQM Widgets Manually

Earlier, a set of navigation links was placed on the home page as a launch point for the user. Initially styled as just a list of links, this set of navigation links is now an excellent candidate for a jQM widget: This library excels at taking relatively standard pieces of markup and rendering the element in a larger, more button-like format, which is good news for mobile users who need a target that's easy to hit with a thumb.

The change to the `render()` function in the Home panel is simple:

```
render: =>
    @html require('views/home/index')()
    @el.addClass('ui-page').find(".nav-list").listview()
```

Ordinarily, using jQM's progressive enhancement, this type of widget will be automatically enabled using a bit of declarative markup along these lines:

```
<ul data-role="listview">
    <li><a class="nav-item">…</li>
    …
</ul>
```

This use of data attributes is very common. The extremely popular Dojo JavaScript library takes a similar approach, for example. But because the automatic system has been turned off to work properly with Spine's render framework, the widget needs to be instantiated manually. In general, the `data-role` of a jQM declarative widget is the same as the function call that jQM extends jQuery with. So you just need to find the element and call `listview()` on it.

As shown in Figure 12-5, the home page now looks slightly spiffier with the addition of the jQM widget.

Figure 12-5: The app now has large navigation buttons.

Adding the Shopping Cart

The add to basket action was left hanging on the product page, and indeed the all-important cart hasn't yet been completed. You can remedy that now.

The first step is to use jQM to render buttons and then pass the information about the product through to the cart:

```
class ProductView extends BasePanel

    events:
        'click .addToBasket': 'add'

    render: =>
        return unless @item
        @html require('views/product/view')(@item)
        @setTitle @item.name
        @el.find('.productview button').button()

    add: (e) =>
        @navigate '/cart',
            item: @item
            trans: 'right'
```

Every time `render` is called, the button is upgraded with jQM. That's because every time the template engine is run, the previous markup is entirely replaced. This sounds somewhat wasteful, although the truth of the matter is that Spine goes to great lengths to reduce this.

When the Add button is clicked, the item in question has already been saved. It's set to `this.item` when this panel is activated, so the job is merely to communicate that information to the cart. In this instance, it's done via the navigate system.

A few different schools of thought exist on how best to do things like this. Generally, putting an ID in a URL request and expecting that to change the state of something (like a cart) would be pretty bad form, but this is a closed navigation system, and URLs aren't really being used.

You can add the item directly from this controller. This is poor design: The product page would be coupled closely to the cart implementation, and if the cart ever needs to change, the product page must also change.

Another, much better solution is to use a synthetic event. Previously, I advocated listening for these on the `<body>` of the main document as convention. In the mobile environment, these can be bound to the global stage instead. For simplicity here, though, I've used the navigation to pass through the data.

As yet there's no cart controller; however, this again is not a complex affair:

```
Spine = require('spine')
BasePanel = require 'controllers/basepanel'
```

```coffeescript
CartItem = require 'models/cart'

class Cart extends BasePanel
    constructor: ->
        super

        @list = new CartItemList

        @routes
          '/cart':  (params) -> @list.active(params)

        CartItem.fetch()

module.exports = Cart
```

Again, an umbrella-style controller panel is used to bring the cart panels together. To begin with only one is listed, although it's probably appropriate to have the checkout be another panel within this system.

The shopping cart is a simple list of products and, in a sense, is much like the product listing page, but the functionality ends up being quite different. The basic panel to list the items in the cart makes a slightly more sophisticated use of templates:

```coffeescript
class CartItemList extends BasePanel
    constructor: ->
        super
        CartItem.bind('refresh change', @render)

    className: 'cart list listView'

    title: 'Shopping Cart'

    render: =>
        items = CartItem.all()
        container = $('<div></div>')

        container.append require('views/cart/items')(items)
        container.find(".group a").button()
        container.find(".group").controlgroup
            type: "horizontal"
            mini: true

        if items.length > 0
            checkout = require('views/cart/checkout')()
            container.append checkout
            $(container).find('button.checkout').button()

        @html container

    active: (params) =>
        super
```

```
    if params.item
        CartItem.create
            product: params.item
            quantity: 1
```

As with other controllers, `render()` can be triggered at several points during its lifetime, but in this case, the panel rerenders anytime the `CartItem` data changes. This model hasn't yet been defined but will represent the application's idea of a shopping cart. As items are added or removed, the cart is rerendered.

Items are added into the cart via the navigation, but the route setup doesn't contain the identifier of the product the user has requested. Instead, the actual item is passed through in the `params` object. The `active()` implementation on this panel looks for the item and, if it exists, creates a cart item that references the product. The mere act of creating this new `CartItem` causes the cart to rerender.

The implementation of `render()` calls for a little bit of description. The cart is a series of items, so a `.jeco` template is used to produce that list, but a checkout action is also required below the items so that they can be purchased. If the cart is empty, though, the checkout button shouldn't be present.

It's possible to write a single eco template that performs the looping manually and contains all the various pieces of logic. This approach loses the main benefit of the `.jeco` system though: The cart items are no longer automatically related to the data that produces them. This means you have to write supporting code to work out which item is which. The easier alternative is to use a couple of different views and join them with a single container.

Thus, the `views/cart/items.jeco` template is still quite simple:

```
<div class="item">
  <div data-role="controlgroup" data-type="horizontal" class="group">
    <a href="#" data-role="button" data-iconpos="notext" data-icon="delete"
  class="del">Del</a>
  </div>

  <span class="quantity"><%= @quantity %> x</span>

  <%= @product?.name %>
</div>
```

The users can remove items from the cart using the provided button and can also see the quantity of the items they're ordering. As a `.jeco` template, the `<div class="item">` is associated with the individual `CartItem`.

The `views/cart/checkout.eco` template (notice it's eco, not jeco) is even simpler:

```
<div>
    <button class="checkout" data-icon="arrow-r"
            data-iconpos="right">Checkout</button>
</div>
```

It's possible to include this template every time and write logic to add the button or not in the template; not much of a saving is made either way, and it's a matter of taste. I personally prefer not to have logic in the template unless it's required.

Although the two slightly different types of templates have been used, they both output DOM nodes, and thus the output can be combined using a containing <div>, which is then put onto the panel.

Wiring the cart item Delete button into the controller code takes little effort because the .jeco template generates that section of the DOM:

```
class CartItemList extends BasePanel

    events:
        'tap .del': 'remove'

    remove: (e) =>
        e.preventDefault()
        item = $(e.target).parents('.item').data('item')
        if item
            item.destroy()
```

Finding the item associated with the node is slightly more difficult: The event arrives via a button that is deep in the body of the template, and the data is associated with the top level containing the <div> node. Walking the tree of parent nodes is the easiest way to find it. However, it's worth ensuring that the class used to identify the container will not get confused with other nodes on the page because bugs that are difficult to correct will ensue.

If the associated data is found, the destroy() method is called on it. This removes the relevant CartItem model, which in turn triggers the model event and then causes the panel to rerender. With event triggers like this in place, there is no need to manually call render(). To do so duplicates logic and ends up making the code more complex than it needs to be.

JUMPING AND HISTORY

One of the last tasks to bring this application together is to put in place some consistent navigation on the various panels so that users can move backward and forward through the application smoothly and quickly. The main launching point has been put on the home page, but two toolbars are on each page that so far have remained relatively unexploited.

If you have more than a passing familiarity with user interface design principles, you're probably familiar with *Fitt's Law*. This is a rule about user interface for mouse users and, in essence, states that the farther the pointer is from an object, the bigger the object ought to be to make it easy to hit. The corners of the screen are particularly prized under this law because the action of blocking further pointer progress when it hits the edge increases the effective size of the button underneath. This is why operating systems tend to put key functions in the corner of screens.

Mobile design has a similar principle: When users are using a device in a one-hand mode, prodding at buttons primarily with their thumb, there is an arc across the device where it's relatively easy to hit the screen. The bottom-left corner is generally quite easy to hit, the bottom-right is slightly less so, the top-right is not too bad, but the top-left is a bit of a stretch (making the bold assumption, of course, that the user is right-handed: largely, but obviously not always, true).

For two of the most important buttons in the application, then, I place a link to the home page on the bottom left in the footer area and a link to the cart bottom right. Additionally, I want the cart button to show the users just how many items are currently in their cart.

Since the footer is attached to the global stage, the `app/index.coffee` file is the place to go to add these new features:

```
class App extends Stage.Global
    events:
        'tap footer .home': -> @navigate '/home', trans: 'left'
        'tap footer .cart': -> @navigate '/cart', trans: 'right'

    constructor: ->
        super

        new Home
        new Cart
        new ProductPanel

        Spine.Route.setup shim: true

        CartItem.bind 'change', @update_title

        @cart_button = $("""<div class="button cart right"></div>""")
        @home_button = $("""<div class="button home">Home</div>""")
        @footer.append @home_button, @cart_button
        @update_title()

        @navigate '/home'

    update_title: =>
        quan = 0
        if CartItem.count() > 0
            quan = (item.quantity for item in CartItem.all()
                    ).reduce (a, b) -> a + b
        @cart_button.text "Cart (#{ quan })"
```

Putting the buttons into the footer is a simple matter for the constructor. Because the footer is essentially a fixture for the entire app, there's no rendering process to worry about. Events are wired up for the buttons being added, and for once a transition to the left is being used. In general, when the user hits the Home button, it feels like going back to the start, so that transition is appropriate.

For the purposes of putting the logic together in one single place, the stage is watching the cart for changes so that it can update the number of items in the footer button; however, this is again coupling and would be better done using synthetic events (with the cart issuing an updated event that carried the total quantity as part of the metadata).

The application now looks like the one in Figure 12-6.

Figure 12-6: The Cart button reflects the number of items in the cart.

On the top bar toward the left, the user expects some kind of back button. For some panels, there's an obvious panel to go "back" to since only one place will send users to the panel. For others, like the cart, the user can come from a number of places, so some kind of navigation history also needs to be maintained.

If the navigation shim is not being used, the history can simply be the browser history. However, implementing a navigation history gives me an opportunity to show you how to further utilize the `BasePanel` class.

Because many panels are in a system, maintaining a consistent history requires that individual panels do not keep their own history. This means that `BasePanel` cannot be used for this task directly; however, a simple navigation history can be set up on the global stage:

```
class NavigationHistory

    constructor: ->
        @buffer = []
        Spine.Route.bind 'navigate', @push

    push: (path) =>
```

```
        @buffer.push path

    pop: =>
        @buffer.pop()
        @buffer.pop() ? '/home'
```

This class listens to navigation changes, stores them as an ordered list, and gives callers the ability to pop them off the end of the list, too. In fact, it pops two off: the last item is the current page, and the penultimate item is the page the application wants to go back to. When the navigation is called to visit that page, it's pushed back onto the stack again.

You need to be sure only a single history exists for the application so it is only instantiated once as part of the constructor for the global stage:

```
        @history = new NavigationHistory()
```

The history is now accessible to the `BasePanel` implementation, which you can use to create a `back` event handler to navigate the application back to the previous page:

```
    back: (e) =>
        e.preventDefault()
        @navigate @stage.history.pop(), trans: 'left'
```

Every panel has access to its parent stage as `@stage`, which will usually be the global stage. Complex applications can have more than one stage though, in which case the panel's parent stage is not assured to be the global stage. The panel can instead call `@globalStage()` to get the reference to the global stage. In this case, I know that the parent stage of all my panels is the global stage.

It's possible to have `BasePanel` add the Back button to the header; however, your application may have pages where such a button is not desired (such as the home page), so there are two alternatives:

- Add the button in the `BasePanel`, but make it configurable.
- Add the button in the subclass.

Either approach is fine. If there are several panels and most of them have the Back button, the first choice leads to the least code. If there are only a few panels or only a few of them have the Back button, the second option is better. Regardless, the final addition to the appropriate panel is simple:

```
    constructor: ->
        super
        @addButton 'Back', 'back'
```

SUMMARY

Developing HTML 5–based applications for mobile devices is a style of web development that will seem unfamiliar and is certainly one of those areas of web technology that still feels immature and cutting edge. It is increasingly important though, and this chapter covered these major areas:

- Comparing mobile devices to standard computers in terms of the facilities available
- Understanding how touch events work in mobile devices and how they can be emulated
- Architecting and writing mobile applications using the Spine.mobile framework
- Enhancing the user interface using the jQuery Mobile library

ADVANCED COFFEESCRIPT

13

DATA BINDINGS AND FORM ELEMENTS

DEVELOPING SLICK INTERFACES for web applications is all very well and good. However, rather than developing the next shiny web 2.0 application, often what's really needed is an application that allows users to perform large-scale day-to-day data processing. Although much less enthralling to programmers, this kind of application is the meat and potatoes of web development.

Working with a large amounts of data is one of the areas in which the web browser is weakest, in terms of both the development platform offered and the ability of the browser to store and manipulate data sets. The challenge of working in this area involves bringing browsers up to the standard desktop applications set, while addressing the unique problems faced operating on the web.

ONE-WAY BINDINGS ONTO FORM VIEWS

Desktop application developers are familiar with the concept of a binding. Binding brings together a data model sitting in the background—perhaps a simple data structure or some more complicated object—and a user interface designed to somehow represent all or part of that structure. It breathes life into the user interface by injecting the data in all the right places.

To some extent, web developers will be familiar with one-way bindings already. When an HTML form is created on a page, it's generally submitted back to the server. The browser comes with a binding built in, which takes the data out of the user interface controls and turns them into the body of an HTTP request that the server will readily understand. Moreover, these bindings can actually be quite complex:

- Form elements are given names, and the values of those elements are submitted back to the server with those names.
- Individual elements are given a name, but a name may be used once or more times within a given form—leading to the submission of different data items with the same name.
- Form elements can present a label to a user that reflects the value they store, which is submitted. An obvious example is a `select` control.

There are also rules about whether an input has been set, whether its value is passed back to the server, and a host of different encoding issues. In short, the browser is capable of doing a lot of work on behalf of the humble web page.

Does the browser do quite enough, though? Getting the data from the page and onto the server is useful; however, nothing allows the data to go in the opposite direction. While, from the start, web browsers were designed to be smart and capable, they were also designed to communicate with smart servers. The general idea was that if a form needed to be populated with data, the server was in the ideal position to do so. Of course, this design hails from the days before AJAX, and although that notion still holds, it's not the only way to design this sharing of data.

To do something a bit more fitting with the Web 2.0 world, you need to slightly sidestep some of the built-in binding machinery. A first good step is to have a binding that, given a JSON structure, can populate a form with data and then later do the reverse—turn the data in the form into a JSON structure.

A SIMPLE BINDING INTERFACE

In the first instance, all that is required is little more than an interface composed of two steps: set the form data; get the form data. Here's an example of how to work out an HTML 5 form:

```
<!DOCTYPE html>
<html lang="en">
<head>
    <meta charset="utf-8">
    <script src="js/jquery-1.8.1.min.js" type="text/javascript"></script>
    <script src="1_binding_oneway.js" type="text/javascript"></script>
```

```
</head>
<body>
    <h1>One-way binding</h1>

    <button id="set">Set Data</button> <button id="get">Get Data</button>

    <form id="test">
        <p>Text field: <input type="text" name="field_text" value=""></p>
        <p>Radio buttons:
            <label><input type="radio" name="field_radio"
value="1">One</label>
            <label><input type="radio" name="field_radio"
value="2">Two</label>
        </p>
        <p>Check box:
            <label><input type="checkbox" name="field_check" value="1"> value
 is 1</label>
        </p>
        <p>Drop-down: <select name="field_select">
            <option value="1">One</option>
            <option value="2">Two</option>
        </select></p>
    </form>
</body>
</html>
```

This is obviously a contrived example, but even here some of the real complexity of forms is visible. A selection of different controls, which behave in very different ways, is present. Outside the main form are two controls, one to set data on the form and the other to retrieve it.

For one moment, assume that the binding is already written. In real life, of course, such things are rarely true—but it's often useful to start from the perspective of how something might look, in an ideal world. The alternative of getting stuck in the implementation of minutiae early in the process is often a recipe for overly complex and over-engineered solutions. In this case, the ideal solution for the one-way binding is simple:

```
$ ->
    data =
        field_text: "Text value"
        field_radio: "2"
        field_check: "1"
        field_select: "2"

    binding = new Binding()

    $("#set").click ->
        binding.set_value "#test", data

    $("#get").click ->
        console.log binding.get_value()
```

The implementation, within the class `Binding`, isn't there yet, but how it would operate is immediately obvious. A straightforward JSON structure holds the data and is passed into the binding along with a reference to the form. The binding then does the work of transferring data from the structure it has been given into the form.

In reverse, the process is even simpler—the binding needs only the name of the form. It extracts the data being held in the form, and then passes that back out as a data structure in the same format.

Is the binding now going to be incredibly complex? Sometimes, starting out from the ideal position leads you to an implementation that's complex at best and impossible at worst, but in this case it's not so. First, with the help of a little jQuery, retrieving the data from the form is easy:

```
class Binding

    get_value: =>
        result = {}
        for elem in @form.find(":input")
            result[$(elem).attr("name")] = $(elem).val()
        result
```

jQuery's `val()` method is incredibly useful for retrieving the value of form elements. As a rule, it will deal with the different types of elements correctly and return effectively what the browser would send if the form were to be submitted.

The `":input"` selector in use is pseudo-CSS, matching all types of HTML input. It would be nice if such a thing did work in CSS in general, but alas no, this is jQuery-only.

SETTING FORM DATA

The implementation of `set_value()` is less straightforward:

```
    set_value: (form, data) =>
        @form = $(form)
        for input in ($(e) for e in @form.find ":input")
            name = input.attr "name"
            if name of data
                if input.attr("type") in ["radio", "checkbox"]
                    if input.val() == data[name]
                        input.prop "checked", true
                else
                    input.val data[name]
        return null
```

The implementation is now complete, but I want to note a couple of points here. The first is the slightly tricky use of a loop on a comprehension. In this instance, it's being used for the slightly mundane purpose of finding all the inputs in the form and then wrapping them in jQuery. In general, this type of pattern is broadly useful—particularly where the comprehension involves matching or some other type of filtering, using CoffeeScript's ever-useful when keyword.

The second key point is the distinction of different types of input. Unfortunately, in terms of setting a value on an input, jQuery's `val()` implementation is slightly overloaded:

- When operating with input types such as the standard text box, setting a value with `val()` simply sets the value attribute of the input, which becomes immediately the set value of the text box.
- When operating with input types that involve selection, such as a check box, `val()` again sets the value attribute of the input, but it does not make any change to the input selection.

This last scenario is crucial. When the value of the input and the concept of the input being selected are two different things, it's important to understand that `val()` is only setting the value of the input. It will not affect whether the input is selected; that has to be handled separately.

The actual operation the binding is performing isn't exactly as described earlier. It's not simply transferring the data into the form; it's also looking at each element and adjusting its value and selecting or checking it as necessary.

There is a lot to say for an implementation this simple. For the straightforward needs of many AJAX-style applications, a more sophisticated setup will be unnecessary. True, this implementation does impose limitations. By using an object as a key-value store, for example, the form is now limited to containing elements with unique names because otherwise the binding would not know which element of a duplicated name to set a specific piece of data on.

In some other applications, though, it becomes important to work with both the data and the user interface, and the most painful limitation of a one-way binding becomes obvious: Before data can be changed or accessed, it needs to be retrieved from the form. While the data is being changed, the form must then be locked to ensure that the data doesn't change and that it is then put back before the user can progress. The solution to this situation is to implement two-way binding.

TWO-WAY BINDINGS

It is possible to use the one-way binding to retrieve and set data as required, but in practice, coordinating this process generally ends with user experience limitations—for example, disabling a form while data is loaded in the background, leaving the user with little else to do but perhaps watch a spinning "loading" graphic.

What is really desired is a way of linking the form control to the data at a slightly deeper level so that the current state of one always reflects the current state of the other, and if one changes, then the other one changes in response.

THE INFAMOUS "GETTER SETTER" PATTERN

Before delving into two-way bindings, here's is a question to consider. If a data structure is going to be linked to a piece of user interface, what mechanism will enable changes to the data structure to be noticed? Simply using `some_var = 1` in CoffeeScript won't set off any particular alarms or triggers.

This type of problem is often called a *gatekeeper problem*. That is, some kind of gatekeeper, or intermediary, is required to generate an event that can be listened for. Without an event, the only other possibility is a system called *polling*, which checks every few moments to see if a change has been made. Much like a child in the back seat of a car demanding to know "Are we there yet?" polling becomes boring very quickly.

Such patterns have been seen in object-oriented circles for many years as a method for controlling access to a piece of data and, in particular, for ensuring that only valid data can be written, if indeed such write access is even allowed. These patterns tend to look something like this:

```
class WithGetterAndSetter

    getName: =>
        @name

    setName: (newName) =>
        @name = newName


obj = new WithGetterAndSetter()
obj.setName("test")
console.log obj.getName()
```

On the face of it, this doesn't look like a huge additional burden—instead of accessing `obj`. `name` directly (which is, in fact, possible), two helper or *ancilliary* functions are added to the class to get and set the attribute. In this example, the additional functions are quite obedient, but, for example, it would be possible for the setter to check a user's login credentials and decide that they are not sufficiently authorized to change the data.

As a rule, this is not regarded highly, as patterns go. The additional functions are effectively a form of boilerplate—that is, additional, repetitive code that serves very little purpose. Such code is certainly not DRY.

What would be more useful would be a way of simply writing a single implementation of a getter and a setter that can then be reused for each property of interest on a class. This is actually quite simple to achieve:

```
class Observable

    @attribute: (name, options={}) ->
        @schema ?= {}
```

```
        @schema[name] = options

    constructor: (attributes) ->
        @attributes = {}

        for name, options of @constructor.schema
            @attributes[name] = attributes?[name] ? options.default

    check: (name) =>
        unless @constructor.schema[name]
            throw Error("Property '#{name}' not defined.")


    get: (name) =>
        @check name
        @attributes[name]

    set: (name, value) =>
        @check name
        if value != @attributes[name]
            @attributes[name] = value


class WithGetterAndSetter extends Observable

    @attribute "name"

obj = new WithGetterAndSetter()
obj.set("name", "test")
console.log obj.get("name")
```

As with many solutions, once they start becoming more abstract, they become instantly less comprehensible—so now look at this implementation piece by piece.

The implementation of `WithGetterAndSetter` is, this time around, an extension of `Observable`, which is the abstract class that holds the getter/setter functionality. This functionality is a mix of static and instance methods, and the first one of note is a static method—`attribute()`.

By using a static call within the body of the class definition, it's possible to set up data that will be true for all instances of this class. Within the body of a class definition—that is, not within functions defined on the class—the @ denotes this static-ness. `attribute()` is a function defined in the superclass, `Observable`, which registers an attribute into the schema for that class. Within this implementation, each attribute can have a series of options (that's not in use in the preceding example, but it will come into play later when each attribute needs a much richer set of metadata to describe it).

The other methods of interest in regard to `Observable` are instance methods. Upon construction, the object sets up internal attributes according to the schema. Two generic functions are available, `set()` and `get()`, to modify these attributes. Before allowing their use, each function checks the names of the attributes to ensure they're defined as part of the schema.

Why is this class called `Observable`? Well, at this point, there are only two functions to set and retrieve data for any attribute defined on the object. These functions are ideal candidates for the gatekeeper role discussed earlier. However, they're still slightly unwieldy. In order to use such an implementation, code must be written to call `set()`, instead of simply using = as it would on a normal object. One more step can be taken, though!

IMPLICIT GETTER/SETTER

By reducing the amount of boilerplate to a generic implementation of `get()` and `set()`, it's possible to build an implementation of two-way binding. The gatekeeper entry points that will be monitored for changes are there, but all the other code calling this implementation will be required to abide by the special convention of using those two specific functions. That's not ideal. Anytime there's a requirement to do something "special" with a piece of code, it's generally a safe bet that a developer will forget and bugs will ensue.

The better approach is to make this implementation more invisible or transparent, but that can only be achieved with a bit of platform support. The good news is that such platform support exists; the bad news is, unfortunately, it's not particularly consistent, and right now there are no good solutions to hide that inconsistency. It's possible to move forward with a solution though:

```coffeescript
class Observable

    @attribute: (name, options={}) ->
        @schema ?= {}
        @schema[name] = options

        Object.defineProperty @, name,
            get: -> @attributes[name]
            set: (value) ->
                if value != @attributes[name]
                    @attributes[name] = value

    constructor: (attributes) ->
        @attributes = {}

        for name, options of @constructor.schema
            @attributes[name] = attributes?[name] ? options.default


class WithGetterAndSetter extends Observable

    @attribute "name"

obj = new WithGetterAndSetter()
obj.name = "test"
console.log obj.name
```

The form of the implementation is relatively similar, except that now the resultant attributes can be accessed as any normal object property. `obj.name` can now be used to get and set, and somewhere behind the curtain this access is still being mediated.

In this new implementation of `Observable`, the key piece of functionality is where `Object.defineProperty()` is called in the static context. This is a generic function that modifies a named property on an arbitrary object, in this case the `Observable` object is modifying itself. Instead of having specific named functions that are called from within the code manually, two anonymous functions are provided, and the underlying JavaScript interpreter uses them in place of normal object access.

Also, the implementation is incredibly similar, with the same reliance on a predefined schema within the class definition in question. Although, as I said, the support for this type of feature is not consistent across different platforms, it is true that all the key platforms in use today have some implementation of `Object.defineProperty` available, including Internet Explorer 9 and above. There is often support for the same feature in older browsers too, albeit with different syntax forms—for example, the proprietary and now deprecated `__defineGetter__` API.

OBSERVING CHANGES

With a useful implementation of `Observable` in place, it's now possible to define a subclass of it that can be used as the basis for a two-way binding. First, working from the perspective of "What would this look like in an ideal world?" consider the end result.

A two-way binding still needs to link a data structure with an implemented HTML form, so some kind of description or *mapping* of how the two connect is needed. For simplicity, the binding assumes that one attribute maps directly onto one input, and that the two-way binding joins them via this unique binding:

```
class DemonstrationForm extends FormMapper

    @attribute "text", input: "field_text", default: "Hello there!"
    @attribute "radio", input: "field_radio", default: "0"
    @attribute "check", input: "field_check", default: "0"
    @attribute "select", input: "field_select", default: "0"
```

That's a relatively good description of the requirements. This is a two-way binding consisting of four attributes, which are linked to four inputs and which also have a default value set. The definition of `attribute()` hasn't changed at all—the `options` argument, which was previously unused, is now being used to store additional metadata about each mapping within this binding.

Now it's possible to consider the actual implementation. With `Observable` as a base, a single gatekeeper (the setter) exists that can be used to watch for changes in the data. To make it straightforward, this setter can be augmented with an abstract method that will be called when the data changes:

```
@attribute: (name, options={}) ->
    # getter etc. removed
```

```
@::__defineSetter__ name, (value) ->
    if value != @attributes[name]
        if @attribute_change(name, @attributes[name], value)
            @attributes[name] = value

attribute_change: (name, old_value, value) =>
    return true
```

To make the most of `Observable`, it must be subclassable, but it would be a mistake for each subclass to need to know how the setter was defined. By putting this additional method in the setter, to be called when the data is changing, a subclass needs to know only that this method exists and that it's called when data changes.

In addition, to make it even more useful, this extra method can return `true` or `false` to control whether the data can actually be modified. The default implementation, which is empty, always allows the data to be modified.

All the pieces to write the two-way binding are now in place:

```
class FormMapper extends Observable

    set_form: (form) =>
        @form = $(form)

        for name, options of @constructor.schema
            continue unless options.input
            for el in @form.find ":input[name=#{options.input}]"
                options.nodes ?= []
                options.nodes.push el
                $(el).data "attr_name", name
            if options.default
                @attribute_change name, null, options.default

        @form.on "keyup change", ":input", @element_change

    element_change: (event) =>
        event.preventDefault()
        name = $(event.target).data "attr_name"
        value = $(event.target).val()
        @[name] = value

    attribute_change: (name, old_value, new_value) =>
        options = @constructor.schema?[name]
        return false unless options
        return true if old_value == new_value

        for node in options.nodes
            input = $(node)
            if input.attr("type") in ["radio", "checkbox"]
                if input.val() == new_value
                    input.prop "checked", true
```

```
            else
                input.prop "checked", false
        else
            input.val new_value

    data: =>
        result = {}
        for name, options of @constructor.schema
            result[name] = @[name]
        return result

    reset: =>
        for name, options of @constructor.schema
            if options.default
                @[name] = options.default
```

This implementation has a lot of moving parts. Not least of all is that change can come from two directions, either from the data being changed or from the form being modified.

The form side of the system is the simpler side. When the binding is created, it needs to be set up on a form, and jQuery is already capable of setting up event handlers that fire when the form element is changed. So, in `set_form()`, a simple change handler is created that calls `element_change()`—this latter function is doing the dirty work of taking the new value from the form and setting the appropriate attribute on the underlying data object.

The object attributes are observable, so changes to them are passed through to `attribute_change()` when they occur. This function does the opposite of `element_change()`: It takes the new data value, finds the relevant input in the form, and changes the value and/or selection on that input.

It's well worth thinking about the actual logic at this point because there's an obvious bug:

- When a form element is changed, that change is passed through to the underlying data.
- When the underlying data changes, that change is passed through to the relevant form element.

In theory, there's an infinite loop here—the changes get passed from one side to the other and back again, indefinitely. In this instance, that's not actually going to happen: When data is passed back into the form element, it's not changing the data, so the change event won't fire, thus breaking the loop—which is perfectly reliable in this case, so long as the data is being passed accurately!

Finally, a couple of utility functions are defined on this binding—one to retrieve the data as it is currently, and another to reset the data (and thus the form) to its initial state. Using this new binding is now really simple:

```
$ ->
    obj = new DemonstrationForm()
```

```
obj.set_form("#test")

$("#output").click ->
    console.log obj.data()

$("#reset").click ->
    obj.reset()
```

This implementation is surprisingly close to the original one used earlier for the one-way binding. In practice, there will often be a start point when data is loaded into a form and an end point when it is sent back to the server; however, the behavior between those two points is now very different, with changes to the form being reflected immediately in the data, and vice versa.

DYNAMIC FORM BUILDING

By putting together a schema for validation and binding, you have an almost complete description of the form. It's possible to take this one step further, though, and effectively have the form build itself from the description given in the class.

To begin with, the attributes describing the data schema need to be extended somewhat to bring in the additional data needed to build the form:

```
class ContactForm extends FormMapper

    @attribute "phone", {input: "phone", validate: "phone_number",
                         label: "Phone number", type: "phone"}
    @attribute "date", {input: "date", validate: "future_date",
                        label: "Date", type: "date"}
    @attribute "message", {input: "message", label: "Message",
                           type: "textarea"}

    @attribute "_meta", action: "/thanks", submit: "Request a call back!"
```

The additional pieces of data are mainly UI-based, describing the type of form element that should be used, and any labels that might be used. In principle, other metadata could also be included in here, such as the CSS class to apply, the type of container in which to place the input, and so on.

Instantiating the form will then be slightly different. For these purposes, there will be a separate class to render the form:

> *Another approach is to ask the form to render itself, but I'll discuss later why I think that's not as useful a methodology:*

```
$ ->
    obj = new ContactForm()

    renderer = new FormMapperRenderer()
    renderer.render "#form_container", obj
```

The form, having been created, is then passed straight through to the renderer—no other actions are required. The renderer will be responsible for putting the form on the page in the appropriate container and also for initializing the binding.

So far so good. The last piece of the puzzle is the rendering class:

```
class FormMapperRenderer

    render: (container, object) =>
        inputs = []
        meta = object.constructor?.schema?._meta

        for name, attribute of object.constructor?.schema
            if name == "_meta"
                continue
            if attribute.type == "textarea"
                input = $("<textarea></textarea>")
            else
                input = $("""<input type="#{ attribute.type }">""")
            input.attr "name", attribute.input

            layout = $("""<p>#{ attribute.label }: </p>""").append input
            inputs.push layout

        content = $("""<form method="post"></form>""")
        content.append inputs
        if meta
            content.attr "action", meta.action
            content.append $("""<p><input type="submit" value="#{ meta.submit }"></
 p>""")

        $(container).html content
        object.set_form content
```

For the sake of simplicity, here I use a combination of string building and DOM manipulation, though there's no reason why it can't all be done one way or the other or, in fact, by using a true templating system to create the form from existing markup.

Looking at the schema and then building the form elements appropriately is an effective way of creating the markup suitable for the form binding—so that within the HTML page nothing except a container is required. This approach can be useful in a number of scenarios:

- Where there are a large number of forms in a common format but with slightly different data requirements
- Where the attributes of a form could vary depending on the type of user accessing the form or on data previously entered into the form
- Where the server-side is effectively creating class definitions on the fly for the client-side to work with

The downside is that without a great deal of flexibility in the layout and the styling attributes given on the form, it will tend to look formulaic and manufactured, but for many tasks, that's actually more of a feature than a problem.

FORM AS MODEL, VIEW, AND CONTROLLER

When defining objects like these, where a data schema is driving the view of something, as well as business logic such as validation, and potentially the data storage or other tasks, you need to keep the concerns carefully separated. Otherwise, the end result is a kind of super object that's performing a variety of different tasks and getting bigger and more complex as development proceeds.

It's possible to make the form mapper class create its own HTML markup, and in some ways that may seem preferable. This rendering class is very closely coupled to the implementation of FormMapper—because it's inspecting the schema attached to the constructor—and such a close coupling is usually a sure sign that the classes should be merged.

In this instance, though, it would be difficult to cleanly separate the different tasks into different logical units. Rendering is a relatively crucial task to separate because often the same form definition will be needed in different contexts where the visual presentation of the form on a page must be very different. The additional look and feel data can be passed into the renderer, which will encapsulate the logic for deciding which HTML markup to use in the different scenarios.

However, that said, the close coupling causes the classes to be highly reliant on each other. In a sense, it's better to think of mapper and renderer as a suite of related classes, even though there is no inheritance or other technical link between them.

SUMMARY

This has been a relatively in-depth look at different ways of working with forms in HTML. Although an unexciting topic, forms continue to be the bedrock of many web applications, and you looked at some techniques that make handling forms easier and the use of form data more dynamic.

Binding data to forms, whether in one direction or two, is a familiar concept for desktop application programmers, but web browsers have tended to have relatively poor support for it as a concept. However, you've seen with smart use of browser features and the important observable pattern it's not difficult to build, and this can be used to make applications more interactive.

14

SERVER-SIDE COFFEESCRIPT

THE COFFEESCRIPT YOU'VE seen so far in this book is best described as *client-side*, Coffee-Script is designed as a solution to the various problems that web developers face, which usually means code working within the environment of the web browser. Although many of the facilities and features of CoffeeScript are designed to solve client-side problems, it's not the whole story.

JavaScript has exploded as a server-side scripting language over the past few years, and the reason for this is a project called Node.js, or simply *node*.

Taking a different approach to the technical architecture of a web server, node asks the JavaScript developer to write highly event-driven and function-oriented code.

It turns out that the event-driven style of coding required by node suits CoffeeScript down to the ground: all of the features that make CoffeeScript compelling in the client-side environment transfer directly to the server-side environment, and development of node-based servers is even more straightforward.

PUTTING COFFEE IN THE SERVER

Before delving too far into the details, I want to take a few moments to recap some of the long and glorious history of JavaScript, starting with the early days of Netscape . From the beginning, JavaScript was intended to be a server-side language and a client-side one, and one of the earliest versions of Netscape Enterprise Server included support for it. By 1996, Microsoft also had included support for the language in its web-server product.

JavaScript was potentially poised to become big, but it simply didn't take off for many reasons, the biggest hurdle being that the server-side implementation was even less standardized than browsers were. A web developer could write script and stand a fair chance of it working in the major browsers of the time; no such feat was possible with the wildly incompatible server implementations.

With the arrival of Web2.0, two important things happened. First, new life was breathed into JavaScript, and its popularity as a language and a development platform exploded. Second, web developers became ever-more concerned with their platforms, and as cloud computing took off, the challenge to develop "web scale" applications that could serve many users simultaneously was taken up by many.

JavaScript always had a natural inclination toward event-driven programming. Google released a super-fast JavaScript implementation in its Chrome browser called *V8,* and an enterprising developer called Ryan Dahl put two and two together to get four. He recognized that, with V8, JavaScript was not only fast enough to drive sophisticated server applications but also the event-driven design was a natural solution to the scaling challenge of dealing with thousands of network clients (the so-called *C10k problem*—adapting web servers to handle as many as ten thousand clients at one time, consequently the term *C10k*). This solution was named Node.js, and its growth in popularity since its release has mirrored the incredible resurgence of interest in JavaScript.

NODE.JS AND COFFEESCRIPT

This chapter focuses on using Node.js on the server-side, using CoffeeScript instead of the traditional JavaScript. Many of CoffeeScript's benefits aren't immediately as evident as those in JavaScript. Node.js provides an advanced JavaScript platform that not only offers excellent language support but also a wealth of libraries and tools to build software. However, the addition of more naturally classful object support and other facilities for programming-in-the-large that CoffeeScript brings to the table are a huge boon in this environment, and are regarded by many enthusiasts as nearly essential for the development and ongoing maintenance of large server codebases.

The Node.js library package manager npm should be familiar to you at this stage. I continue to use it in this chapter to assemble the various dependencies required to put together a functioning web-server application.

In addition, I use the MongoDB document database, which is available on all major platforms at www.mongodb.org. The installation and set up of this database is a little beyond the scope of this book, but the process is straightforward in most instances.

I use the feature set of this database sparingly; my reason for choosing it is the simplicity and maturity of the API for Node.js. A database speaking a dialect of SQL is another good choice, and in many cases, the transition to such a system isn't complicated.

WRITING A SIMPLE SERVER

In chapter 4, I examined the detail of an HTTP request from the point of view of the client. From the perspective of the server, things are much the same:

- Incoming HTTP requests are primarily identified by a verb such as GET or PUT and a URL including hostname and document path, but they also include a variety of headers and potentially a request body.
- The server deals with the request and issues a response, which consists of headers and a response body.
- A client may issue a few requests simultaneously, and as HTTP is generally stateless, some mechanism such as cookies are required to correctly identify the same client over a number of requests (simultaneous or not).

From experience with asynchronous server-side calls, you probably won't be surprised that the response on the server-side is also asynchronous—and then some. To deliver the scalability for which it is famous, Node.js requires that software give up the thread of execution as early as possible (known as *yielding*) so that other parts of the software can run.

At first, this may seem jarring. Although server-side calls are asynchronous in the browser, not much else is. For example, storing data in a cookie or using local storage is generally synchronous. On the server-side, any operation that cannot be immediately fulfilled is a candidate for an asynchronous interface—for example, reading from disk, which from the perspective of a computer is an interminably slow process, is asynchronous.

USING MONGODB

To illustrate the requirement to write code as asynchronously as possible, you begin your exploration of the world of server-side Node.js deep in I/O territory—in the database. Although requests to a database are generally quite easy to state (for example, *Fetch me all the documents for this user*) the computation and calculation that the database undertakes is often significantly more difficult and may take tens or hundreds of milliseconds. While that doesn't sound like a lot, add thousands of clients, and suddenly it becomes tens or hundreds of *seconds*, which is an altogether different proposition.

Unlike other database systems, MongoDB doesn't require a formal schema for the data it holds—it can be passed a set of data in JSON format, and it will store it. This document-oriented approach is at odds with the traditional relational approach of the SQL database server and may be better or worse, depending on the type of workload.

Rather than accessing MongoDB directly, though, I demonstrate the use of Mongoose, which is known as an object document mapper (or ODM). Using an ODM requires the specification for the data schema upfront, but once you supply a schema, it creates much of the scaffolding needed for accessing a database, including saving and intelligent querying of data.

The primary example I show in this chapter is a microblogging application, along the lines of a service such as twitter.com or identi.ca. Since there is a lot of code, I'll break it down into chunks, and I recommend downloading a complete copy of the application from `wiley.com/go/smashingcoffeescript`.

The main data to capture for this application is information about user accounts and the microblogs posted from those accounts. This is how the initial interface with Mongoose looks:

```
mongoose = require 'mongoose'
db = mongoose.createConnection 'localhost', 'demo'

User = db.model 'User', new mongoose.Schema
    name: 'string'
    password: 'string'
    follows: [ type: mongoose.Schema.Types.ObjectId, ref: 'User' ]

Blog = db.model 'Blog', new mongoose.Schema
    author: type: mongoose.Schema.Types.ObjectId, ref: 'User'
    blog: 'string'
    date: type: Date, default: Date.now
```

After the Mongoose library is imported into the code, a connection is opened to the MongoDB server. In this instance, the assumption is that the database is running on the local host and that there is a "database" within Mongo called demo available for use. Mongo's internal structure is simple: Documents (which are a lot like files) are read and written from collections (which are a lot like folders), and collections live in databases (which, stretching the analogy slightly too far, are like disk partitions).

The schema in use here defines two classes, although not with anything that resembles standard CoffeeScript syntax. Three pieces of information are stored about a user: name (a string), password (also a string), and a list of other users the user follows.

Actually, four pieces of information are stored here. As well as the three explicit fields listed, each object is given an attribute _id that uniquely identifies the object within the collection. These identifiers are used to refer to objects, so when a user has a list of other users (*followers*), what it actually has is an array of object identifiers.

The microblogs have a similar structure: a single author, the blog text, and a post date that defaults to the time the Blog object was created. So far, so good.

ARCHITECTING WITH MVC

Before going much further, it's worth spending a little bit of time on some architectural considerations. You may have come across the acronym MVC before. It stands for Model, View, Controller and is a software design pattern that dates from some of the earliest graphical user interfaces.

As developers started writing graphical desktop applications, they constantly encountered a number of similar issues. Logic for retrieving data and business rules about how to treat the data were often coded so that they were embedded in the user interface code. This meant that whenever the user interface needed to be updated, all the code that fetched data for the interface needed to be reimplemented.

Clearly, this was not the right way to go. *Separation of concerns* became the watchwords, and when developers analyzed their software, they found three major concerns:

- The handling of data, validation, and business logic (models)
- The display and editing of data (views)
- The logic that tied the various functionalities of the software together (controllers)

By separating certain tasks into specific parts of a piece of software and then ensuring that those different parts weren't too closely coupled, developers structured their software in such a way that they were able to make major changes—for example, changing how the software wrote data to disk—without those changes impacting the front-end user interface, and vice versa.

As web development, particularly on the client-side, became more sophisticated, developers who were creating software for browsers took those lessons from the big desktop applications and started to apply them to the new environment. The MVC pattern in particular has become so popular that not only is a framework for any language you can think of that implements the MVC pattern guaranteed, you're almost sure to have a selection of such frameworks to choose from!

INTRODUCING EXPRESS.JS

Rather than implement all the parts of a framework that you might need to write a substantial application in CoffeeScript, I've chosen to demonstrate a lightweight but popular framework—Express.js.

By no means a full MVC framework, Express provides a standardized library of most of the common requirements for a server-based application. Express isn't what is commonly known as an *opinionated framework;* instead, it concentrates on providing a flexible selection of functions to build a server. In this example, I use those features in an MVC–style. All of the ideas and principles embodied in my code are transferrable to other frameworks.

In my opinion, the most important part of any application is always the model, and because the model contains the storage and the business logic, that seems a relatively natural conclusion to draw. However, there is some disagreement about this, and you will find examples of software with relatively "skinny" models that end up having a good degree more logic built into their controllers.

This is particularly obvious when a developer uses a system such as Mongoose, which automatically handles the loading, saving, and querying of data. Because so much of the data structure is built into that layer, the developer considers that layer alone to be the model, and anything that cannot be placed in those models ends up being placed in the controller because there's nowhere else to place it.

In my experience, this is a poor design. The smarter a controller becomes, the more coupled the various sections of the application become—the separation of concerns breaks down. Instead, my instinct is to build on the models in the application, to the extent that I often treat a database layer as simply a storage mechanism and build my "real" models on top of that as a separate series of classes. This is the design that I use in this example—so beware, it does appear slightly contrived, because in an application so small, such a layer is hardly required. As with most structural considerations, though, the decision to spend time reinforcing the foundations often pays dividends later on.

So, the model layer for this application is designed as a straightforward CoffeeScript class:

```
class Database

    fetch_user: (user_id, callback) =>
        User.findById user_id, (err, user) =>
            if err
                return callback status: "error", reason: "No user #{ user_id }"
            return callback status: "ok", user: user
```

This first method on the model—`fetch_user(id, callback)`—illustrates all the general principles of asynchronous programming that are used again and again throughout the rest of the code. The function signature alone is typical. As well as a number of arguments like any other function, a final argument is provided that refers to a function to be called later on when all the work has been done.

A simple implementation to fetch the user is given here. The function is passed the identifier of the user, so the function calls the Mongoose interface to the database to fetch the document in the User collection with that identifier.

Make sure you understand thoroughly what's happening at this point. If there is code elsewhere that calls `fetch_user()`, all that happens in the function is that it calls `User.findById()` and passes it a function, and `findById()` will do no work and return immediately; the code leaves `fetch_user()` almost as quickly as it entered.

Entering and leaving almost immediately doesn't sound very useful, and it's not; there is no result at that point. The Node.js mongo driver is off consulting the database and only later comes back with an answer that is passed through to the anonymous callback function provided to `findById()`. The original `callback` function is finally triggered, with data indicating whether the call was successful.

Simple functions like `fetch_user()` have one layer of call back internally. However, things don't need to become much more complicated for more layers to be required. To store users' passwords securely, some hashing functions must be available:

```
bcrypt = require("bcrypt")
bcrypt_rounds = bcrypt.genSaltSync(10)
```

The function to create the user in the database needs a number of layers:

```
create_user: (name, password, callback) =>
    hashed_password = bcrypt.hashSync password, bcrypt_rounds
    User.find name: name, (err, users) =>
        if err
            callback status: "error", reason: err
        if users?.length > 0
            callback status: "error", reason: "That user already exists"
        user = new User name: name, password: hashed_password
        user.save ->
            callback status: "ok", user: user
```

`create_user()` in this example is doing two I/O operations. First, it looks up the user to ensure that the user doesn't already exist. If not, the function attempts to create them, which triggers the second database operation. With both those requests operating asynchronously, two anonymous callbacks are involved, one nested within the other. And this isn't even fully asynchronous: the various `bcrypt` calls to generate a password hash are executing synchronously (synchronous functions are often suffixed `–Sync`) and they're actually pretty slow. To make this genuinely asynchronous, another two layers of callback would be required to await the result of each bcrypt operation.

This process of nesting callbacks is sometimes uncharitably referred to as *callback hell.* It's the modern event-driven equivalent of spaghetti programming. Imagine a function that requires some ten or twenty different Mongo requests. If each request is nested, the code ends up severely indented, affecting readability and, more importantly, maintainability. In Chapter 15, I cover some style rules you can use to mitigate this situation and some technical approaches to avoid the problem.

So far, I've covered how to find Mongoose models by identifier or by a parameter, but there hasn't really been an example of a substantive query. The function to retrieve the list of microblogs for a user remedies that:

```
get_blogs: (user, callback) =>
    blog_author_list = (u for u in user.follows)
    blog_author_list.push(user._id)
    User.where('_id').in(user.follows)
        .sort('name')
        .exec (err, following) ->
            usermap = {}
            usermap["#{user._id}"] = user.name
            usermap["#{u._id}"] = u.name for u in following

            Blog.where('author').in(blog_author_list)
                .sort('-date')
                .limit(20)
```

```
          .exec (err, posts) =>
              callback
                  status: "ok"
                  blogs: posts
                  following: following
                  usermap: usermap
```

This function is passed a `user` object to begin with, and from that user's *follows* list (the other users they've followed), a new list of identifiers is created using a comprehension, including the user's identifier. This list is utilized as part of a query to return all of the `User` documents that those identifiers represent and to create a mapping from identifier to username.

Then a query is run to find the microblogs authored by a user on that list, limited to the most recent 20. In practice, most queries on the database are more sophisticated than this example, but one interesting takeaway is that the fluent interface style has been copied here and makes perfect sense. Each additional filter is another call in the chain, until `exec()` is used to retrieve the final result (as always, using an asynchronous callback).

Armed with all of this knowledge, you can now comprehend the rest of this model, which is mainly made up of other utility functions to manipulate the two key MongoDB document types, `User` and `Blog`:

```
verify_user: (name, password, callback) =>
    hashed_password = bcrypt.hashSync password, bcrypt_rounds

    User.find name: name, password: hashed_password, (err, users) =>
        if err
            console.log err
        if users?.length
            callback users[0]
        callback null

post_blog: (user, status, callback) =>
    blog = new Blog author: user._id, blog: status
    blog.save ->
        callback status: "ok", blog: blog

delete_blog: (user, blog_id, callback) =>
    Blog.findById blog_id, (err, blog) =>
        if blog.author != blog_id
            callback status: "error", reason: "You don't own this post"
        blog.remove ->
            callback status: "ok"

get_people: (user_id, callback) =>
    @fetch_user user_id, (result) =>
        if result.status == "error"
            callback result
        user = result.user
        follow_list = ("#{id}" for id in user.follows)
```

```
        User.find {}, (err, people) =>
            result_list = []
            if err
                callback status: "error", reason: "Couldn't find users"

            if people?.length
                for person in people
                    result = { user: person, following: false }
                    if "#{person._id}" in follow_list
                        result.following = true
                    else
                    if "#{person._id}" != "#{user._id}"
                        result_list.push result

            callback status: "ok", people: result_list

    set_follow_status: (user_id, follow_id, status, callback) =>
        @fetch_user user_id, (result) =>
            if result.status == "error"
                callback result
            user = result.user
            user.follows = user.follows.filter (other_id) ->
                "#{other_id}" isnt "#{follow_id}"
            if status is true
                user.follows.push follow_id
            user.save ->
                callback status: "ok"

module?.exports =
    Database: Database
```

The functions that make up the model are now complete. All of the logic pertaining to the two key data structures—from validation of user passwords up to and including allowing users to follow other users—is included in this class.

As mentioned earlier, it's possible to directly extend the base storage models `User` and `Blog` with this type of functionality. However, this example makes it clear that a large amount of logic is involved when using that data and that this logic doesn't need to be tied to any specific implementation. This model could be refactored easily to make use of an SQL database instead of MongoDB, with the only real problem being translation of the query code.

RESPONDING TO CLIENT REQUESTS

Now you can move on to the real heart of the matter: writing the web application code that communicates directly with the browser. Following the rough guide of the MVC architecture, the model part is already taken care of, leaving the controllers and the views.

Again, a number of members within the MVC community adhere to slightly different interpretations of these terms. My perspective on this is that views should be side-effect free (that is to say, code within a view should never change any application state) and have as little logic built into them as possible. Controllers should orchestrate the various model changes in response to a request and then render the appropriate view to the client, while ensuring that only the logic required in a controller is present and that application state or business rules that rightfully should belong in the model do not seep into them.

That said, like any good rules, there are always exceptions. My experience is that different applications require at least slightly different designs, and there are sometimes good reasons to make some of these sections less separate than they ought to be. My firm principle is to avoid building anything that will be difficult to refactor later. I've broken these rules and later come to regret my decision!

RENDERING VIEWS

The view is really the simplest component of the application, and the easiest to describe. However, before looking at a view, take a look at the simplest possible controller:

```
app.get '/', (req, res) ->
    res.render 'index.eco',
        locals:
            title: 'Home'
```

A lot is happening in this few lines of code. `app` is the object that represents the entire application, and for the moment, you don't have to know precisely how it's set up. Suffice it to say, the `get()` method is defining what's known as a *route*.

It's no coincidence that the method is named the same as the HTTP verb—`app` also has `post`, `delete`, and `put` methods—and this call links the verb and path used in the request to a function that handles that specific request, the controller. Each such controller has a (`req`, `res`) signature. The first argument represents the HTTP request, the second the response.

This controller is essentially doing no work. It's calling the `render()` method on the response, telling it which template file to use and what variables to pass through to the template. This is the final stage of the process, where the client's request has been acted upon, and the response is being generated.

In these examples, I'm using a templating system called Eco. Much like MVC frameworks, templating systems are available to meet all needs and tastes. I chose Eco for this exercise primarily because it allows CoffeeScript expressions within the templates, but also because it's written in CoffeeScript. The source is very instructive, and I recommend taking a look to appreciate just how simple a system it actually is.

The template file is nice and simple:

```
<!DOCTYPE html>
<html lang="en">
    <head>
    </head>
```

```
    <body>
        <h1><%= @title %></h1>
    </body>
</html>
```

The `title` variable, set in the controller as a local variable to the view, is output by using Eco's `<%= %>` tag, which evaluates the expression contained within and prints the escaped result. `<% %>` is used for simple evaluation (nothing is output), and `<%- %>` can be used to output raw unescaped code (which is generally a no-no, and what's known in the trade as *bad code smell*; its presence indicates a poor design decision elsewhere).

Small amounts of logic can be used; as Eco evaluates any CoffeeScript expression there is conditional logic and looping available:

```
<% if @following?.length > 0: %>
    <ul class="following">
        <% for user in @following: %>
            <li><%= user.name %></li>
        <% end %>
    </ul>
<% else: %>
    <p>You aren't following anyone!</p>
<% end %>
```

Unlike CoffeeScript, indentation alone is no good for marking the end of a block in an HTML template, so there are some small additions with the use of colons to mark the start of a block and a new `end` keyword to mark the end. In every other respect, expressions are the same, including the ever-useful existential soaking.

CONTROLLING RESPONSES

Now that you know how the model is defined and how the views are rendered, the only aspects left to look at are the controllers and the overall definition of the application. For this application, all you need is a simple setup for Express.js. Unfortunately, by simple, I don't mean brief. There is some degree of boilerplate code here:

```
express = require 'express'
app = module.exports = express()
eco = require 'eco'
csrf = require 'csrf'
flash = require 'connect-flash'

{Database} = require './model'
db = new Database()

port = 8015
secret = "some long string with random characters"app.configure ->
    app.engine ".eco", render
    app.set "views", "#{__dirname}/views"
```

```coffeescript
    app.use express.logger()
    app.use express.bodyParser()
    app.use express.methodOverride()
    app.use express.cookieParser(secret)
    app.use express.session
        key: 'sid'
        cookie:
            maxAge: 60000

    app.use csrfMiddleware
    app.use flash()
    app.use app.router

app.configure 'development', ->
    app.use express.errorHandler
        dumpExceptions: true
        showStack: true

app.configure 'production', ->
    app.use express.errorHandler()

app.get '/', (req, res) ->
    if req.session.user_id
        req.flash 'success', "Authenticated"
        res.redirect '/dashboard'

    res.render 'index.eco',
        locals:
            title: 'Home'

if not module.parent
    app.listen port
    console.log "Express server listening on port #{port}"
```

That feels like quite a large chunk of code and it's not even working yet, but it's the core of an Express.js application and I'll explain it piece by piece. Like most apps, it begins with importing the various libraries—including the model that was defined previously—and almost straightaway dives into configuration.

Previously, I said that Express.js was less a framework and more a set of tools. The basic `app` object that is given essentially does nothing, and `app.configure()` is used to run the code that sets up all the facilities that are required.

`app.engine()` is called first, and this defines the templating system to be used to render views. The example here is written in Eco, and `render()` is a function that is defined later to do the actual work of rendering the view into HTML. In addition, a directory holding the actual template files is set; `app.set()` is used to store configuration variables, and there is a matching `app.get()`, as you might expect.

`app.use()` is where the interesting work begins to happen. The various statements here have one thing in common: They define a piece of the middleware. The application actually has a stack of middleware, and each time `use()` is called, a new handler is appended to that stack.

Middleware is nothing special. It's simply a function with a specific signature, and `use()` takes a reference to that function. Then, on each request, each middleware gets to look at the request before the application, in turn. The previous code references non-standard middleware called `csrfMiddleware`. Its definition is simply this:

```
csrfMiddleware = (req, res, next) ->
    res.locals._csrf = req.session._csrf ? "disabled"
    next()
```

Every piece of middleware has this `(req, res, next)` signature, allowing it to see a request (the first argument), alter the response (the second argument), and call the next middleware (the last). It's similar to the controller signature except that a controller is effectively the last function to be called, so there's no need for `next()`.

The main use of middleware is to do a global task that would otherwise need to be repeated in the controllers. Using middleware is a great way of ensuring the code doesn't become too repetitive. In the previous example, the middleware sets a local variable within the response context, which means that every template being written for this application can rely on `@_csrf` being present in the template context. This information is used to prevent cross-site request forgery (CSRF) attacks, a common vulnerability in web applications.

> *CRSF attacks are covered later in this chapter in the section on security measures.*

With the middleware configuration out of the way, the remaining task is to route some URLs through to the right controllers, and `app.listen()` is used to start the entire application. At that point, it opens the port and starts accepting requests from web browsers.

Walking Through Authentication

It can be challenging to take in the design of an entire application at once, so first examine the authentication processes that a user goes through from sign-up to logout. The model is already in place and includes a number of functions for finding and validating user requests. Adding a form to allow the user to create a new account on the system isn't complicated:

```
<h1>Sign up</h1>

<form method="POST" action="/signup">
    <% @_csrf_input() %>
    <p><label>Username:
        <input type="text" name="username" value="<%= @username %>"></label>
    </p>
```

```
    <p><label>Password:
        <input type="password" name="password"></label></p>
    <p><input type="submit" value="Register"></p>
</form>
```

This is a standard form, with only two small additions: a `csrf` input, which is covered later in this chapter in the section on security measures, and pre-population of the form with a username if this is not the user's first attempt (for example, if the user failed to supply a password originally and the sign-up request was then refused).

To process this request, a route and a controller are needed:

```
app.post '/signup', (req, res) ->
    params = req.body

    db.create_user params.username, params.password, (result) =>
        if result.status == "ok"
            req.session.user_id = result.user._id
            res.redirect "/dashboard"
        else
            res.redirect "/"
```

The `db` object is the instance of the model created when the application first starts. The controller is doing little more than orchestrating the required model call, which if successful, directs users to their dashboards. In another application, sign-up may not automatically log a user in to the application (for example, e-mail address validation may be required), but the logic within the controller is still similar. It's differentiating between a successful request and a failed one, and choosing a view appropriately.

`req.session` is a special part of the request, representing the user session that is maintained from one request to the next. By storing the user's identifier in the session, you can retrieve it in subsequent requests and use it to identify the user. In the Express.js configuration section, the session was configured as an entirely cookie-based affair, with data being encrypted on the server-side to prevent nefarious clients from claiming to be someone they're not.

Because the state of being logged on is really just a matter of having the right data available in the user's session, the action of logging out can be considered as a request to clear the current session:

```
app.get '/logout', (req, res) ->
    req.session.destroy ->
        res.redirect '/'
```

Displaying the Dashboard

Once the user is logged on, the application displays the dashboard—the heart of the system that allows the user to view the posts from other users and to create posts. This time, because the controller is more involved, I define it as a stand-alone function:

```
dashboard = (req, res) ->
    user = db.fetch_user req.session.user_id, (result) =>
        if result.status == "ok"
            db.get_blogs result.user, (result) =>
                res.render 'dashboard.eco',
                    locals:
                        user_id: req.session.user_id
                        posts: result.blogs
                        usermap: result.usermap
                        following: result.following
        else
            # couldn't find user
            res.redirect '/'
```

The controller invokes the dashboard view, but as of yet no route is associated with it. So there isn't actually a URL that invokes the controller. Several pieces of information are passed through as a template context: the identifier of the user, the most recent posts by that user and the users he or she follows, and the names and identifiers of those users being followed.

The view template makes use of these different pieces of context to provide the full page:

```
<!DOCTYPE html>
<html lang="en">
    <head>
        <link rel="stylesheet" type="text/css" href="/media/style.css">
    </head>
    <body>
        <div class="sidebar">
            <form method="POST" action="/dashboard">
                <% @_csrf_input() %>
                <textarea name="blog"></textarea>
                <input type="submit" value="Update status">
            </form>

            <h2>Following</h2>

            <% if @following?.length > 0: %>
                <ul class="following">
                <% for user in @following: %>
                    <li><%= user.name %></li>
                <% end %>
                </ul>
            <% else: %>
                <p>You aren't following anyone!</p>
            <% end %>

            <form method="get" action="/logout">
                <input type="submit" value="Log Out">
            </form>
        </div>
```

```
<form method="get" action="/dashboard">
    <input type="submit" value="Refresh">
</form>

<% if @posts?.length > 0: %>
    <ol class="posts">
    <% for post in @posts: %>
    <li>
        <%= post.blog %>
        <p class="footer">Posted by <%= @usermap[post.author] %>
        on <%= post.date %></p>
        <% if "#{ post.author }" == @user_id: %>
            <form action="/post/<%= post._id %>/" method="POST">
                <% @_csrf_input() %>
                <input type="hidden" name="_method" value="delete">
                <input type="submit" value="Delete">
            </form>
        <% end %>
    </li>
    <% end %>
    </ol>
<% else: %>
    <p>You haven't posted anything yet.</p>
<% end %>
</body>
</html>
```

Several activities are available from this page, and the key feature—the ability to post a microblog—is simply a POST request to the same page. So, although the end view should be the same in that case (users see the same page, containing their latest content), that POST path needs extra logic to deal with new content being inserted into the database before the view is rendered. Wire the controller into the routes to make this happen:

```
app.get '/dashboard', dashboard

app.post '/dashboard', (req, res) ->
    params = req.body
    user = db.fetch_user req.session.user_id, (result) =>
        if result.status == "ok"
            db.post_blog result.user, params.blog, ->
                dashboard req, res
```

Both variants eventually defer to dashboard() as the way to render the view, but while the GET path is effectively a straight reference, the POST path executes what is a basic controller before returning the view, in this case submitting new data to the database.

This method of separating controllers into the part that is performing operations in response to the request, and the remainder generating the response, is a useful technique for keeping code DRY.

SECURING THE APPLICATION

So far, the application is designed with *authentication* (the process of identifying the user) but with little regard to *authorization* (checking that users are entitled to access the requested resource) and common security measures to keep out those with ill intentions.

The first job is to define which routes require an authenticated session, and then perhaps which users might be entitled to access those routes. There are a number of different ways to create this kind of architecture, and the best choice is application-dependent. If only a small number of users with the same level of access are accessing a web application, your main goal is ensuring that all the users are successfully authenticated.

On the other hand, if a site is being accessed by a large number of users with different levels of access or with personal data that others shouldn't have access to, your job becomes a lot more complicated. It becomes necessary to create a flexible system that can deal with the different requirements as they crop up within the application.

A sensible choice is to use the idea of separating the task from the controller, effectively building a single controller from a number of parts. To ensure that a user has been authenticated, a single check is needed:

```
secure = (next) ->
    return (req, res) ->
        res.redirect '/login' unless req.session.user_id
        next req, res
```

The internal logic here is simple: If there is no identifier for the user in the request session, which is secure and private to the application, the user has not logged on and should be redirected to a login page.

To deliver this logic, a function that returns a controller is written, which allows the function to wrap another controller so that, if the test succeeds, the function can simply call the controller as the controller would have been called originally—passing in the request and response objects. This check can now be added to the route definition for a resource, with the dashboard for example (leaving out the body of the function to deal with POST data):

```
app.get '/dashboard', secure dashboard
app.post '/dashboard', secure (req, res) ->
```

Blink, and you'd miss it: the `secure()` call is just in front of the "standard" controller and appears almost as a new keyword—it's descriptive of the task it's performing.

You can extend this concept in a variety of ways. For example, if user accounts have roles, it might be useful to limit some resources to not only logged-in users but also to those with specific account roles:

```
secure = (roles, next) ->
    return (req, res) ->
```

```
        role_ok = req.session.user?.role in roles
        res.redirect '/login' unless req.session.user_id and role_ok
        next req, res
app.get '/admin', secure ['admin'] (req, res) ->
```

The ability to configure the behavior based on the route makes this approach highly flexible. In contrast, it is possible to implement the controls as middleware, for example, white-listing those paths that don't require authentication and implementing the role-checking as logic within the middleware. However, that's less flexible and not as self-descriptive as adding the information onto the route definition.

Considering CSRF Attacks

Attacks on web applications are, sadly, numerous. It's entirely beyond the scope of this book to attempt to enumerate them or demonstrate fool-proof methods of preventing them. However, "the perfect is the enemy of the good," and it would be a poor show indeed to ignore this problem. To illustrate some solutions, I'll briefly focus on cross-site request forgery (CSRF) attacks.

The CSRF middleware cropped up briefly earlier, although at the time I didn't explain what it was for. Request forgery is actually a simple attack. By manipulating a website, an attacker can trick a user's browser into making a request for a different website, and with a carefully crafted request, the attacker can do some serious no-good. For example, if a user is logged on to the microblogging application, it's possible to craft requests to delete their blogs (for example), which on the face of it, the system will allow—a logged-on user should have the ability to do that.

An answer to CSRF attacks is to ensure that requests are as difficult to forge as possible. In general, that means putting a piece of information into a form that the system later checks for to ensure that the request it's processing isn't a forged request. A common way of doing this is to place a token in your forms that validates each user. The token is an unguessable piece of information that an attacker could not use without somehow getting the intended victim to fetch the CSRF token on the behalf of the attack.

Express.js already comes with a system for creating and validating such tokens, and the @ crsf middleware shown earlier ensures that the token is placed into the template context so that it's available in all responses. The page templates from earlier also included a form input being placed into forms to pass through this token; the only missing piece is in the view renderer:

```
render = (path, options, callback) ->
    opts = {}
    opts[k] = v for k, v of options._locals
    opts[k] = v for k, v of options.locals

    opts._csrf_input = ->
        """<input type="hidden" name="csrf" value="#{options._locals._csrf }">"""
```

```
fs.readFile path, 'utf8', (err, str) ->
    return callback(err) if err
    callback null, eco.render str, opts
```

The `render()` function wraps the Eco engine and is the function provided to Express.js early in the process of configuring the views. Its job is to implement the view renderer API that Express expects, with an implementation that calls the Eco system to generate the view output.

First it merges all the local variables in the context into a single object, to be later passed through to Eco. It also defines a function on that object. Since Eco templates can contain any CoffeeScript expression, they need not limit themselves to variables and simple expressions. Function calls are possible, although I strongly recommend avoiding them.

In this case, a function is the most appropriate way of exposing the functionality, as it is generating an input for the form and populating the input with the CSRF token for the current user. Then each template with a form that requires protection must include only the call to `<% @_csrf_input() %>` to place the token-containing input in the form.

Other Attacks

There are a variety of other attacks, and it's virtually impossible to give even high-level guidance about the best way to defend against them. However, here's a bit of advice I'd like to offer:

- Never trust input from the remote browser, either when processing it in the first instance or when later reusing it.
- There is virtually never a good reason to output data in a non-escaped fashion, and certainly never a good reason if the data being output contains any user input.
- Don't rely on one single scheme to deliver security; validate input, check forms for forgery, check authentication tokens, defend the application in depth.
- Never send information to the browser unless it's absolutely required; if the information can be retained in session instead, use the session.
- As much as possible, stay up on the state of the art. A few years ago, SQL injections (a form of incorrectly trusted input attack) were all the rage, but there is always a new attack just around the corner.

Sadly, being a CoffeeScript user alone confers little benefit (although many of the various checks that the system performs for you during compilation and at runtime are definitely of value), and if you're just starting to exercise your server-side development skills, many of these design factors will feel slightly unfamiliar. Don't let that put you off; read around the subject, but more importantly, put yourself in the attacker's shoes and think about the weak spots.

SUMMARY

This chapter represents this book's first true foray into server-side programming. Developers are often surprised just how many of the client-side skills they have can transfer to the server-side, and with event-driven systems like node the environment is actually very similar.

You should now be basically familiar with running applications under Node.js, but also with the Express.js framework, which can be used to implement sophisticated server-side web applications. In addition, you looked at:

- Using the MongoDB database server as a method of server-side data persistence
- Creating Express.js views that use Eco as a template rendering engine
- Protection from CSRF attacks in particular, but also some security best practices that generally apply to designing web applications

15

REAL-TIME WEB WITH SOCKET.IO

THE MAJOR SHIFT to client-side technology—loosely referred to as AJAX or Web 2.0—required big changes in the way web developers went about their work. As well as confronting greater performance issues and facing the problem of intermittent network connectivity, developers also must go through a change in mind set in order to appropriately architect an application with extensive client-side functionality.

If there is a "next big thing," real-time functionality is it. However, along with the issues that client-server communications already bring come the special challenges of real time. Rather than using the traditional request-response model, developers need to think more abstractly about what the client is doing and take a more general approach to the design of web services.

DEFINING REAL-TIME APPLICATIONS

Before starting to look at code, it's important to understand what *real-time* actually means. You can find a number of different definitions, some of which describe things that are easier to achieve than others.

However, in traditional computer science, *real-time* has a specific meaning that refers to the ability of a piece of software to complete work in a given time frame. For example, if a computer controls a washing machine, the computer must be able to calculate the level of water in a timely way so that the drum (tub) doesn't overflow. Control computers are the obvious applications for these techniques—for example, car engine control systems or aircraft fly-by-wire control systems—and it's worth being clear that this class of real-time is definitely not what is meant here.

Instead, a real-time system as far as the web is concerned is one that attempts to reflect the current state of affairs as they change, whether it's as straightforward as an e-mail inbox changing the number of e-mails unread as more come in or a stock trading system displaying the correct current share price (which also meets the traditional definition of real-time).

On the web, the traditional architecture has been that a client performs a request, and the server creates a response. Generally, the server wasn't able to contact the client outside of that framework. Unless the client made a request, the server didn't have any type of response to send. So, from a client perspective, this architecture is pretty much useless in terms of displaying up-to-date information.

POLLING THE SERVER FOR DATA

Although HTTP as a protocol wasn't really designed with server-client communication in mind, it was extended to do so almost right from the start. The earliest versions of Netscape Navigator contained a feature called *server push* that could be seen as a forerunner of the current technology. Unlike many of the other features of Navigator, it was rarely used and thus not cloned by the competitors, but allowed the server to keep open the connection to the browser after a request and push new data when required.

In addition, the concept of *polling* is as old as the hills and can be brought to bear here, too. With polling, instead of needing a specific mechanism by which the server can push information toward the client, the client simply keeps in touch with the server by contacting it regularly. Although this means that the client is generally up to date, this approach has a big problem: The more regularly the client polls—therefore, the more up-to-date it is—the more resources the client consumes on the server-side. To give the impression of being truly real time might require updating many times per minute, generating much more load per user than would otherwise be the case. Polling can never be a true substitute for real-time data. If an application polls infrequently, it doesn't cause much load but it doesn't stay up to date well either. By polling frequently enough to look real-time, the application will consume significant server-side resources.

COMET FOR LIGHTWEIGHT POLLING

Around the same time AJAX became popular, a new method of doing real-time updates on the server-side became popular; it was informally known as *Comet* after many different developers starting using the technique. Relying on the fact that a server doesn't need to give a response as soon as possible to a client, Comet takes the architecture of polling but turns it into something genuinely real time: The client opens a connection and makes a request, but the server doesn't respond until it has event data to respond with (or until the connection times out—which may be a very long time indeed).

Consuming fewer resources than polling, but requiring a totally different technical setup, Comet makes a reasonably good fit with AJAX techniques, although it's also possible to implement it with other means (iframes, for example). However, this is still very much a hodge-podge solution. It's effectively still a polling mechanism, still entails additional resource cost, and can tend to cause unfortunate side effects with web caches.

Better solutions didn't arrive until the implementation of HTML 5, and after this wait, two solutions came along at once: Server-Side Events and WebSockets, both of which are being standardized as part of the HTML 5 effort.

SERVER-SIDE EVENTS AND WEB SOCKETS

Server-Side Events, or SSE (not to be confused with the Intel processor instruction technology), were proposed by the makers of the Opera web browser. They are the simpler implementation of an event-driven design and are really unidirectional. Once the browser has opened a connection to the server, the connection is used by the server to send updates to the browser, but not for two-way conversions. Supported by all A-grade browsers other than Internet Explorer, SSE events are trivial to listen for:

```
if 'EventSource' of window
    events = new EventSource '/some/url'
    events.addEventListener 'message', =>
        if e.origin == 'example.com'
            console.log e.data
```

This snippet first checks that the browser supports the interface and then connects to a known URL to listen for events. A simple event handler is used to listen for messages—much like clicks or other events are handled—and although the origin of the event should always be checked as a security measure, it's very easy to set up a connection as the browser does most of the other management.

There is, of course, much more depth to this interface, with the ability to send custom events and get more detailed status information.

WebSockets are more sophisticated and, as such, a lot more difficult to use. In fact, they have been so difficult to get right that some browsers have taken a number of attempts to implement them in a secure fashion—unlike SSE, WebSockets introduce a full bidirectional communication channel with a web server that, although notionally based on HTTP, is effectively a brand-new protocol. The browser interface to this system is again being standardized through the HTML 5 project, but the protocol is a different matter, going through the IETF process under the cozy name of RFC 6455.

While WebSockets enjoy slightly wider browser support—because of the support built into Internet Explorer 10, although sadly none earlier—there have been a number of different editions of the protocol, and realistically browsers released much before 2012 don't support the latest (more secure) variation. However, the future of the protocol is incredibly rosy, given its broad industry acceptance.

Connecting to a web socket is similar to using SSE:

```
if 'WebSocket' of window
    socket = new WebSocket 'ws://example.com:8080/updates'

    socket.onopen = =>
        socket.send "Some message"

    socket.onmessage = (event) =>
        console.log e.data
```

The first obvious difference here is that, as well as listening for messages, the client-side has the chance to communicate messages back to the server as well. Whether this is a blessing or a curse is difficult to determine. A perfectly serviceable communication channel is already available (standard AJAX), but for it to be of use to the server in the case of SSE, it would need to be able to tie the incoming AJAX request to the outgoing SSE channel in order to provide something approaching WebSocket functionality.

Another major difference is that the URI for the WebSocket end point is not http—it uses the scheme ws:// to indicate that it is RFC 6455 protocol (or it may specify wss:// as the secure, encrypted alternative).

Choosing which type of system to use (whether an up-to-date HTML 5–based system, or something more akin to the earlier polling-style mechanisms) is generally more of a server-side than a client-side consideration. Where an existing web service framework is being used, there may be less choice, particularly in the deployment of WebSockets. However, it's also true that turning an existing service into one that is real-time capable is such a radical step that often a more or less complete redesign is required.

DOING MICRO-BLOGGING IN REAL TIME

Now that I just said choosing a system can be tough, I'm going to show you the way out on the client-side at least: socket.io.

With the myriad options available, you may be thinking there's too much choice and that the different options all do roughly the same thing anyway. socket.io takes that view and provides an abstract interface to a socket so that you don't have to worry about which of the various APIs are available in the browser the code is running on. Much as jQuery abstracts away the specifics of doing DOM manipulation, so socket.io simplifies the process of server-client communication through the browser.

In addition to supporting the various in-browser APIs, socket.io provides a Flash-based alternative—which means that even on the various older editions of Internet Explorer, the chances of having to fall back to polling are pretty slim and that virtually all A-grade browser users will have a genuine WebSocket-like experience.

In addition, socket.io provides namespaces and multiplexing, allowing an application to run many different types of message over the same socket, without you having to worry about implementing custom logic to separate them.

Best of all, socket.io comes with a simple API that is more or less the same on both the client- and server-side. Accessing a server with socket.io from the client is as simple as this:

```
socket = io.connect 'http://127.0.0.1/'
socket.on 'connect', ->
    socket.send 'Initial message'

    socket.on 'message', (msg) ->
        # take some action
        console.log msg
```

A socket.io connection is generally given an http end point on the server, which is either directly a socket.io server or at least a connection that can be passed to socket.io for processing.

Much like AJAX within the client, the initial connection and then the sending and receiving of messages all happens asynchronously, so anonymous functions are once again the order of the day. An application will usually open up the socket early on as part of the page-loading process and then leave it open until the point where it is genuinely no longer needed—so the connect process, although quick, should generally occur only once on a page.

The server-side equivalent is only slightly more complex than this:

```
io = require('socket.io').listen 80

io.sockets.on 'connection', (socket) ->
  socket.on 'message', ->
    socket.send 'This is a response to an incoming message'
```

The API is obviously very similar, except that the server is waiting for connections to come in rather than initiating them itself, so the individual `socket` representing a specific client connection is created when the client first connects, and the various event handlers then attached to the socket get re-created for each incoming connection.

Integrating this into an Express.js application is also pretty straightforward:

```
express = require 'express'
app = express()
io = require('socket.io').listen app

app.listen 80

io.sockets.on 'connection', (socket) ->
  socket.emit 'event', {'initial': 'data'}

  socket.on 'other event', (data) ->
    console.log data
```

In this case, socket.io needs to be given an instance of the application that it's working alongside but otherwise works almost identically to the client-side version. In the preceding code, `emit()` is used instead of `send()`; `send('data')` is simply shorthand for `emit('message', 'data')` and nothing more complex than that. In any substantial application, there will be a requirement for a number of different message types or events, so generally `emit()` is the preferred API.

INTEGRATING STATIC AND REAL-TIME DATA

In the previous chapter, a micro-blogging application was developed primarily as a server-side Express.js application. With socket.io, there is an obvious way to turn the system into one that can publish new blogs in real time so that users viewing their dashboards don't need to refresh the page—the new blogs will simply appear on the page over time, as they're posted.

However, there's a small problem here. The existing rendering is happening server-side to begin with. It's possible to reimplement that logic on the client-side, but that involves duplicating a large portion of code, violating the DRY principle and causing a maintenance headache.

This is a similar problem faced by developers attempting to build a system that is partly server-side rendered, partly client-side rendered. AJAH is an acceptable compromise, but it's relatively limited in terms of the flexibility it offers (the markup being created is still static from the point of view of the client-side application).

RENDERING ON THE CLIENT SIDE

A better solution is to make the system much more AJAX-native to begin with, such that all the key rendering takes place on the client-side. At first glance, this would seem to make the initial page load slightly longer—the page needs to fully load and then make the request for the first tranche of data, and only then will it render. However, there's a neat trick —you can "prime the pump," so to speak, and include the first set of data in the page itself, negating the need for an initial AJAX call.

Further updates to the page may be required—either in response to an AJAX request or to act upon messages received via socket.io—but these are then reusing the same client-side infrastructure as before to render the page in the first place.

So, a small client-side rendering function might look like this:

```
renderPosts = (posts, container) ->
    content = "<p>You haven't posted anything yet</p>"
    if posts.length > 0
        content = '<ol class="posts">'
        for post in posts
            content += """<li>
                #{ post.blog }
                <p class="footer">Posted by #{post.author} on #{post.date}</p>
            </li>"""
        content += '</ol>'

    $(container).html content
```

Then, as part of the static page, instead of rendering the blogs individually, the application injects the data into the page as a JSON data structure and then passes that data to `renderPosts()`.

To listen for updates to the blog, a socket.io event listener is needed, and given that most of the infrastructure is now in place, setting one up is simple:

```
socket = io.connect 'http://127.0.0.1/blogupdates/'
socket.on 'connect', ->
    socket.on 'blog', (data) ->
        posts.unshift data
        renderPosts posts, '#post_container'
```

This is perhaps overly simplified. If left open, the array of posts will simply grow and grow as more blogs come through, and in reality, some kind of limit is needed. However, as a feature, data injection lends itself to a nice architecture:

- Server-side processing generates data structures, which may be injected directly into page templates or sent over AJAX/WebSocket requests.
- Client-side templates are run over data received from the page or other requests to create or update the page.

Of course, this is not always entirely suitable, for example, where parts of templates may render or not depending on the security context of the user, but generally even in those cases, you can design a system that adheres to this architecture without compromising security, performance, or some other desirable attribute.

REUSING SERVER-SIDE CODE ON THE CLIENT

Since the advent of node.js, developers have asked whether the "holy grail" is reachable: a single code base executed partly on the server, partly on the client, with shared code between the two sides to simplify development and speed up delivery.

There are some obvious reasons for optimism. With both the server-side and client-side possessing excellent JavaScript execution environments, and a developer's natural taste for reuse of code, developing code for both client- and server-side execution is seemingly an excellent fit.

Some in the web development community see things differently. Although admitting the theoretical advantages, a number of developers see sharing code between the client-side and the server-side as bad practice, because the two environments are quite different. Still others find the whole idea antithetical, in both principle and practice, because the considerations and work load on the two sides are so radically different.

I tend to sit on the fence on this debate. For most applications, I think there can be either a benefit or a detriment, and this difference may not be clear to many developers until they actually try it. That said, following are some thoughts on my experiences regarding what is likely to produce "a win" or "a lose."

SHARING TEMPLATES

For me, the template code that creates or modifies markup is the strongest candidate for sharing between the client and server side. The examples shown so far in this book have relied on the Eco engine, executing in the node.js environment. In reality, nothing requires that it actually has to execute in that environment, and indeed Eco comes with a compiler that turns templates into JavaScript functions that can be called on directly.

The big advantage here is the ability to generate the same markup for a given template on the server or the client, keeping the template itself DRY, while not significantly increasing the system's complexity as a whole.

The primary downsides here are that passing templates through to the client-side is a more involved affair—the application is effectively creating data that it would ordinarily be processing. If the server-side is passing templates through to the client-side, it's also possible to use server-side templates to generate templates that are then passed to the client. This type of scheme, which may seem clever and flexible at first glance, is an absolute nightmare in practice. It results in fragile applications that occasionally generate invalid template code, leading to frustrating and challenging debugging sessions.

In addition to Eco, a variety of other templating systems are available, many of which are "pure" JavaScript designed for use within the browser but that can also be deployed server-side. These solutions are even more suitable for sharing code, where the primary requirement is on the client-side, but the occasional server-side render is helpful.

SHARING MODELS

Because you are at the business end of the codebase, it can be tempting to allow the key logic of an application to be used on the client-side—for example, to use it to validate data entry before the data is sent back to the server. I've also seen developers attempt to abstract their data storage model sufficiently for it to be used with a server-side technology such as MongoDB and client-side offline technology such as `IndexedDB`. In general—and I don't say this lightly—such attempts are doomed to fail.

This is an excellent example of how the similarity between the platform tends to hide the different considerations. On the server side, where many requests are coming in from different users, performance is pretty crucial, in terms of speed of execution and memory consumption. The potential cost here might be disk space needed to ensure that queries complete as quickly as possible—for example, when the database indexes a large data set.

On the client-side, the requirements are almost entirely the opposite. The performance doesn't matter so much, because there's a single user and only that user's data is on the system, rather than multiple users and their associated data. Equally, the amount of storage *does* matter a fair amount, because all the local storage mechanisms have limits on how much data they can store—extraneous data that isn't absolutely needed by the client in offline mode shouldn't be stored.

It's very difficult to make the argument that shared model or model-level logic makes sense for most applications. The requirements in the server and client environments are very different, and sooner or later one side or the other—or even both—will end up the worse because of the compromises made to ensure that the code remains compatible for both consumers.

DEALING WITH CALLBACK PYRAMIDS

Developing an event-driven application usually means making use of asynchronous APIs—function calls that take a callback function as an argument, and complete immediately without having done any work. The callback function is later called when the work requested is done. This is true in the browser and you saw in Chapter 14 that server-side code running under node.js is heavily event-driven. For an application working in real-time on the server side, it becomes even more important: every piece must be asynchronous. This results in heavy use of callbacks.

A callback pyramid refers to a block of code that relies on a number of callbacks that are dependent on each other. Usually this would be where there are a number of separate calls to read files or access a database. Imagine a server-side view that would automatically log users into their account, creating an account if one did not exist and then updating the "last logged in" time:

```
auto_account: (req, res, next) =>
    params = req.body
```

```
@db.verify_user params.username, params.password, (user) =>
    if not user
        @db.create_user params.username, params.password, (result) =>
            if result.status == "ok"
                user = result.user
                req.session.user_id = user._id
                user.update_last_logged_in()
                @db.save_user user, () =>
                    res.redirect "/dashboard"
            else
                next req, res
    else
        req.session.user_id = user._id
        user.update_last_logged_in()
        @db.save_user user, () =>
            res.redirect "/dashboard"
```

As you can see, with each successive callback the code is getting further indented to the right. This is often referred to as *callback hell*. There are only so many levels of callback that can be used before the code is too indented.

One good approach to this type of problem is to remember that functions can be created within other functions. The previous example could be written this way:

```
auto_account: (req, res, next) =>
    params = req.body

    onLogin = (user) =>
        req.session.user_id = user._id
        user.update_last_logged_in()
        @db.save_user user, () =>
            res.redirect "/dashboard"

    @db.verify_user params.username, params.password, (user) =>
        if not user
            @db.create_user params.username, params.password, (result) =>
                if result.status == "ok"
                    onLogin result.user
                else
                    next req, res
        else
            onLogin user
```

By extracting out the logic into the `onLogin` function, the code is actually simpler than the previous version. There is a slight loss of readability with this type of solution since the code being executed later is defined first, but my experience is that separating callbacks into standalone functions ends up making the various code paths better isolated and less interdependent. The scope of each function is clearer, and data not already in the enclosing scope (such as user in the last example) has to be explicitly passed through.

Another approach to solving this issue would be to re-use the $.Deferred support in jQuery. In Chapter 4, you saw how building a wrapper around the standard jQuery functions could be used as a support to handle asynchronous callbacks: There's no reason why that approach can't be used here, too. Using promises is a potentially limited answer because they can't replicate the various different logic branches that might be needed in practice, but they provide a native way of chaining callbacks together and critically providing useful failure paths in the case something goes wrong.

One project worth mentioning at this point is Iced CoffeeScript, available here: http://maxtaco.github.com/coffee-script/.

This is a fork of the main CoffeeScript compiler, with two additional keywords added to the language syntax: await and defer. Examining this fork in detail is beyond the scope of this chapter, but the benefit of this extension to CoffeeScript is that it allows callbacks to be created by the compilation process. For many asynchronous designs, this can result in much cleaner code.

There is no one-size-fits-all approach to managing callbacks. Different applications will have different patterns of file or database access for example, resulting in different internal structures and callback requirements. In my experience, spending time up-front thinking about the architecture of an asynchronous application pays off in spades.

REAL-TIME COLLABORATION WITHIN A SINGLE APP

Collaboration can mean very different things to different people. For example, for some people, the idea of e-mailing documents to each other is collaboration enough. However, I find that once you place the words *real time* before the term, it starts to have a specific meaning: getting work done with multiple people at the same time.

Although technology has always been about bringing people together and allowing them to communicate better, it wasn't until relatively recently that this kind of communication was actually delivered; and many of the most interesting products that have developed our collective understanding of collaboration on the web have actually fallen by the wayside.

Google has probably done more in this area than most others. You are probably familiar with the Google Apps series of products, which are styled as an office suite in a web environment, but also offer strong real-time collaborative features: the ability to see someone else working on a document at the same time you work on it, for example, or to host a chat room of sorts to discuss a document that's being worked on.

However, the most interesting product they released in this area was called Google Wave. Somewhat like chat rooms or e-mail, it allowed users to hold conversations in real time and, unlike any other product, to develop pieces of content at the same time. (I use the past tense because unfortunately, like many similar products before it, Google Wave was cancelled.)

Although Wave continues on at the Apache Foundation as an open source project, it was slightly before its time and something of a solution in search of a problem. But it did highlight an extremely important development pattern that is crucial to distributed multiuser real-time collaboration: *the Operational Transform.*

OPERATIONAL TRANSFORMATION

No textual description of Operational Transformation, or OT, is wholly adequate because the system is really, at its heart, a form of algebra. Don't let this put you off though! Originally developed as a way of allowing more than one user to work on a text document at once, OT is a way of thinking about how information is used within an application.

For a simple example, imagine two users collaborating on the sentence, "The cat sat on the mat." The first user may want the cat to be brown; the second user may want the mat to be red, in which case, the end result would be, "The brown cat sat on the red mat." However, there are two possible intermediate stages, depending on the timing of who makes the first edit. If the software worked in whole sentences, it would not be possible to make two simultaneous edits like this—one would get lost.

The point of OT is to describe the changes made by a user in a way that allows for variations in sequence and timing. Changes to a document are broken into their smallest appropriate description—for example, "Insert the word *red* between *the* and *mat*". This approach makes it easier to combine them even when the order changes, and the changes themselves are less likely to conflict (although, of course, if two users attempt to change the same word at the same time, a conflict of edits is inevitable).

OT is not a single technology per se. It, or something like it, can actually be implemented in a variety of ways, and the *primitive operations,* the small units of change that are the currency of OT, will be different from application to application. For a text document, inserting and removing characters may be enough; for a graphical application, a broader range of potential operations is required.

SEPARATING INPUT FROM OPERATION

The key takeaway from OT is that input and operation should be almost entirely separated. If an application has multiple simultaneous users, it's almost as though a single computer has an number of different keyboards at which users are typing different things. Some way of managing those different inputs and turning the stream of keystrokes from each user into an ordered process is required.

To do this, OT asks that you consider the changes that an application might make to the data it has as a series of transforms and that input into the application is nothing more than a request for a specific operation that does the transformation.

Viewed in that way, an architecture for this kind of application begins to suggest itself naturally. Starting with a model for the data in question, an interface is created that trans-forms the data in certain ways using a series of primitives (such as insert or remove a charac-ter, or perhaps add/remove/resize/rotate a graphic). The application translates input—whether it is local input via mouse, touch or keyboard, or remote input via some network socket—into a series of primitive operations and sends those operations that originated locally to the network for other users to access.

The question of conflict has been studiously avoided so far, so let me address it now. With any system where multiple users can request simultaneous changes, it is virtually always certain that the system (in principle at least, even if it is difficult in practice) will allow users to make requests that cannot be reconciled with each other—for example, the two users changing the same word in a sentence.

So in general, the question is not "how do I avoid conflicts?" but really "how do I deal with conflicts?" And, like many other problems, the correct solution is in the eye of the beholder. Developers should do whatever makes the most sense for their application. That said, here are some common strategies:

- **The software picks a winner.** Usually, the first change wins, and later changes that conflict are backed out. This requires sufficient centralization to be able to determine reliably which change was actually made first.
- **Both changes lose.** In the case of conflict, both changes are rolled back and the users will have to reenter them to try again.
- **A user picks a winner.** Usually this is done by conflict resolution (that is, making a further change that resolves the conflict), but also potentially by picking one of the changes.

There is no obvious right or wrong to any of these, although (for example) if the data is important and throwing out changes that conflict is highly undesirable, the manual conflict-resolution process might be attractive. Equally, if changes are generally unimportant, it might be best to simply throw them away.

Ideally, in all situations, users on the losing end of the algorithm will be warned in some manner—at least showing them the change that has not been made. However, by this point, the user interface is beginning to resemble something closer to a version control system—certainly not simple and easy to use, and users as a rule tend to have difficulty with the concept of conflicting editing and an ordered history of changes.

BUILDING A MEETING WHITEBOARD APP

To demonstrate collaboration in the wider sense of the word, a more down-to-earth example is appropriate, and to do this, I'll walk you through the idea of providing a real-time conference whiteboard. Using socket.io and HTML 5's `<canvas>` widget, the idea is straightforward. You provide a whiteboard for a user, but transmit the user's drawing to a server, which broadcasts those same drawings out to other users connected to the same drawing.

The starting point for this application is a single-user whiteboard that demonstrates the mode of drawing and the data structures at play. As a general rule, this is exactly the wrong way to go about the process of design, and this example demonstrates why—as is often the case, examining the mistakes made along the way is more instructive than the final solution itself!

To implement the whiteboard on a page, you just create an instance of a class and give it a containing `<div>`:

```
<body>
    <h1>White Board</h1>
    <div id="whiteboard"></div>
</body>


$ ->
    whiteboard = new Whiteboard('#whiteboard')
```

Then the main work to create the canvas will happen when the object is created. This is the constructor for the class:

```
class Whiteboard

    width: 800
    height: 400

    constructor: (@container) ->
        @canvas = $("<canvas>")
            .css(height: @height, width: @width, border: "1px solid black")
            .attr(height: @height, width: @width)[0]
        $(@container).append(@canvas)

        @ctx = @canvas.getContext "2d"
        @is_drawing = false

        $(@canvas).on "mousedown mouseup mousemove", (event) =>
            offset = $(event.target).offset()

            x = event.pageX - offset.left
            y = event.pageY - offset.top

            @draw(x, y, event.handleObj.type)
```

Although the canvas element may be new to you, the rest of this construction should be familiar. The `<canvas>` node is created, given some basic styles, and appended to the document via the provided container. The *drawing context* of the canvas is also taken—this is used to perform the drawing operations—and an event listener is set up so that any mouse movements on the canvas may trigger drawing.

All of the interesting logic is contained within the `draw()` function of the class:

```
    draw: (x, y, type) =>
        switch type
            when "mousedown"
                @ctx.beginPath()
                @ctx.moveTo(x, y)
                @is_drawing = true
```

```
when "mousemove"
    if @is_drawing
        @ctx.lineTo(x, y)
        @ctx.stroke()
else
    @ctx.closePath()
    @is_drawing = false
```

This is a nice simple implementation. Depending on the event that has occurred, some slightly different actions are taken. The initial state of the whiteboard is that the mouse is not drawing and doesn't go into a drawing mode until the user holds down the mouse button, triggering the initial `mousedown` event, setting `this.is_drawing`, and moving the context to the current mouse position for the start of drawing.

Mouse movement is ignored if the whiteboard is not in a drawing mode, but if it is, then a line is drawn to the current mouse position. If this is the first movement, the line is drawn from the initial coordinates; otherwise, the line is drawn from the point at which the previously drawn line finished. Once the mouse button is released, the drawing mode stops, and the "current path" is closed—so that future lines are drawn from the next set of coordinates, not simply from the end of the last line.

Compiling and running this results in a display similar to Figure 15-1.

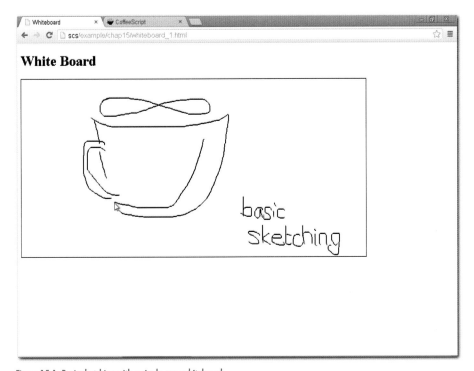

Figure 15-1: Basic sketching with a single-user whiteboard.

Although this is not the prettiest system in the world, the initial goals are met! The user is able to draw on the surface, and in principle, nothing is stopping that information from being communicated to a server in order to be broadcast to other users.

MODELING INFORMATION ACCORDING TO OT

I made the claim earlier that starting from a single-user application design like this was probably the wrong way to start, so now let me explain that statement more fully, taking the design for the whiteboard given so far and incorporating the ideas of operational transformation.

In any system where collaboration occurs in real time, careful thought must be given to how updated information arrives into the system and into individual clients, and how those clients resolve the problem of receiving the same data as other clients but potentially in a different order or at a slightly different time.

There is a specific issue in this case: the canvas drawing context. The system, as coded, draws shapes by effectively joining short lines end-to-end, where the next new line is drawn from the point at which the last one stopped. This has two implications:

- Drawing more than one of these segments simultaneously is going to be impossible.
- Entire segments must be communicated to the server; otherwise, a client that closed before sending a *line end* signal would effectively block the drawing from receiving any more updates.

Neither of these are useful features, and in fact, it gets slightly worse. If the system can communicate only with whole segments, it means that the real-time nature is effectively lost. A user's screen is effectively frozen until the end of their current drawing operation, at which point, it updates with any changes that happened in the meantime. That could easily be achieved with polling as well.

So, in fact, a different model is required. Rather than rely on the context of the canvas to join these lines up, each individual line being drawn should be its own segment, and the information being passed to clients should be the entire line being draw—effectively, two *x, y* coordinates—ensuring that drawing operations are atomic and completed quickly so that the real-time nature of the system is apparent. If three people are drawing simultaneously, their drawings should update instantly in each user's view of the whiteboard.

This is an excellent example of where a data model that makes sense for a single-user application makes little sense in a multiuser context—or, in fact, impedes what the desirable design would look like. Although the technical limitation of the canvas context has been used as a convenient hook on which to talk about these types of design consideration, they come into play in many different scenarios:

- When designing a chat server, is it important that text from users is properly ordered? Does it matter that user B's response to user A's question is seen in the wrong order by user C?

- When designing a game, does the order in which things happen matter? If a player is shot, but then a later update says the player moved out of the way, how is that resolved?

- If two users are collaborating on a document, what happens if they both attempt to change the same piece of text?

Unfortunately, there are no simple solutions to any of these questions. For example, with computer gaming, there is more emphasis on protocol and client security, since cheaters are adept at altering both their game and the data their game senses in such a way that it benefits them. Building highly distributed applications that work in something approaching real time is an incredibly difficult challenge in many instances.

SERVING SIMPLE SOCKET.IO INFORMATION

Before moving forward with a new implementation that uses socket.io to communicate between different whiteboard users, take a look at the server-side implementation that will be used to facilitate the collaboration:

```
io = require('socket.io').listen(8016)

current_drawing = []

io.sockets.on 'connection', (socket) ->

    socket.emit 'initialize', current_drawing

    socket.on 'draw', (segment) ->
        current_drawing.push segment
        socket.broadcast.emit 'draw', segment

    socket.on 'clear', () ->
        current_drawing = []
        socket.broadcast.emit 'clear'
```

As you may appreciate from that short listing, this is definitely an overly simplified version of the application. In particular, there is a severe limitation in that this server supports only one collaborative drawing at a time. The drawing is modeled internally as an array, although this could be extended a number of ways to support many drawings at the same time.

The server sits listening for incoming WebSocket connections, and on receipt of a connection, the first thing it does is emit() the current drawing to the client—that is, it sends the client all the current data it has for a drawing. This doesn't do anything for the first user connecting, but for users who connect after others have started drawing, it allows their whiteboards to be updated to reflect all the previous drawing.

This demonstrates an important principle: With any type of client-side programming, it is dangerous to assume that the state of the software is in some way static or reliable. After all, it only really takes a second for the user to press the Refresh button in his or her browser and to return the page to a clean slate. Whenever possible, have a system that restores visiting clients to a known state so that, for example, if their browser crashes, they don't lose their existing work (or at least, lose as little of it as possible!).

The `clear` event implemented by the server is similar; it returns clients to the known state of having an entirely clear canvas. Again, this is very much over-simplified. Depending on the context, this type of function will at least be protected by some measure of security and an authorization mechanism of some sort.

Before moving on, I want to note quickly that, although the initial data is sent to the client using `socket.emit()`, the later calls are all to `socket.broadcast.emit()`.

HANDLING REMOTE UPDATES

With a server in place, it's now possible to look at how the whiteboard application needs to be rewritten to take advantage of this new framework. There is no real need to change the API, but the constructor for the class will need to be updated:

```coffeescript
constructor: (@container) ->
    @canvas = $("<canvas>")
        .css(height: @height, width: @width, border: "1px solid black")
        .attr(height: @height, width: @width)[0]
    $(@container).append(@canvas)

    @ctx = @canvas.getContext "2d"
    @is_drawing = false

    $(@canvas).on "mousedown mouseup mousemove", (event) =>
        offset = $(event.target).offset()

        x = event.pageX - offset.left
        y = event.pageY - offset.top

        @canvas_handler(x, y, event.handleObj.type)
```

Up to this point, the constructor is basically the same, although the previous `draw()` function has been changed to `canvas_handler()` to emphasize the split between dealing with the event and actually performing a drawing operation. After this point, though, comes the socket.io:

```coffeescript
@socket = io.connect('http://localhost:8016/')

@socket.on 'initialize', (drawing) =>
    for segment in drawing
        @draw_segment segment

@socket.on 'clear', =>
    @clear()
```

```
@socket.on 'draw', (segment) =>
    @draw_segment segment
```

In a sense, this can be viewed as entirely the inverse of the server-side code, and it's worth having a look at both pieces of code side by side to because it becomes clear quite quickly how they match up.

On initial connection, the server will send back the information for the drawing in its current state. It's possible to send these as a series of separate `draw` events, but that would be somewhat wasteful in terms of resources (because it would trigger a large number of client-side events, which could end up being slow for larger drawings); however, it's reasonable to view them as batched `draw` events, and that's how the code treats them.

Two other events are set up, one for the `draw` event and one for the `clear` event. The main logic for these events is, of course, elsewhere, so first look at the new `canvas_handler()` function, which also uses the `draw_segment()` function:

```
canvas_handler: (x, y, type) =>
    switch type
        when "mousedown"
            @last_x = x
            @last_y = y

            @is_drawing = true
        when "mousemove"
            if @is_drawing
                @draw_segment([@last_x, @last_y, x, y])
                @socket.emit "draw", [@last_x, @last_y, x, y]
            @last_x = x
            @last_y = y
        else
            @is_drawing = false
```

Previously, the equivalent handler relied on the canvas context to remember the finishing coordinates of the last drawing operation—that is no longer possible, so this handler is remembering `@last_x` and `@last_y` specifically, based on previous events.

Although now it's mostly just tweaking internal state, when the handler is in the drawing mode, it does two things. First, it draws a line from the previous coordinates to the current coordinates of the mouse pointer; second, it sends that information directly to the server so that it will be instantly rebroadcast to the other clients connected to the drawing.

Now, only two remaining functions defined in this class need to be examined:

```
draw_segment: (segment) =>
    [x1, y1, x2, y2] = segment
    @ctx.beginPath()
    @ctx.moveTo(x1, y1)
    @ctx.lineTo(x2, y2)
```

```
        @ctx.stroke()
        @ctx.closePath()

    clear: =>
        @ctx.clearRect 0, 0, @width, @height
```

Here, the `clear()` implementation is pretty straightforward—using the known width and height of the canvas, it simply clears a rectangular area across the entire canvas.

The logic within `draw_segment()` is very different from that used previously, though. Rather than a segment beginning with mouse down and lines being drawn to reflect mouse movement and the segment being closed with mouse up, there is now just a short segment to reflect the line being drawn at this exact moment. Destructuring assignment is used to pull the coordinates out of a four-element array, which is being used as the basic data type here (to represent a line segment).

With the server running and the same drawing opened in two different browser windows, the real-time nature of this system is clearly demonstrated in Figure 15-2.

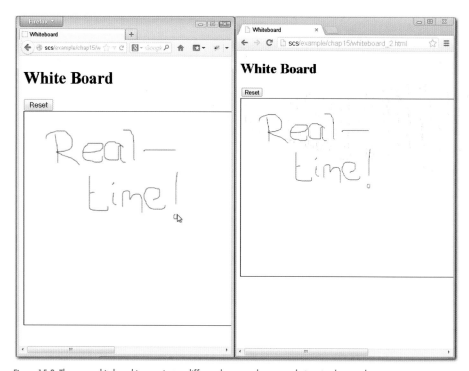

Figure 15-2: The same whiteboard is open in two different browsers that are updating simultaneously.

SUMMARY

Writing real-time applications takes understanding and care, but really isn't too difficult. This chapter has given you some insight into:

- How real-time connections work between the browser and the server
- The importance of thinking about the data structures being used by an application and how they might change for a real-time application
- Structuring the different logical parts of an application between the client and the server

I expect over the next five to ten years that many (if not most) applications developed for web browsers will have some element of real-time functionality, and as support for the modern websockets becomes more widespread it will lead people to think about how applications work in different fashion.

INDEX